The Policy Makers

The Policy Makers

Shaping American Foreign Policy from 1947 to the Present

Edited by
Anna Kasten Nelson

ROWMAN & LITTLEFIELD PUBLISHERS, INC.
Lanham · Boulder · New York · Toronto · Plymouth, UK

ROWMAN & LITTLEFIELD PUBLISHERS, INC.

Published in the United States of America
by Rowman & Littlefield Publishers, Inc.
A wholly owned subsidiary of The Rowman & Littlefield Publishing Group, Inc.
4501 Forbes Boulevard, Suite 200, Lanham, Maryland 20706
www.rowmanlittlefield.com

Estover Road
Plymouth PL6 7PY
United Kingdom

British Library Cataloguing in Publication Information Available

Library of Congress Cataloging-in-Publication Data

Nelson, Anna Kasten.
The policy makers : shaping American foreign policy from 1947 to the present / Anna
Kasten Nelson.
    p. cm.
Includes bibliographical references and index.
ISBN-13: 978-0-7425-5041-4 (cloth : alk. paper)
ISBN-10: 0-7425-5041-9 (cloth : alk. paper)
ISBN-13: 978-0-7425-5042-1 (pbk. : alk. paper)
ISBN-10: 0-7425-5042-7 (pbk. : alk. paper)
ISBN-13: 978-0-7425-6471-8 (electronic)
ISBN-10: 0-7425-6471-1 (electronic)
    1. Statesmen—United States—Biography. 2. Cabinet officers—United State—
Biography. 3. Legislators—United States—Biography. 4. Political consultants—United
States—Biography. 5. United States—Officials and employees—Biography. 6. United
States—Foreign relations—1945-1989. 7. United States—Foreign relations—1989– I.
Title.
    E840.6.N45 2009
    328.73092—dc22   2008019953

Printed in the United States of America

⊗™ The paper used in this publication meets the minimum requirements of American
National Standard for Information Sciences—Permanence of Paper for Printed Library
Materials, ANSI/NISO Z39.48-1992.

To the Men in My Life
Paul, Eric, and Michael

Contents

Introduction

$\mathcal{T}$wo years after the end of World War II, as the United States became a global power, its foreign policy began the metamorphosis into national security policy. It had brought the world into the nuclear age, established a large military presence throughout the world and resolved never to allow another Pearl Harbor.

The National Security Act of 1947 reflected those changes by creating a united military establishment, a Central Intelligence Agency (CIA), and a National Security Council. No longer did presidents and secretaries of state sit down together to determine the course of American policy. The secretary of defense, director of central intelligence, and first and foremost, after 1960, the president's own assistant for national security affairs were now at the table. Absent but not forgotten was the U.S. Congress, the generous appropriations of which were essential for a global presence.

These chapters, which pair policies and the policy makers, reflect the importance of these new players in national security policy. Colin Powell is the only secretary of state in the collection, and he is included only because he also played an important role in American policy as chairman of the Joint Chiefs of Staff.

The book begins with a discussion of the drafting of the seminal Cold War paper, NSC 68, by the head of the State Department Planning Staff, Paul Nitze, and a small interdepartmental group. As Steven Rearden notes in his chapter, to understand Nitze and NSC 68, it is also necessary to understand the views of his predecessor, George Kennan. Analyzing the substance of NSC 68, it becomes clear that Nitze, encouraged by Secretary of State Dean Acheson, turned away from Kennan and deliberately changed U.S. policy.

The next chapter is also devoted to a State Department figure, Robert Bowie, who served as head of policy planning under John Foster Dulles during the Eisenhower administration. As the loyal assistant, Bowie stayed in the shadows, but his influence was keenly felt in relations between the United States and Europe during the formative years of the North Atlantic Treaty Organization.

That the first two chapters are on policy makers and policies that were conceived largely in the State Department is a reflection of the difficult transition to the new national security system. In spite of inroads from the military and intelligence agencies, both Nitze and Bowie served under strong secretaries of state. No other member of either the Truman or the Eisenhower administration gained the positions of influence achieved by Dean Acheson and John Foster Dulles.

But 1961 marked the end of that era as presidents began turning to their national security assistants for advice on foreign policy. Two chapters discuss their role in developing important policies. The first one is Walt Whitman Rostow. Although he served both President John F. Kennedy and President Lyndon B. Johnson, Rostow was especially important to Johnson in his role as national security adviser during the Vietnam War. As Lloyd Gardner notes, he never lost his belief that the war could be won and continued to encourage Johnson.

The other national security adviser is Zbigniew Brzezinski, President Jimmy Carter's White House assistant. When the Soviets invaded Afghanistan, his was the principal voice among Carter's advisers. His hardline views toward the Soviets greatly influenced Carter's reaction to that defining event. Patrick Vaughan provides insight into the forces in Brzezinski's life that determined his reaction to the Soviet action.

Between these chapters is one on a U.S. senator, Henry "Scoop" Jackson. Foreign policy has been and continues to be the domain of the president and executive branch, but a forceful, influential senator, from time to time, can manage to challenge White House policy. Jackson was a firm believer in maintaining the military supremacy of the United States and never lost his suspicion of the Cold War enemy. To the dismay of both Kissinger and Nixon, he managed to unravel their efforts toward establishing détente with the Soviet Union.

John Prados's chapter on William Casey illustrates the ease with which neutral intelligence can lapse into policymaking. For fifty years, presidents and their advisers have depended on the neutral intelligence gained by the CIA and other intelligence agencies to inform their policymaking. But William Casey had his own agenda. This chapter on Casey, who advised Ronald Reagan during the Iran-Contra controversy, illustrates the way in which the intelligence agencies can sometimes exert influence very damaging to the nation's security.

The policy maker in the final chapter, Colin Powell, is almost unique because he was involved in two wars and advised two presidents named Bush. As head of the Joint Chiefs of Staff, he was a critical adviser to George H. W. Bush during the Gulf War. He then served as the secretary of state for George W. Bush during the first years of the Iraq War. In this chapter, Walter LaFeber contrasts his strong position as a policy adviser to the senior Bush with his inability to influence George W. Bush.

No one discussed in this book is truly unknown, but most garner few paragraphs in textbooks or popular histories even though in every instance the policies they influenced were of vital importance to the country. I hope these chapters will help illustrate that important policies were also the result of men behind the scenes as well as those whose status allowed them to stand at the president's shoulder.

Anna Kasten Nelson
American University

• *1* •

Paul H. Nitze and NSC 68: "Militarizing" the Cold War

Steven L. Rearden

$\mathcal{T}$he history of NSC 68 and the life of Paul Henry Nitze are so closely intertwined as to be practically indistinguishable. Submitted to President Harry S. Truman in the spring of 1950, NSC 68 was a broad analysis of national security policy recommending major revisions in U.S. politicomilitary strategy toward the Soviet Union. Appearing on the eve of the Korean War, NSC 68 called for an all-round strengthening of the country's defense posture and more proactive measures to contain the Soviet threat. As the State Department's senior representative to the interagency drafting committee that produced NSC 68, Nitze was a leading figure in shaping its content, analysis, and recommendations. A controversial paper, even at the time it was written, NSC 68 has since earned both praise as a realistic assessment of the problem and condemnation for what critics view as the "militarization" of American foreign policy after World War II. As historian Ernest R. May characterized the change. "Before mid-1950 containment seemed to involve primarily an effort to create economic, social, and political conditions assumed to be inhospitable to communism, whereas from mid-1950 onward, the policy seemed primarily one of preserving military frontiers behind which conditions unsuitable to subversion could gradually evolve."[1]

Although Nitze is often celebrated as the "author" of NSC 68, his role in the project was not what he later considered his most significant accomplishment during a lifetime of public service and philanthropy. As far as Nitze was concerned, his most significant and enduring contributions were his involvement in arms control from the late 1960s on and his role in establishing and nurturing the Johns Hopkins School of Advanced International Studies, which today bears his name. Yet for historians, it was his involvement in NSC 68 that stands out both in the evolution of postwar

American foreign policy and in the development of Nitze's personal philosophy of national security.

THE CONTAINMENT STRATEGY

Nitze emerged as a significant figure in the policy process in the aftermath of World War II. Shaping the atmosphere at the time were escalating tensions between the United States and the Soviet Union and growing concern at home over the menace of communist subversion. By 1948, repeated run-ins between Washington and Moscow over the political future of Eastern Europe, the security of the Near East, access to Berlin, the control of atomic energy, and other issues pointed to an increasingly sharp divergence of interests. Meanwhile, a White House–instigated loyalty program and a wide-ranging investigation by the House Un-American Activities Committee fed speculation and suspicions that communist penetration of the American government and American institutions was rampant and widespread. In short, the Cold War had come to dominate both the international and domestic political landscapes.

Prior to NSC 68, Nitze was a relatively obscure midlevel State Department bureaucrat who had spent most of his time since World War II grappling with the financial and economic problems of European recovery. Until 1950, the reigning expert on the Soviet threat—the man assumed to know the most about the problem—was his colleague, George F. Kennan, a career Foreign Service officer and head of State's Policy Planning Staff. Steeped in Russian history and culture and fluent in the language, Kennan had spent much of the 1930s and most of World War II at the American embassy in Moscow, observing the Soviet Union firsthand during one of its most fateful periods. Despite the wartime alliance between the United States and the Soviet Union, Kennan found the deterioration in U.S.–Soviet relations that followed the defeat of Germany and Japan hardly surprising and wholly predictable. For practical reasons, he downplayed the possibility of a war between Russia and the West, feeling that the Soviet Union was in no position after the sacrifices it had made in World War II to pose a serious military threat; however, he cautioned that relations between Moscow and the West were likely to remain unsettled, even antagonistic, for some time to come and that the solution lay in "a long-term, patient but firm and vigilant containment of Russian expansive tendencies."[2]

As the director of policy planning from 1947 to 1950, Kennan was well positioned to make his views heard and felt in official circles. During the critical policy debates in the spring of 1947, Kennan took exception to the "sweeping language" of the Truman Doctrine, arguing that it placed aid to Greece and Turkey "in the framework of a universal policy rather than in that of a specific decision addressed to a specific set of circumstances."[3] His preferred approach was that incorporated into the European Recovery Plan (ERP), which Kennan played a major part in drafting and which Nitze helped to organize and steer through Congress. In contrast to the Truman Doctrine, the ERP downplayed ideology in favor of concrete economic, political, and social programs. The net effect, Kennan was pleased to see, was a more focused and balanced program directed at reversing the dislocations that were breeding misery and discontent and providing opportunities for communists to make significant inroads into European politics.

While Kennan and Nitze were in accord on the need to promote European recovery, they often differed on other issues. Most significant was the relative importance of military power in American foreign policy, which Nitze accorded a higher priority for the purposes of containing Soviet expansion. Although Kennan readily acknowledged that military forces were a vital diplomatic tool, he routinely warned against excessive reliance on armed strength. The United States, he argued, should maintain sufficient strength and enough varied units to operate effectively in two separate theaters simultaneously, a rule of thumb that would dominate U.S. military planning more or less continuously for the duration of the Cold War.

Despite his tendency to downplay the role of military power, Kennan's advice carried considerable weight in the senior echelons of the armed services and was especially important in shaping Secretary of the Navy James V. Forrestal's perception of the Soviet threat. In Kennan, Forrestal saw much of himself—a sensitive, perceptive mind, always probing with questions and never fully satisfied with the answers. Impressed by Kennan's insights and familiarity with Soviet behavior, Forrestal did much to publicize his ideas and arranged for his writings to be part of the curriculum of the National War College and other service schools.

Following passage of the 1947 National Security Act that unified the armed services and Forrestal's appointment as the first secretary of defense, Kennan became a regular participant in Pentagon policy discussions. As State's designated representative, he routinely sat in on meetings of the War Council and the Committee of Four Secretaries, Forrestal's principal in-house advisory bodies on military policy and strategy. Forrestal faced two serious problems at the same time: the need to develop a postwar force structure, tailored to limited fiscal resources, that could effectively support the expanding demands of American foreign policy and the reorganization of the armed services into a more cohesive, integrated defense establishment. Interservice rivalry and competition for funds were rife, and in the aftermath of the bitterly contested unification debate, cooperation and collaboration among the services were in short supply. Especially intense and controversial were the quarrels between the air force and the navy over the control of atomic weapons and whether the country should rely on long-range land-based bombers or carrier-based aviation as its first line of defense. Seeking help, Forrestal turned to Kennan in the spring of 1948 in the hope that he and the Policy Planning Staff, working in collaboration with the new National Security Council (NSC), could provide policy guidance that would clarify strategic objectives, establish priorities for the armed forces, and ultimately quell the interservice bickering over the allocation of funds.

Both Kennan and his boss, Secretary of State George C. Marshall, sympathized with Forrestal's predicament. A career military officer, Marshall had ably served as Army Chief of Staff in World War II and knew firsthand the pitfalls of interservice rivalry and competition for scarce resources. Not surprisingly, neither he nor Kennan had any desire to become embroiled in the Pentagon's internecine quarrels. Moreover, despite a war scare in March 1948, the ensuing coup d'état that brought down the pro-Western government of Czechoslovakia, the Soviet blockade of access to Berlin, and the rising tempo of communist agitation in Italy and elsewhere, President Harry S. Truman wanted defense spending, for domestic economic reasons, held to $15 billion per year. In these circumstances, as much as they may have wanted to help, there was not a lot that either Kennan or Marshall could realistically do to make Forrestal's life any easier.

Kennan's main contribution to this debate was a comprehensive report (NSC 20/4) to the NSC in November 1948 setting forth basic U.S. national security policy, the first such report of its kind and the forerunner of NSC 68. Prepared in response to Forrestal's request for guidance, NSC 20/4 was a broad-brush treatment. As such, it was practically useless for the purposes Forrestal had in mind of evaluating the various threats the country faced and the relative merits of competing weapons systems and strategies. Notably absent from the report was any mention of nuclear weapons, which the United States continued to monopolize, or the role they should play in American policy and strategy. Although the paper acknowledged that Soviet behavior remained ominous and could precipitate a conflict through miscalculation by one side or the other, it downplayed the immediate danger in view of the Soviet Union's still fragile, war-ravaged economy. In true Kennanesque fashion, NSC 20/4 warned against "excessive" U.S. armaments and recommended instead "a level of military readiness which can be maintained as long as necessary as a deterrent to Soviet aggression."[4]

While the guidance in NSC 20/4 was less specific than Forrestal had sought, it was better than nothing and helped give strategic credibility to the administration's military budget for fiscal year 1950, submitted to Congress early in 1949. Unable to persuade Truman to lift the ceiling on military spending, Forrestal had to look elsewhere to shore up what he and his military advisers, the Joint Chiefs of Staff, considered weaknesses in the country's defense posture. He did so by coming down on the side of the air force and placing increased reliance on nuclear weapons and long-range strategic bombers. Not everyone in the Pentagon agreed with this solution, certainly not disgruntled admirals in the navy, nor in some ways was it the most practical approach to take since atomic bombs and suitably equipped delivery aircraft were as yet in relatively short supply. But it seemed the most viable option at the time and held considerable appeal to an economy-minded president and Congress.

NEW FACES, NEW IDEAS

It was against this background of unrelenting tensions with the Soviet Union, fiscal restraint, and growing reliance on nuclear weapons that Paul H. Nitze became deputy director of the State Department's Policy Planning Staff in the summer of 1949, officially succeeding Kennan as head of the organization on January 1, 1950. In contrast to Kennan, whose entire career had been in the Foreign Service, much of it overseas, Nitze's training and background had been in American high finance, in bond trading as a junior partner of Forrestal's during the interwar years at the New York investment house of Dillon, Reed and Company. At the outset of World War II, Nitze followed Forrestal to Washington to work on economic mobilization matters for the Board of Economic Warfare. Toward the end of 1944, at the age of thirty-six, he joined the War Department's newly organized U.S. Strategic Bombing Survey (USSBS) and spent the next year in Europe and Japan assessing the impact of strategic airpower and the use of nuclear weapons against Hiroshima and Nagasaki. Nitze, though duly impressed by the atomic bomb's destructive force, disagreed with those who saw it as ushering in a revolution in modern warfare and pointed to the equally devastating effects that conventional fire-bombing raids had had on Dresden and Tokyo. "The significance of the atomic bomb," he concluded from his work on the USSBS, "was that it compressed the explosive power of many conventional bombs into one and thus enormously enhanced the effectiveness of a single bomber."[5]

After the war, Nitze postponed returning to his business career and stayed in Washington to work in the State Department on trade matters, economic assistance, and the European Recovery Program. He bought a comfortable brick home on Woodley Road in the fashionable northwest part of Washington, added a new wing to accommodate his growing family, and settled in for what would become a new career in government and public service. Even so, he remained active in his family's extensive business affairs and always considered his tenure in Washington to be temporary, expecting to return someday to Wall Street. In fact, he never did, and while he continued to dabble in business, amassing a substantial fortune in the process, he found that his heart lay in trying to make sense of the intricate details of national security policy.

Nitze owed his appointment as director of policy planning to Truman's new secretary of state, Dean G. Acheson, who replaced the ailing George C. Marshall in January 1949. Among the personnel changes he made was Kennan's transfer from the Policy Planning Staff to the more or less honorific job of counselor. In his memoirs, Kennan characterized his departure from the planning staff as voluntary, the product of bureaucratic procedural changes that threatened to deny him direct access to the secretary of state. However, it also seems clear that, as far as Acheson was concerned, Kennan had outlived his usefulness. Faced with a growing array of foreign policy problems, Acheson wanted to broaden the department's professional base and bolster its analytical capabilities. As secretary of state, he relied increasingly on "outsiders" like Nitze, with backgrounds in business, law, or academia. In effect, the "philosophers" like Kennan found themselves displaced by the "pragmatists" like Nitze. One side effect was to alienate many of the department's careerists, especially its elite circle of Soviet affairs specialists that included Kennan and Charles E. Bohlen, who felt they alone had the experience and credentials for interpreting Soviet behavior. Later, when they were virtually excluded from the preparation of NSC 68, they believed their worst fears confirmed and dismissed the paper's treatment of the Soviet Union as crude and uninformed.

The policies that Acheson and Nitze pushed were not, in fact, much different from those Kennan advocated. All three viewed the containment of Soviet power and influence as the central problem of American foreign policy. Where they parted company was over the role of military force, which Acheson and Nitze viewed as far more integral to the effective conduct of diplomacy. This is not to say that they sought a military showdown with the Soviet Union—far from it. But they wanted as many instruments at their disposal as they could possibly muster. A top priority throughout Acheson's tenure as secretary of state was to strengthen ties between the United States and Europe, a process that included the completion in April 1949 of a military alliance that created the North Atlantic Treaty Organization (NATO) and a companion measure, the Mutual Defense Assistance Program (MDAP), to bolster Western Europe's confidence and depleted military capabilities. To Kennan, these measures placed excessive trust in responses of a military nature and would only antagonize the Soviet Union into more belligerent behavior. Acheson and Nitze, on the other hand, saw them as essential forms of insurance to preserve the gains made under the Marshall Plan.

Looking down the road, Acheson and Nitze were of a mind that the United States needed a more flexible defense posture than the one taking shape by 1949 around an arsenal of nuclear weapons and long-range bombers. However, they received little cooperation from Forrestal's successor at the Pentagon, Louis A. Johnson. A prominent figure in the Democratic Party, Johnson was said to have had ambitions of becoming president of the United States. During the 1948 election, he had headed Truman's fund-raising campaign and, according to the president's daughter, had "proceeded to accomplish miracles."[6] In gratitude for Johnson's help, Truman named him secretary of defense in March 1949 and gave him carte blanche to impose discipline on the armed services and make them toe the line on fiscal policy.

Johnson pursued his mandate with uncommon vigor and in so doing further exacerbated interservice tensions and rivalry. In the spring of 1949, justifying his decision on cost-containment grounds, he peremptorily canceled construction of the USS *United States*, the navy's prototype for a new generation of atomic-capable flush-deck "supercarriers" intended for missions similar to those of the air force's long-range bombers. Seeing their future in jeopardy, many of the navy's senior officers staged a protest and in "leaks" to the press and public hearings before Congress denounced the secretary's policies as an injustice to their service and a danger to national security.

Relations between State and Defense suffered as well from Johnson's advent. While Acheson sought closer collaboration with the Pentagon, Johnson narrowed the opportunities by requiring his subordinates, the secretaries of the military departments, and the Joint Chiefs of Staff to clear all business with the State Department, including even routine contacts, through his immediate office. Secretaries of defense since Johnson's time have customarily issued similar directives, but in 1949 it seemed a sharp departure from the collegial atmosphere and close collaboration between State and Defense that Forrestal had tried to encourage. Many of Johnson's prohibitions on State–Defense contacts were impossible to enforce, and some were simply ignored as a matter of necessity. Yet their overall effect was a severe strain on State–Defense relations that fueled press speculation of an Acheson–Johnson feud. A frustrated Acheson eventually concluded that Johnson must have been "mentally ill." "His conduct," Acheson insisted, "became too outrageous to be explained by mere cussedness. It did not surprise me when some years later he underwent a brain operation."[7]

THE IMMEDIATE ORIGINS OF NSC 68

In the autumn of 1949, two events convinced Nitze and Acheson that the time for a reappraisal of American foreign policy had come. The first was the discovery in early September 1949 that the Soviet Union had recently tested an atomic device and would probably soon have an arsenal of nuclear weapons that could threaten Western Europe or even the United States. Although not unexpected, the Soviet test came several years ahead of predictions, an error in intelligence caused by the Central Intelligence Agency's gross underestimation of the Soviet Union's access to high-grade uranium ore.[8] Heretofore, the United States had relied on the atomic bomb as one of the mainstays of its postwar security posture. "As long as we can outproduce the world, can control the sea and can strike inland with the atomic bomb," Secretary of Defense Forrestal had once observed, "we can assume certain risks otherwise unacceptable."[9] Now, with that formula rendered suspect, it was no longer clear whether the United States could continue to mount effective deterrence and containment of the Soviet Union with the resources it had on hand.

The other development was the creation of the People's Republic of China on October 1, 1949, the culmination of a steady series of military victories by the communist forces of Mao Tse-tung over his Nationalist rival, Chiang Kai-shek. Like the Soviet atomic test, Mao's triumph was foreseeable to those familiar with the situation but a shock to others who had been counting on the Nationalists under Chiang Kai-shek to bolster the American position in the Far East. The result was a backlash of second-guessing and recrimination in Washington. Acheson and Nitze had no doubt that the United States would continue to enjoy a dominant position in Japan and the western Pacific. But along the rim, on the Korean peninsula and in Southeast Asia where East and West were in direct contact, the potential for friction and conflict seemed to go up enormously.

While the need for a reassessment of American policy was self-evident to Acheson and Nitze, it met with stubborn resistance from Secretary of Defense Johnson, who viewed it with suspicion, as if it might become an infringement on his power and authority over the Pentagon. Matters came to a head during an internal debate that took place toward the end of 1949 over whether to develop a so-called superbomb, or thermonuclear bomb, as one means of countering the Soviet atomic test and strengthening U.S. nuclear deterrence. While discussing the issue with Nitze, the chairman of the Atomic Energy Commission, David E. Lilienthal, expressed deep reservations about developing a superbomb without some idea of the effect it might have on the overall international situation and the future of U.S.–Soviet relations. Lilienthal deemed such weapons morally objectionable and regretted the growing role that the nuclear arsenal was coming to play in American defense policy. Nitze concurred that there were legitimate grounds, including moral ones, for concern. But he disagreed with Lilienthal's contention that the superbomb should be delayed until its full implications could be evaluated and ascertained. Stressing the possibility that the Soviets might already be at work on a thermonuclear weapon, Nitze argued that it was only prudent that the United States launch its own H-bomb project concurrently with a review of basic national security policy. "The upshot of this," he found, "was to satisfy Lilienthal's basic argument."[10]

On January 31, 1950, President Truman announced two fateful decisions. First, he authorized accelerated work to determine the feasibility of a thermonuclear weapon, and, second, brushing aside objections from Louis Johnson, he wanted the secretaries of state and defense to collaborate on a reexamination of basic U.S. security policy in light of the changed circumstances arising from the Soviet Union's acquisition of atomic weapons and a possible thermonuclear bomb capability. From the outset, Nitze and his colleagues on the policy review group formed to conduct the inquiry knew that, to do justice to the problems they faced, they would have to interpret their mandate loosely. The resulting report—probably much broader and more detailed than Truman expected—would replace NSC 20/4 as the blueprint of basic American security policy and serve as the guide for similar policy papers generated over the next decade. In Nitze's view, this in itself was perhaps NSC 68's most significant and lasting contribution. "The papers up to the date," he explained, "dealt largely with the major components of policy rather than policy as a whole. . . . I think the important thing about the paper was the comprehensiveness of the approach rather than the particular recommendations contained therein."[11]

Although a collaborative effort between the State and Defense departments, NSC 68 was mainly the product of State's Policy Planning Staff, with Nitze closely overseeing the project from start to finish. Years later, as one of his protégés characterized his work habits, Nitze was "an inveterate problemsolver . . . result-oriented to a fault."[12] Others from the Planning Staff who worked on the project included Robert W. Tufts, George H. Butler, Carlton Savage, Harry H. Schwartz, Dorothy Fosdick (later a key foreign policy adviser to Governor Adlai Stevenson during his campaigns for the presidency and foreign policy adviser to Senator Henry Jackson), and John Paton Davies Jr., who prepared the first draft. Armed with the president's directive, Nitze insisted on full cooperation from the Pentagon. Inputs from the military side came principally from the Joint Chiefs of Staff through their representative, Major General Truman H. Landon, USAF. Nitze remembered Landon as "a wise, straightforward, and competent collaborator."[13] But he was also utterly loyal to his superiors and not inclined to challenge Johnson's economy program. Initially, Landon presented modest proposals to shore up weaknesses here and there, expedite the procurement of new equipment, and correct minor deficiencies in the existing force structure. But after a few weeks, Nitze recalled, Landon become persuaded that "we were serious about doing a basic strategic review and not just writing some papers which would help people promote special projects of one kind or another." Given the change in Landon's outlook, Nitze suspected that "there was, in fact, a revolt from within" the Pentagon taking shape against Johnson's policies of placing economy over preparedness.[14]

After proceeding through six weeks of work and several drafts, Nitze felt it was time for Acheson and Johnson to meet to examine the review group's progress. This meeting, held on March 22, 1950, at the State Department, nearly killed the project. While Nitze had kept Acheson up to date on almost a day-to-day basis, Johnson received only intermittent reports from his personal representative, Major General James H. Burns, an army retiree who worked part time as coordinator for politicomilitary affairs in the Office of the Secretary of Defense. Whether Johnson even bothered to read Burns's reports is problematic. When Johnson arrived for the meeting, he cut short Nitze's oral briefing, denounced the State Department for numerous past discourtesies, and declared that he would take no position until he had time to read the review group's papers in detail. Acheson took Johnson aside, but their inability to hold a civil discussion led to the collapse of the meeting. After Johnson stalked out, the executive secretary of the NSC, James S. Lay, relayed word of the impasse to the White House. "Within the hour," Acheson later recalled, "the president telephoned me, expressing his outrage and telling me to carry on exactly as we had been doing."[15]

From this point on, Johnson's influence within the administration declined steadily as his differences with Acheson became more pronounced. While Johnson was out of town a week later attending a meeting of the NATO defense ministers at The Hague, the review group circulated its report and slipped a bootleg copy to Truman. The Joint Chiefs and the service secretaries uniformly supported its recommendations. Faced with the choice of concurring or of offering an embarrassing lone dissent, Johnson endorsed the report and urged Truman to place it before the NSC for further action. In April the report entered the council's serial number file as NSC 68. Unable to suppress the report, Johnson decided to accept it, though he remained skeptical about whether it would produce any significant change of policy.

ASSESSING THE THREAT

NSC 68 opens with a dramatic comparison of the American and Soviet political systems, underscoring the inherent conflict between them and, by extension, between East and West. The purpose of the American system, as enunciated in the preamble of the Constitution, is "to assure the integrity and vitality of our free society, which is founded upon the dignity and worth of the individual."[16] The purpose of the Soviet system, in contrast, is to assure the supremacy of communist leaders and their "absolute power, first in the Soviet Union and second in the areas now under their control." Characterizing the Soviet Union as a "slave state," pursuing ruthless policies of oppression and exploitation at home and abroad, NSC 68 depicted the world as being divided between two irreconcilable philosophies—one committed to the preservation of freedom, as pursued in the West, and the other committed to the perpetuation of a totalitarian dictatorship bent on nothing less than world domination controlled from Moscow. "What is new," the report argued, "what makes the continuing crisis, is the polarization of power which now inescapably confronts the slave society with the free."

Critics have since tended to dismiss the opening sections of the report as hyperbole, intended either to capture readers' attention (Truman's especially) or to give vent to pent-up Cold War frustrations. Yet a close reading of this part of the report suggests a more serious purpose. Indeed, it suggests a redefinition of the Soviet threat as an almost permanent menace to the American way of life. Up until NSC 68, the prevailing assumption, nurtured by Kennan's optimism, was that containment of the Soviet Union over time would produce internal changes that would alter Soviet behavior, causing a mellowing of Soviet hostility toward the West and eventually the emergence of new Soviet leaders who would be less antagonist, less paranoid, and less bent on expansion. NSC 68 holds out no such hope or little at best. It views the Soviet Union as an implacable foe whose internal political system is self-perpetuating and whose dangerous policies and philosophy are therefore likely to threaten the West for years to come, perhaps indefinitely. Instead of being a transient phenomenon, as depicted by Kennan, the Cold War as viewed in NSC 68 had become the more or less permanent state of Soviet–American relations. It might ease up from time to time, or it might intensify, but it would not go away, even under the pressures brought to bear on the Soviet Union by continuing American containment.

The report then surveys the strengths and weaknesses of the Soviet system. Most dangerous and menacing were the Soviet Union's military capabilities, which NSC 68 found to be "far in excess of those necessary to defend its national territory," leading to the conclusion that their only possible purpose was to help further Moscow's "design for world domination." Military expenditures in the Soviet Union consumed nearly 14 percent of the gross national product (GNP), as against 6 to 7 percent in the United States. Only in atomic armaments did the United States hold a commanding lead, though as time went on this advantage was expected to diminish. Citing the most recent coordinated intelligence estimate, the report predicted a "year of maximum danger" by mid-1954, the point at which, theoretically, the Soviet Union would have a sufficient stockpile of atomic bombs (around 200) to inflict "serious damage" on the United States. Should the Soviet Union successfully develop a thermonuclear capability, the threat would be "tremendously increased."

To counteract this threat, the review group looked at four possible courses of action. Two of these—a return to isolationism and the initiation of a preventive war—the group dismissed as impractical and inadvisable. The historic and traditional role of the United States, the report argued, was to provide world leadership and to forestall wars, not start them. A third option—to pursue a continuation of current policies—seemed no less ill advised. "From the military point of view," NSC 68 said, "the actual and potential capabilities of the United States, given a continuation of current and projected programs, will become less and less effective as a war deterrent." This left the fourth and final option, the only one the report found realistic and prudent— "a substantial and rapid building-up of strength in the free world . . . to support a firm policy intended to check and roll back the Kremlin's drive for world domination."

To preserve credible deterrence and to prepare for any possible future emergency, NSC 68 urged the United States to step up nuclear weapons production and to "increase as rapidly as possible our general air, ground and sea strength and that of our allies to a point where we are militarily not so heavily dependent on atomic weapons." Within the next four years, the United States should have forces in being or readily available to defend the Western Hemisphere, protect the mobilization base at home, conduct offensive operations on a scale "sufficient to destroy vital elements of the Soviet war-making capacity," defend lines of communication, and provide aid to allies. Additionally, and as part of a "comprehensive and decisive program," the report endorsed the development of "an adequate political and economic framework for the achievement of our long-range objectives," a "substantial increase" in American military expenditures, an enlarged program of foreign military assistance, increases in foreign economic aid, intensification of intelligence activities and covert operations, and stronger measures for internal security and civil defense.

The need for these measures followed logically from what the policy review group perceived as the principal source of danger—"a strong surprise blow" similar to the Japanese attack on Pearl Harbor in 1941. The warning implicit in NSC 68 was that the United States could ill afford a similar disaster, least of all one mounted by an enemy using nuclear weapons. The purpose of rearming, therefore, was not merely to deter the Soviets from launching an attack but to be able to absorb the first strike if it should come and to have sufficient conventional and nuclear forces survive to respond effectively. Hence, the call for a peacetime buildup that would reduce the need for protracted mobilization in wartime and assure the successful conduct of military operations until the enemy capitulated or reinforcements arrived.

While the authors of NSC 68 had a healthy respect for nuclear weapons, they did not view them as necessarily decisive or likely to become so in the foreseeable future, given the limited size of nuclear arsenals at the time. If the United States could take steps to absorb a nuclear attack, so could the Soviet Union. A surprise atomic attack would indeed be devastating but not decisive if the necessary precautionary steps were taken and forces-in-being were sufficiently dispersed and survivable. Here, Nitze's influence becomes strikingly apparent. Of those who served on the NSC 68 policy review group, Nitze had more firsthand experience with the effects of nuclear weapons than anyone. As vice chairman of the USSBS in 1945, he was among the earliest to inspect Hiroshima and Nagasaki. Although the USSBS investigation confirmed the awesome destructive power of the atomic bomb, it also turned up some surprising findings that left Nitze skeptical: in Hiroshima rail traffic had resumed forty-eight hours after the attack; tunnel shelters in Nagasaki had provided effective protection from the attack, even at ground zero; nonradioactive vegetation was soon growing again immediately under the centers of the explosions; and factories on the periphery of the cities were virtually undamaged, out of operation only for lack of materials. "Frankly," Nitze later recalled, "the emotional effect of seeing what had happened at Darmstadt was greater, in a surprising way, than it was at Hiroshima and Nagasaki."[17]

Yet in the final analysis, it was not a military confrontation with the Soviets that the authors most feared. Rather, it was the prospect that over time there might occur a weakening of "the integrity and vitality of our system" brought on by a progressive erosion of values or a deteriorating willingness to defend them. "Even if there were no Soviet Union," the report contended, "we would [still] face the great problem of the free society, accentuated manyfold in this industrial age, of reconciling order, security, the need for participation, with the requirements of freedom." In other words, the defense of freedom was a constant, ongoing battle. That it now involved the Soviet Union, a country with immense military assets, did not in any way alter the nature of the struggle, though it did necessitate a redoubling of American awareness, dedication, and effort. Increased military power was of primary importance because it represented the most visible demonstration of will, a signal to Moscow that the United States would go to any length to protect its freedoms and thwart the Kremlin's "design."

The key finding of NSC 68 was its all-encompassing call for "a rapid and sustained buildup of the political, economic, and military strength of the free world." The key word is *sustained*, which implied a sharp departure from previous assumptions governing national security policy. Above all, NSC 68 demanded a reassessment of Marshall's dictum that the American people would not tolerate open-ended foreign commitments or heavy defense expenditures year after year. During the preparation of the report, the members of the policy review group held lengthy discussions about whether the program they envisioned could be sustained and whether the American people had the will to pursue it. The members were confident that the United States could mobilize the necessary resources but less sure whether the American people would be willing to bear the burdens for an indefinite time and make the necessary sacrifices. Marshall's response, had be been asked to comment, would probably have been "no." The review group, perhaps knowing what it was likely to hear, apparently made no attempt to solicit Marshall's advice. However, it did consult with others, including former Undersecretary of State Robert A. Lovett; J. Robert Oppenheimer, who had overseen the Los Alamos atomic bomb project in World War II; Harvard president and chemist James B. Conant; Ernest O. Lawrence, winner of the 1939 Nobel Prize in physics; Henry D. Smyth, a former member of the Manhattan Project and author of a 1945 study of the program's accomplishments; and Chester I. Barnard of the Rockefeller Foundation. All agreed that public acceptance of the program could not be taken for granted and that the government would need all the assistance it could get to mobilize and sustain public support.

Initially, however, it was President Truman's acceptance rather than the public's that the policy review group needed. One way of doing this was to delete financial estimates from the report and leave the president free of any binding prior commitments should he choose to approve the report for implementation. Privately, Nitze and others who worked on NSC 68 estimated the cost at between $35 billion and $50 billion annually over the next several years. While Nitze made his personal estimate known to Secretary Acheson, there is no evidence that Acheson ever conveyed it to Truman. Given the president's tough-minded approach to money matters, it followed logically that if he could be persuaded that the danger was as great as it seemed, requiring all the necessary sacrifices, so could most other people. The report conceded that the program it outlined would be "costly" and probably require higher taxes to avoid deficit budgets. But it simply did not belabor these points.

Much of the subsequent criticism of NSC 68 has focused on its rhetoric, which for a "top-secret" policy document seems unduly sharp and harsh, as though the paper may have had some propaganda purpose. Throughout his lifetime, Nitze asserted that the report was meant solely for internal consumption and that the phrasing and choice of words was purely for illustration purposes. "We wrote it that way for clarity," Nitze insisted.[18] Be that as it may, the paper still relied heavily on questionable generalizations that gave East–West relations the aura of a black-and-white struggle. The idea that there was a distinct dichotomy in the world between the "slave" society in the East and a "free" society in the West was a gross oversimplification since very few countries outside the Soviet bloc were at that time free by American standards of democracy. Many countries in Asia and Africa remained colonial holdings from the days of European imperialism. In Latin America, right-wing authoritarian regimes abounded. Moreover, communism was by no means the monolith as NSC 68 portrayed it. Yugoslavia's defection was already an accomplished fact, and Acheson was counting on a similar occurrence in China to thwart the extension of Soviet power and influence in the Far East. Yet the picture of communism in NSC 68 is that of a galvanized movement, directed from Moscow and virtually impervious to accommodation with the West.

Perhaps the most disturbing part of NSC 68 was its treatment of nuclear weapons. Even though it urged substantial increases in conventional forces, NSC 68 regarded nuclear weapons as crucial to American security and likely to remain so as the Soviets expanded their atomic arsenal. This implied that the more weapons the Soviets stockpiled, the more the United States should stockpile—a classic action/reaction phenomenon. Where this process might lead or be expected to end, the report failed to say, though it did suggest that both sides eventually would acquire offsetting nuclear capabilities. Until that point was reached, however, the report cast doubt on the probability that U.S. reliance on nuclear weapons would significantly diminish. Acheson wanted a better balance between conventional and nuclear forces. But he could not have been overly reassured that such a balance would soon be achieved.

Yet for all its faults and weaknesses, NSC 68 was still a remarkable document, distinctly representative of the troubled, uncertain times in which it was written. An emotional yet analytical paper at the same time, it addressed an issue that was without precedent in American experience—the rise of an adversary with seemingly limitless ambitions, committed to an ideology that claimed the tide of history was on its side, willing to allocate enormous resources to carry out those ambitions. Since World War II, in facing up to this challenge, the United States had rethought its role in world affairs and had undertaken initiatives—full and active membership in the United Nations, the Marshall Plan, the Greek-Turkish aid program, and NATO—that earlier generations of Americans would have seen as beyond the pale of contemplation. Yet for all the effort and resources that had been expended to counter the communist danger, it seemed only to grow more bold and menacing.

The point that NSC 68 endeavored to drive home was that there was no "quick fix" to the problem of Soviet power, no easy solution that would guarantee peace, prosperity, and international harmony. That a confrontation with the Soviets might escalate into global nuclear war compounded the problem, making it all the more urgent for the United States to raise its level of preparedness. The American people were not accustomed to such continuous psychological exposure to these dangers; NSC 68 clearly implied that they would have to adjust lest they risk losing the values and freedoms they cherished.

REACTIONS AND IMPLEMENTATION

Despite the impression that Acheson conveyed in his memoirs, Truman did not approve NSC 68 as soon as he officially received it in April 1950. In fact, his initial reaction to the report was one of typical caution. Reluctant to commit himself to new or enlarged programs without knowing what they might cost, he directed the creation of an ad hoc interagency committee, including his economic and budget advisers, to assess the report's requirements and potential impact. At the same time, Secretary of Defense Johnson ordered the Joint Chiefs of Staff to prepare itemized listings of force-level deficiencies. These studies were still in progress when the Korean War erupted on June 25, 1950. Confronted with the sudden outbreak of hostilities and fearing an escalation of communist aggression, Truman sent U.S. combat troops into Korea and notified Congress that he would need supplemental appropriations for defense and military assistance totaling $10 billion, the first of several such requests he would make before the end of the year. Finally, on September 30, 1950, he got around to signing a memorandum (NSC 68/1) approving NSC 68 "as a statement of policy to be followed over the next four or five years."[19]

This sequence of events raises the intriguing question of what Truman would have done about NSC 68 had the Korean War not intervened. Most involved in policymaking at the time, including Nitze, recognized that NSC 68 presaged a major departure of policy that would radically alter priorities at home and drastically expand the scale and scope of American commitments abroad. Even if Truman had not approved the report, however, it seems likely that the results would have been more or less the same because of the worries generated by the Korean War. NSC 68 provided a new rationale that effectively subordinated most other concerns to meeting the needs of national security. Presidents invariably hedge major decisions of this sort as long as possible, and Truman, despite his celebrated motto that "the buck stops here," was no exception. He took more than five months to make up his mind on the report and then acted only after events seemed to fix his course.

Nitze believed that, sooner or later, events would have forced the president's hand. As early as February 1950, when NSC 68 was still in its early gestation stage, Nitze expressed growing concern over signs of "a boldness that is essentially new" in Soviet behavior—an apparent willingness on the part of the Soviet Union, emboldened by its new nuclear capability, to assume risk that it had eschewed previously. While not ruling out the possibility of general war if the Soviets miscalculated and went too far, Nitze anticipated that they would localize their aggression in areas where the United States had marginal interests and would be hard pressed to respond. Among the areas in which the Soviets seemed most likely to foment troubles, Nitze singled out Indochina, Berlin, Austria, the United Nations, and Korea.

Nitze's assessment was essentially a hunch. He had no solid proof that the Soviets were planning something, nor did intelligence reports predict a general worsening of the world situation. According to the U.S. embassy in Moscow, in its annual tour d'horizon report that reached Washington just a few days after NSC 68 went to the president, the situation was no better and no worse than a year before. If anything, despite the Soviet A-bomb test and the fall of China, the signing of the North Atlantic Treaty and the preliminary implementation of MDAP had yielded "a slight net gain for the West."[20] In other words, there seemed nothing to provoke undue alarm, comparable to the situation two years earlier when the Soviets overthrew the Czech government, made menacing gestures toward Norway and Finland, and launched the Berlin blockade. At that time, the United States still had a monopoly on nuclear weapons. Even so, this had not stopped the Soviets from seeking to make gains and to exploit weak spots where they could. Given this perspective, it seemed to Nitze only logical that with a nuclear capability, the Soviets would feel more confident than ever and would try somehow to capitalize on their newly acquired strength.

Nitze's most disturbing "evidence" of Soviet malevolence came from Alexander Sachs, an economist with Lehman Brothers. Sachs arrived at Nitze's office one day in the spring of 1950 with a set of papers warning that the Soviets saw the "correlation of forces" as having turned in their favor.

Sachs believed the Soviets would act cautiously at first, probably through one or more reliable satellites. From this he further deduced that an attack on South Korea loomed in the very near future. But as accurate as Sachs's warning proved to be, it was not the first such report to cross Nitze's desk. Indeed, similar assessments had recurred regularly in official channels ever since the first signs of a North Korean military buildup in 1947. In any case, Nitze doubted whether much could be done to forestall a conflict until Truman reached a decision on NSC 68.

Even without Korea, Truman probably would have approved NSC 68, if only to demonstrate his support for and confidence in Acheson's policies and advice. However, it seems clear that he would not have given it the full funding that Nitze and his collaborators on the review group had in mind. Historians generally agreed that, without the impetus of Korea, an increase of between $3 billion and $5 billion annually was about as much as Truman would have approved. This was a piffling amount, to be sure, compared with subsequent appropriations brought on by the Korean War, but it appears to follow from the instructions Truman issued to his budget director, Frederick J. Lawton, at a meeting on May 23. "The President indicated," Lawton recalled in his diary, "that we were to continue to raise any questions that we had on this program and that it definitely was not as large in scope as some of the people seem to think."[21]

Still, any increase would have served Acheson's immediate purpose, for it would have represented a tacit repudiation of Johnson's economy program and, with it, the beginning of the end of policies predicated on economic feasibility rather than security objectives. This in itself would have been a significant departure from the prevailing practice since World War II. But it probably would not have been enough to guarantee the continuation of a "sustained" buildup as called for in NSC 68. Only with the onset of the Korean emergency did Truman accept the full range of NSC 68 recommendations and, more importantly, the thinking behind them.

By all standards, the Korean War buildup was an impressive accomplishment. From a prewar base of less than $13 billion in fiscal year 1950, national defense spending soared to $48 billion in fiscal year 1953, nearly a fourfold increase that consumed 13.5 percent of the GNP, compared with 4.8 percent three years earlier. At the same time, the United States poured additional billions into a greatly expanded military assistance program, added new facilities to accelerate the production of tactical and strategic nuclear weapons, built a chain of overseas air and sea bases that virtually encircled the Soviet Union and China, and strengthened its covert operations and psychological warfare capabilities. The rearmament of Germany began, NATO acquired an integrated multinational high command, and four divisions of

American combat troops deployed to Europe. Elsewhere, the United States signed a mutual security agreement with Japan, concluded a similar arrangement with Australia and New Zealand, and assumed much of the financial burden of keeping French forces fighting communism in Indochina, while American troops did the same in Korea.

Despite a lengthy list of accomplishments, however, the job seemed never ending, the goals almost always beyond reach. At one point late in 1950, Nitze expressed astonishment at "the enormous cost" of the buildup and the "rather small forces" it had yielded thus far.[22] Yet it was not simply the cost of rearmament that gave Nitze cause for concern. With clever budget management, a surge in the economy from defense orders, and acceptance of the need from time to time for deficit financing (eventually to become an almost routine part of the budget process), fiscal problems took on relatively less importance than before. Rather, it was the continuing uncertainty over the public's willingness to sustain the buildup that most worried Nitze and its other supporters. One result was the emergence of public interest groups like the first bipartisan Committee on the Present Danger, which dedicated itself to educating the public on the need for a strong defense posture. Still, it was an uphill struggle, one made all the harder by the stalemated war in Korea and seemingly fruitless negotiations with an inscrutable enemy. The outbreak of the war had elevated NSC 68 to the status of national policy, yet, ironically, the longer the war continued, the harder it became to rally a national following for that policy. As Acheson soon realized ,the war diverted attention from the true danger. "We are fighting the second team," he conceded, "whereas the real enemy is the Soviet Union."[23]

The backlash came in November 1952 with the election of a new administration that promised to end the Korean War as its first order of business. Once in office, Eisenhower went even further, reimposing ceilings on military spending and reverting to defense policies that again stressed primary reliance on nuclear weapons, now more heavily than ever. Rejecting the notion in NSC 68 that the nation should prepare itself for a "year of maximum danger," Eisenhower wanted policies and programs suitable for the "long haul." As Kennan had experienced three years earlier, Nitze saw his power and influence wane, as his views on national security policy grew to be more and more at odds with those of Eisenhower and his secretary of state, John Foster Dulles. Although Nitze was conditionally offered a new job in the Defense Department, the appointment never materialized because of the opposition of Republican conservatives in Congress who felt that Nitze had too closely identified with Acheson and the Truman administration. As much as he disagreed with the new administration's philosophy, friends of his said he deeply regretted not being kept on.

THE LEGACY OF NSC 68

The Eisenhower administration was by no means the end of Nitze's career in national security. Although out of public service for the remainder of the 1950s, he returned to serve in subcabinet posts in the Defense Department during the Kennedy and Johnson administrations and as a senior adviser and negotiator on arms control matters in the 1970s and 1980s. Throughout, Nitze remained the champion of a robust defense posture along the lines laid out in NSC 68. Equally if not more important, he became convinced that NSC 68's most useful contribution lay in its "organized approach," which became almost standard procedure from 1950 on, to the development and implementation of national security policy.[24] Not every administration followed the same practices or procedures or came up with the same solutions. Yet all agreed, to one degree or another, that having a general blueprint of goals and priorities was a useful asset. Even President John F. Kennedy, who disdained the prescriptive policy approach used by the Truman and Eisenhower administrations, came to realize that it was practically impossible to manage the allocation of resources without a governing concept, hence his reliance on Secretary of Defense Robert S. McNamara's annual "posture statements" and draft presidential memorandums setting forth not only the details of politicomilitary programs but also the philosophy and ultimate purposes behind them.

The institutionalization of national security became NSC 68's most enduring—and controversial—legacy. Where Nitze saw NSC 68 fostering a more sensible and systematic approach to policy and the allocation of resources, critics later deplored it for giving rise to a national security state and a foreign policy increasingly dependent on military power. Obviously, opinions have differed considerably over NSC 68's long-term impact. Yet all would agree that it profoundly reshaped the federal government's management of national security. Prior to NSC 68, during the interwar years and in the immediate aftermath of World War II, expenditures for defense and national security were calculated on the "remainder method," a procedure that gave priority to meeting domestic needs and fixed charges before determining the available resources for defense and national security. But from NSC 68 on, the ground rules changed. Although presidents continued to set ceilings or use other devices to control costs, they treated national security as another line item in the budget, with a more or less equally valid claim on resources as domestic programs. Technically, the military budget fell under the category of "discretionary" spending. But over time, as a growing number of programs in the defense budget became fixed expenditures, there was less and less "discretionary" room left.

The result was a vast expansion of the national security system, including not only the military but also the intelligence community, foreign military assistance, arms control, atomic energy, and other related programs. Largest of all was the Pentagon's share. On average during the 1950s and 1960s, the military budget consumed 10 percent or more of the nation's GNP, compared with less than 5 percent prior to the run-up to World War II. Even though the authors of NSC 68 had warned that the country might eventually rebel against such expenditures, lobbying and information groups like the first Committee on the Present Danger did an effective job of getting the message across and mobilizing sustained support. What emerged was a broad, bipartisan national consensus that kept the Soviet threat in the forefront and the NSC 68 commitment to national security alive, thriving, and in some ways unassailable.

By the mid- to late 1960s, however, the consensus was breaking down along lines still recognizable more than three decades later. Opposition to the war in Vietnam and the emergence of costly, high-profile domestic programs like the Great Society challenged the underlying assumptions governing basic national security policy and the allocation of resources. Technological breakthroughs in guided missiles, strategic defense, and other areas once seen as the panacea for national security now threatened an alarming, open-ended strategic arms competition with the Soviet Union. Some, Nitze among them, turned to arms control as a possible solution. But others, most notably in the liberal wing of the Democratic Party, became disillusioned and suspicious of practically anything that smacked of national security or the armed forces.

Despite challengers, the military's claim on resources was hard to dislodge. Even under the constrained spending of the 1970s, defense continued to consume on average 5 percent of the country's GNP, rising to more than 6 percent during the Reagan buildup of the 1980s. At the same time, the defense establishment invested heavily in theoretical studies of new strategic concepts and research and development of new weapons and other systems. Ronald Reagan's Strategic Defense Initiative (SDI)—derided as "Star Wars" by its critics—was a notable outgrowth of this process, though only one of many such projects.

Most of the work done on SDI and other technical programs was carried out by defense contractors and consulting firms that grew up and prospered during the Cold War in the shadow of the Pentagon. Many were private, profit-making enterprises; others were semipublic and operated under the auspices of major universities. While it was clear that the number of consultants and defense contractors increased enormously in the decades following World War II, no one was ever able to determine with much accuracy how many there were, who they were, or how much they cost taxpayers. According to a

General Accounting Office audit in 1988, the Department of Defense devoted anywhere between $2.8 billion and $15.9 billion for consulting services in fiscal year 1987, excluding individual consultants earning less than $25,000.

Whether these developments constituted the creation of a "national security state" and all that that implies remains a matter of judgment. Certainly, from 1950 on, military power played a larger role in American foreign policy than it did before. But was this change truly the watershed that Ernest R. May and others have made it out to be? Or was it not a continuation, albeit at a more intense and sustained level, of events already in motion? As dramatic and consequential as the post-1950 expansion of the defense establishment may seem, it had its roots in decisions taken earlier and was wholly consistent with the transformation ushered in by the 1941 attack on Pearl Harbor and the ensuing experiences of World War II. By the time the war ended, it was practically an article of faith in the executive and legislative branches that the United States needed a larger, stronger, and more closely unified military establishment than it had had prior to the war. Operating on this premise, the armed services planned and proposed a permanent peacetime military structure of unprecedented size—ideally, an army of twenty-five active and reserve divisions, a seventy-group air force, and a two-ocean navy of over 300 combatant vessels organized around powerful carrier battle groups.

Although the fate of this proposed postwar force remained in flux, the peacetime military establishment that emerged after the war was still substantially bigger and more formidable than any the country had known, with a budget more than three times larger than before the war. The collapse of the wartime Grand Alliance and deteriorating relations between the United States and the Soviet Union gave advocates of a strong defense posture a further boost. With the outbreak of hostilities in Korea in the summer of 1950, the worst-case scenario that Nitze and others had been arguing seemed fully confirmed. Although Truman was slow to come around until events in Korea forces his hand, his acceptance of NSC 68 reflected not so much a change of basic policy as a recognition that that policy needed more substance behind it.

Nitze never liked the idea, suggested by some, that NSC 68 was the product of its times and, as such, subject to obsolescence as the Cold War evolved and eventually wound down. He preferred to think of it as a timeless, objective analysis, standing on its own merits, a guide to the long-term preservation of American institutions and values. Critics countered that those institutions and values became endangered, to one degree or another, by the very process of defending them. But from Nitze's standpoint, the Soviet threat outweighed all other dangers. What worried him most of all was whether the country had the will to stand up to that danger as long as it took to defeat it.

Worst of all would have been the failure to act and do nothing. Although Nitze and his colleagues might have framed their arguments differently, toning down the rhetoric and qualifying their recommendations, they elected to portray the Soviet threat in stark black-and-white terms to draw the utmost attention to the problem and the solutions they proposed. That events conveniently conspired to support their arguments doubtless assured NSC 68 greater credibility and impact than it otherwise would have enjoyed.

NOTES

1. Ernest R. May, "The Cold War," in Joseph S. Nye Jr., *The Making of America's Soviet Policy* (New Haven, Conn.: Yale University Press, 1984), 221.

2. [George F. Kennan], "The Sources of Soviet Conduct," *Foreign Affairs* 25 (July 1947): 566–82.

3. George F. Kennan, *Memoirs, 1925–1950* (Boston: Little, Brown, 1967), 320–21.

4. NSC 20/4, "U.S. Objectives with Respect to the USSR to Counter Soviet Threats to U.S. Security," November 23, 1948, U.S. Department of State, *Foreign Relations of the United States 1948*, vol. I (Washington, D.C.: U.S. Government Printing Office, 1976), 662–69 (hereafter cited as *FRUS*).

5. Paul H. Nitze, *From Hiroshima to Glasnost: At the Center of Decision—A Memoir* (New York: Grove, Weidenfeld, 1989), 43.

6. Margaret Truman, *Harry S. Truman* (New York: Morrow, 1973), 20.

7. Dean Acheson, *Present at the Creation: My Years in the State Department* (New York: Norton, 1969), 374.

8. See Donald P. Steury, "How the CIA Missed Stalin's Bomb," *Studies in Intelligence* 49, no. 1 (2005), 19–26.

9. Forrestal to Chan Gurney, December 8, 1947, in *The Forrestal Diaries*, ed. Walter Millis and E. S. Duffield (New York: Viking Press, 1951), 350–51.

10. Interview no. 2 with Nitze by Richard D. McKinzie, July 17, 1975, Arlington, Virginia, Oral History Collection, Harry S. Truman Library, Independence, Missouri, 8.

11. Nitze testimony, June 17, 1960, in U.S. Congress, Senate, Committee on Government Operations, Subcommittee on National Policy Machinery, *Hearings: Organizing for National Security: The Department of State, the Policy Planning Staff, and the National Security Council* 86, no. 2 (Washington, D.C.: U.S. Government Printing Office, 1960), pt. 6, 879.

12. Richard Perle quoted in Strobe Talbott, *The Master of the Game: Paul Nitze and the Nuclear Peace* (New York: Alfred A. Knopf, 1988), 168.

13. Nitze, *From Hiroshima to Glasnost*, 93.

14. McKinzie interview with Nitze, no. 4, 11, 14.

15. Acheson, *Present at the Creation*, 373.

16. Quotations are from the official version of NSC 68 that appears in U.S. Department of State, *FRUS 1950*, vol. I (Washington, D.C.: U.S. Government Printing Office, 1976), 234–92.

17. Interview with Nitze by Walter Miale, April 14, 1976, Nitze Papers, Library of Congress.

18. Interview with Nitze by John N. Dick and James C. Hasdorff, Part I, October 25–28, 1977, Washington, D.C., U.S. Air Force Oral History Program, 247.

19. U.S. Department of State, *FRUS 1950*, vol. I, pt. 1, 400.

20. U.S. Department of State, *FRUS 1950*, vol. IV (Washington, D.C.: U.S. Government Printing Office, 1980), 1171.

21. Lawton Diary, May 23, 1950, Papers of Frederick J. Lawton, Harry S. Truman Library, Independence, Missouri, quoted in Samuel R. Williamson Jr., and Steven L. Rearden, *The Origins of U.S. Nuclear Strategy, 1945–1950* (New York: St. Martin's Press, 1993), 138.

22. U.S. Department of State, *FRUS 1950*, vol. I, 420.

23. U.S. Department of State, *FRUS 1950*, vol. VII (Washington, D.C.: U.S. Government Printing Office, 1976), 1326.

24. Nitze, "Postscript to NSC 68," in *NSC-68: Forging the Strategy of Containment*, ed. S. Nelson Drew (Washington, D.C.: National Defense University, 1994), 131.

• 2 •

"The Devil's Advocate": Robert Bowie, Western European Integration, and the German Problem, 1953–1954

Chris Tudda*

*O*n August 30, 1954, the French National Assembly rejected the European Defense Community (EDC) treaty, seriously jeopardizing the conception of collective security envisioned by President Dwight D. Eisenhower and Secretary of State John Foster Dulles. Eisenhower and Dulles believed that the EDC could solve four important national security problems. First, the EDC would serve as the military component of the North Atlantic Treaty Organization (NATO), the collective security organization aimed at protecting Western Europe from the Soviet Union. Second, U.S. policymakers believed that Western Europe could not be successfully defended without German participation. The Joint Chiefs of Staff (JCS) even preferred full German membership in NATO to the EDC. The absorption of German forces would prevent it from attacking either Western Europe or the Soviet Union again. Third, a supranational army in Western Europe, including the western half of Germany, would end the conflict between France and Germany that had plagued the Continent for generations. Finally, the EDC would allow the United States to reconfigure its defense strategies and priorities and ultimately reduce its defense budget. The administration would provide "security" with fiscal "solvency."[1]

Two days later, Robert Bowie, the director of the State Department's Policy Planning Staff (PPS), asked his European specialist, Lewis Fuller, to examine the European reaction to the treaty's defeat. Fuller reported widespread "shock and emotional reaction to the event" but "little evidence of a considered appraisal of the situation in Paris and elsewhere." While publicly

*Note: The views presented here are my own and do not necessarily reflect those of the U.S. Department of State or the U.S. government. I would like to thank my colleague Kristin L. Ahlberg for her helpful comments and suggestions.

angry, the allies actually seemed content because this kept Germany divided and West German troops out of the alliance. Germany, on the other hand, was furious and now "demanded restoration of full sovereignty, including the right to rearm," the one result the allies had wished to prevent.[2]

This chapter focuses on how Robert Bowie contributed to the Eisenhower administration's oftentimes painful and exasperating and only moderately successful attempts to bring Western Europe together and present a united front against the Soviet Union. I concentrate on 1953 and 1954, when he, the PPS, and the White House wrestled with how to integrate West Germany into the EDC.

Strengthening U.S.–NATO relations became the most crucial component of President Eisenhower's approach to national security policy. Picking up from where the Truman administration had left off, Eisenhower and his secretary of state, John Foster Dulles, labored to ensure that Western Europe developed a sustainable means of self-defense, in particular through the mechanism of the EDC. Even before he became president, Truman had asked and Eisenhower had agreed to serve as supreme commander of NATO. There he urged the French and Germans, with only limited success, to overcome their hostility in favor of political and military European integration. Other NATO countries, in particular the Netherlands, endorsed the EDC because of Eisenhower's support for the program.[3]

The two leaders understood that the French and Germans would not readily bury the hatchet between them, and they worried that too much political pressure from Washington might backfire. Yet they also knew that the public in both countries had tired of war and hoped that this sentiment could be communicated to each nation's leadership. If Western Europe remained fractured, the Soviet Union would probe the inherent weaknesses within the alliance, try to turn European public opinion against the United States with tempting offers of "neutrality" and conditional German reunification, and try to peel off wavering NATO nations with promises of the establishment of a "nuclear-free" Western Europe. This concern only increased after Soviet Premier Josef Stalin died in March 1953 and his successors embarked on a "peace offensive" toward the West. The administration then faced a potential public relations crisis because many Europeans argued that the United States should engage the new Soviet leadership and settle the German problem.

A lawyer by profession, Robert Bowie served in the U.S. Army during World War II. In 1945, at the conclusion of the war, he became the personal assistant to General Lucius Clay, the military governor of Germany, and became directly involved in German reconstruction. Bowie's optimistic report about German efforts at denazification convinced Clay and the Truman administration to turn over control of day-to-day activities to Germans. A year later, he left the government and spent the next four years as a professor at Harvard Law School, returning to government service in 1950 as legal adviser to John J. McCloy, the U.S. high commissioner to Germany (HICOG), where he wrote early drafts of a constitution for West Germany.

Documentary evidence strongly suggests that Bowie and McCloy independently supported the creation of the EDC. In 1952, McCloy said that "there is just no other way open" to the path of European integration. In a long personal report to McCloy, Bowie observed that "dangerous complications in the local political situation and tremendous forces from the East . . . actively" opposed "German integration with the West." Each man reinforced each other's commitment to Western European integration. McCloy forwarded Bowie's report to President Truman's secretary of state, Dean Acheson, and argued that the United States must back European integration in order to maintain U.S. involvement on the Continent.[4] Bowie also played a vital role in the legal "dismantling" of the German coal and steel cartels in the Ruhr, "the essential condition" for the "free trade of coal and steel" in Western Europe and a key element in the development of economic and political interdependence in the region.[5]

In 1952, he returned to Cambridge and joined Harvard President James B. Conant, a prominent Eisenhower supporter, in backing the Committee on the Present Danger (CPD). Conant created the CPD to gin up public support for a sustained international role for the United States against the Soviet Union and also to combat what he and Eisenhower considered Truman's ineffectual policies. Even though he was a Democrat, Bowie supported Eisenhower in both the Republican primary (where he faced the anti-internationalist Ohio Senator Robert Taft) and the general election against Democrat Adlai Stevenson.[6]

After Eisenhower's election in 1952, both McCloy and Clay recommended Bowie to Dulles and Eisenhower. McCloy told Dulles's special assistant, Roderick O'Connor, that Bowie was "very intelligent, highly articulate," and possessed "a sharp incisive mind." But he was not a yes-man. Prone to be "contentious in argument," Bowie had an "intelligent intolerance for the stupid" and "a certain little curl to his lip." But, McCloy added, "if you are looking for incisive thinking, he is top-grade." Impressed, Dulles asked Erwin Griswold, the dean of the Harvard Law School, to release Bowie from his faculty contract so he could join the State Department. Dulles wanted Bowie to fill "one of the most important assignments there is"—the director of the PPS—and serve as State's representative on the National Security Council (NSC). Policy Planning, created by former Secretary of State George Marshall and its first director, Soviet specialist George F. Kennan, was responsible for long-range planning and became the office known for its independent thinking and willingness to diverge from the department's consensus. In other words, the director could not be a yes-man, and Bowie filled the bill perfectly. In May 1953, after the end of the spring semester, Bowie officially joined the State Department as director of the PPS.[7]

He quickly developed a reputation for being Secretary Dulles's "devil's advocate." In tandem with his staff members, which included future ambassador to the Soviet Union Jacob Beam, he developed numerous "think pieces." These illustrate that Bowie possessed the backbone to both challenge Dulles's policies and bare many uncomfortable truths about the challenges of European integration. Bowie, Townsend Hoopes has argued, "became an important catalyst on a range of major issues," including Germany. "Bowie's imagination and relative liberality" and his rigorous devotion to logical reasoning forced Dulles to confront some disturbing realities about the domestic and foreign policies of European states that directly clashed with U.S. interests. Andrew McFadzean, who also called Bowie a devil's advocate, refers to him as an "institutionalist" who, like Clay, McCloy, Conant, and Eisenhower, believed in "international cooperation, the resolution of conflicts through mediation and the changes from the emphasis and use of military force to a greater recognition of political, economic and popular power and economic interdependence."[8]

Dillon Anderson, Eisenhower's national security adviser from 1955 to 1956, recalled that Bowie helped formulate foreign policy by "question[ing] Dulles from below." Richard Immerman has noted that Dulles was so well prepared during NSC meetings because he had been extensively briefed by "the equally argumentative" Bowie, who continually bombarded his boss with contrary advice. Their "epic debates . . . became legendary inside the State Department, although unknown outside of it."[9]

In spite of these qualities, for the historian Robert Bowie remains an elusive figure. His name appears on relatively few of the voluminous documents available in Department of State records at the National Archives and in the John Foster Dulles collection at Princeton University. As a result, there is little written evidence of his "epic battles" with Dulles, at least on the subject of European integration. The researcher must extrapolate his beliefs from these sources. The oral interviews that he gave to the Eisenhower Oral History Project at Columbia University and for television programs such as CNN's series *The Cold War* and his monograph *Waging Peace* are policy oriented and therefore similarly unrevealing. He barely mentions his role in any of the decision-making processes. While his refusal to engage in self-promotion is as admirable as it is unusual and his loyalty to Dulles unquestionable, by all accounts he played an important role as he questioned department orthodoxies.

PPS records indicate that he orally directed his staff to prepare studies on subjects such as Germany, the EDC, nuclear and national security strategy, and long-term policy analyses. The staff then prepared papers and reports that he read and approved and then passed on to Secretary Dulles in what can only be described as terse, no-nonsense language. Of course, this is exactly what Dulles (and former General Eisenhower, who valued short, to-the-point memoranda rather than long-winded analyses) wanted from his PPS director and why Bowie was chosen to fill this crucial post. But like his public interviews and writings, the researcher must read into these short memoranda and the PPS reports in order to provide a more complete picture of Robert Bowie the foreign policymaker.

In his first State of the Union Address in January 1953, Eisenhower had lamented that "the problem of security demands closer cooperation among the nations of Europe than has been known to date." He reiterated the link between U.S. national security and European security and pressed for passage of the EDC in Europe. Indeed, every sector of the U.S. government wanted the EDC because they believed that Western Europe could not be successfully defended without German participation. As noted earlier, the JCS actually preferred "full German membership in NATO" to the EDC. The EDC would absorb German forces, which would prevent Germany from becoming the preeminent military force on the Continent.[10]

Soon after Bowie's arrival at the PPS, he directed Fuller to examine the prospects for a European union. In a long analysis that Bowie passed on to Dulles, Fuller explained that unification, "although immediately inspired by the Soviet threat to the West, is of vital, long-term significance for averting situations which in the past have made Europe a focal area of international unrest." Fuller cautioned that even though union "is a relatively untried device," it nonetheless could not "be viewed as a panacea for the organic ailments of European society." These included centuries-long distrust and conflict; seemingly irreconcilable economic, political, and military differences between nations; and, most important although not as readily apparent on the surface, domestic unrest within the two biggest continental powers, France and Germany.

The United States, Fuller advised, must use "exceptional tact and restraint" with the allies. The administration should seek out "projects initiated spontaneously by Europeans" instead of "quick results forced by US direction." Washington should allow the process to occur naturally—even if that meant short-term erosion of unionist sentiment as nations satisfied internal political demands—because U.S. national security depended on European cooperation and integration. If this meant standing quietly by while French and German nationalists let off steam by railing against the EDC, then so be it.

If this also meant temporarily turning a blind eye to German neutralist sentiment, the United States should grin and bear it. The key to security was to rebuild Germany so that it would be a "bulwark" against the Soviets and not "menace" the European community. This would require a delicate balancing act that relied on *political*, not military, confrontation with Moscow.[11]

Bowie, in a perfect manifestation of the devil's advocate, worried about the implications of a united Germany fully integrated within the Western alliance. He set up an Interagency Working Group (IWG) consisting of representatives from the State Department, NSC, and the Department of Defense (DOD) to examine this problem in more detail.[12] As Fuller noted, the IWG laid out, with "calculated realism, rationally adapted to the existing situation," the challenge that the administration faced. In order to achieve a viable European defense, the French would have to accept German troops in a European army, with a U.S. guarantee of France's security.

Fuller explained that the IWG seconded the JCS's assessment of Germany's importance to Western European defense and called Germany "potentially the strongest continental power west of the USSR." Politically, West German Chancellor Konrad Adenauer had convinced the Parliament to ratify the EDC. However, the infant democracy faced many challenges, including "maladjusted and, to some extent, disaffected elements," such as former Nazis, refugees streaming west from East Germany and other Iron Curtain countries, and a vibrant socialist party (the Social Democratic Party [SPD]) that criticized Adenauer's pro-U.S. attitude and was the party most willing to trade reunification for neutralism. The SPD could be democratically elected if Adenauer slipped.

The IWG also floated another devil's advocate position. German participation in the EDC "would also involve very considerable risks—perhaps greater than the risk that a united Germany would *not* join EDC or equivalent arrangements." If Adenauer, as the IWG suspected, was merely paying lip service to the idea of the EDC and the United States attempted to assuage Soviet fears by providing a security guarantee in the form of U.S. troop participation in the EDC and made "adherence to EDC and other GFR commitments a mandatory precondition for a settlement," the Germans would see this "as a breach of faith and evidence of a lack of sincerity in our professed support of German reunification." This would only "provide fresh fuel to the SPD and other elements of opposition to the Adenauer policy." As before, Bowie passed this paper on to Dulles without comment; presumably, it conveyed Bowie's belief about Germany's importance and the difficulties inherent in bringing it into the European community. Since Dulles was such a strong advocate of the EDC, this position perfectly illustrates Bowie's refusal to be a yes-man on the prospects of European integration.[13]

While he managed the PPS's think pieces on European integration and Germany, Robert Bowie played an ever-larger role in the administration's overall approach to national security policy. He helped formulate NSC Paper 153/1, "Basic National Security Strategy," an important early document completed and approved by Eisenhower on June 10, 1953, that identified "two principle threats to the survival of fundamental values and institutions of the United States": the "formidable power and aggressive policy" of the Soviet bloc and the "serious weakening of the economy" due to the costs needed to counter this threat. The United States must "strike a proper balance between the risks arising from these two threats" by "building up its own and free world strength" through collective security institutions such as NATO and the EDC. These institutions would provide the political and military firewalls necessary for Western and U.S. national security while simultaneously streamlining and, if possible, reducing defense spending.[14]

Bowie also served as the State Department's representative on the NSC's "Project Solarium." President Eisenhower established Solarium after a long May 8, 1953, NSC meeting in which he, Dulles, and the rest of his national security team analyzed how best to establish a long-term strategy that was politically, militarily, and economically viable to deal with the Soviet threat. Both NSC 153/1 and Solarium dovetailed with the philosophy Bowie and the PPS would develop over the next year to deal with the EDC and the German problem.

Solarium began under the assumption that, as the president said in the May 8 meeting, "the present [Truman] policy was leading to disaster." Eisenhower called for a detailed study of all the options the United States could take to counter the Soviets. He directed Cutler to establish three task forces to assess these options. Task Force A, chaired by former PPS Director George F. Kennan, examined how best to use NSC 153/1 "with such improvements and changes in emphasis as might seem desirable." Task Force B examined the establishment of "a continuous line around the Soviet bloc beyond which the U.S. will not permit Soviet or satellite military forces to advance without general war," while Task Force C studied the viability of "rollback," or "forc[ing] the Soviets to shift their efforts to holding what they already have." Solarium reiterated that "our minimum objective . . . is a rearmed West Germany associated with the West" and concluded that the United States must implement the EDC.[15]

NSC 153/1 and Solarium should be examined in light of the decision by the new Soviet leadership to propose a new Four-Power Conference on Germany after Stalin died on March 4, 1953.[16] The Eisenhower administration, however, was split on how to respond to the offer. Ambassador to the Soviet Union Charles Bohlen and the NSC considered it a genuine attempt at a settlement. The offices in charge of psychological warfare, such as the Operations Coordinating Board (OCB) of the Central Intelligence Agency (CIA) and the Psychological Strategy Board, on the other hand, argued that the proposal was a propaganda ploy and that the United States should try to exploit the leadership struggle and launch a propaganda counteroffensive. A week after Stalin's death, Secretary Dulles initially dismissed this advice and warned the NSC that the United States must be careful that "in our attempt to destroy the unity of the Soviet orbit we [do]not jeopardize the unity of our own coalition." Eventually, however, in an April 3 press conference, he rejected the Soviet peace overture and charged that "the basic situation or danger in which we stand" had not changed.[17]

Two months after Dulles's speech, however, Bowie asked the IWG to reassess the effect that Stalin's death and the Soviet peace offensive had on the German problem. "Events since Stalin's death," the IWG responded, "may be leading the Russians to consider making what they would wish to be regarded as a serious attempt at a German settlement." The East German uprising of early June had shown that the new leadership's position was actually tenuous at best—even though the Soviets had easily crushed the workers rebellion—so they "may wish to reduce their commitment" and perhaps trade off German participation in the EDC for a quid pro quo on Berlin. The public relations hit the Soviets had taken for crushing the rebellion could be reversed if the German problem as a whole could be settled, but the IWG cautioned that achieving settlement on U.S. terms would be "difficult, if not unrealistic" because the Soviets would not accede to German revival within a larger Western alliance.[18]

A second study by the IWG further strengthened Bowie's case. The IWG noted that since the Germans wanted democracy and reunification, which the Soviets opposed unless it became a neutral nation, the United States should highlight the benefits already enjoyed by Germans who lived in the Western zone, even if their fellow Germans in the East were stuck under communist rule. While this was a cynical proposal, it enjoyed the advantage of cementing the status quo, which, while far from perfect, at least kept the peace between East and West and kept Germany from threatening either Europe or the Soviet Union. The United States, the IWG argued, should test the Soviet peace offensive and see if the new leadership truly wanted a relaxation of tensions. In this way, the United States could win either at the negotiating table or, should the Soviets demur, in the propaganda battle between the two sides.[19]

While the IWG examined the German problem, it also participated in State Department planning for the upcoming Washington Minister's Conference between Dulles, British Foreign Secretary Lord Salisbury, and French

Foreign Minister Henri Bidault. Bowie and Dulles approved a telegram that notified Conant (who had replaced McCloy as high commissioner of Germany in March 1953) that Germany would be an "important subject for discussion, both within the context of possible quadripartite talks with Soviets and in view of recent developments in Germany which may decisively affect Adenauer's position," in particular the quashing of the East German rebellion. State informed Conant that the United States would tell Salisbury and Bidault that "it is out of question to plan for quadripartite talks with Soviets unless firm tripartite agreement reached in advance." Furthermore, any conference should first settle Austria's status. Only then would Germany be discussed.[20]

State also proposed a "Declaration of Intent respecting Germany" that would create a unified allied front and also "embody West principles for German settlement and peace treaty contrasting favorably with Soviet draft of 1952," in which Stalin had called for a reunified, independent, but neutral Germany prohibited from joining any anti-Soviet alliances such as NATO and the EDC. Adenauer, backed by the United States, had rejected the offer out of hand. Conant should now "consult informally with Adenauer to obtain his views" as soon as possible on the effects of the EDC on his political status.[21]

Two days later, Conant reported that Adenauer "strongly opposed" the idea of quadripartite discussions "unless there is reasonable certainty that they will have positive results" and if the Soviets agreed "to come to a genuine solution of European or German problem." Otherwise, the Soviets would continue to use Germany as "a propaganda platform" that would result in "never-ending talks." After tentatively endorsing the idea of a "Declaration of Intent," he expressed "optimism" that the new French cabinet would endorse the ratification of EDC and asked that Washington continue to "pressure" Paris to convince the French National Assembly to do so. On July 9, David K. E. Bruce, the U.S. observer to the Interim Committee of the EDC, told Washington that the French cabinet authorized Bidault "to join in any statement strongly endorsing European integration projects." Bruce then urged the United States to do all it could to ensure Adenauer's reelection as a way to move EDC and integration forward.[22]

Three days before the Washington Conference, after two months of public debate in Washington over possible defense spending and troop reductions in Europe and a delay in naming a replacement for William Draper, the recently recalled U.S. representative to NATO's North Atlantic Council (NAC), Livingston Merchant of the European desk at State notified Bowie and Dulles of a palpable "decline in enthusiasm for the EDC" because the United States had been unable to match the Soviet peace offensive with a "psychological or propaganda counteroffensive" of its own. The constant press stories about budget cuts and the like indicated that the United States had lost interest in living up to its defense responsibilities. Merchant detected a "crisis" within NATO and advised the administration to

> make crystal clear that the declared purpose of the North Atlantic Treaty is in fact our European policy; that NATO supplemented and supported by EDC is its shield; that we consider Europe defensible if attacked and that we will do our share in making it possible for our partners to earn a self-respecting living in the world.[23]

Bowie attended but did not speak during the July 1953 Washington Conference, which lasted for four days. He played an important role, however, because he essentially wrote Dulles's July 10 opening statement since the secretary repeated the talking points he had prepared for the conference. Dulles emphasized the importance of Western European "solidarity and military and economic power" through NATO and the EDC, which he said would not only protect the Continent—and the United States—from the Soviet threat but also act as a "magnet" to the captive peoples of Eastern Europe. "Keeping alive their hopes and aspirations," Bowie had advised Dulles, would eventually weaken the Soviet Empire from the inside in the long run. However, Dulles ignored one of Bowie's most important points—that the United States should eschew the reunification of Germany—and instead again endorsed re-unification.

Bidault's opening statement at the conference, however, portended a rocky road to European solidarity. He did not mention either Germany or the EDC. Instead, he made a rather anodyne statement stating he "had nothing to contradict what Secretary Dulles had said regarding the correctness of the policies which we have pursued." In contrast, Salisbury devoted most of his statement to four-power talks on Germany. Bidault later endorsed integration but repeatedly refused to commit to the reunification of Germany and questioned whether four-power talks would "settle the German question," with the caveat that "no French Government could successfully oppose the talks."[24] Naturally, this hardly reassured Dulles about Paris's commitment.

Despite being the critical component for a strong continental defense, the other NATO countries shared the Soviet Union's interest in a permanently divided Germany. But if German troops were excluded from the EDC, only U.S. troops could fill that gap. The administration remained reluctant to face this reality—no matter how many times the PPS and JCS repeated this politically uncomfortable reality—given that the United States was only eight years removed from World War II and still involved in the unpopular war in Korea.

At the same time, many Europeans, including a majority of Germans, pushed the United States to negotiate with the Soviet Union to achieve a German and European "settlement" that would put World War II to rest. In addition, a near majority of Germans preferred reunification, even if it meant neutralization, over participation in the EDC if it could be achieved. In this climate, how could the United States keep the alliance together? Forcing the Germans to join the EDC would belie its commitment to freedom and democracy.

Meanwhile, Bowie's IWG warned that the Soviets would never accede to West Germany's military revival and its integration into a Western European army. The Soviets wanted Germany to be neutralized or so weakened that it could never start another world war. The United States stood between a rock and a hard place. If it supported German revival, it would "appear as obstructing a settlement by putting forth proposals patently unacceptable to the Soviets" as well as those Europeans who wanted "détente" with the Soviets. In the wake of the post-Stalin Soviet peace offensive, Washington could lose the all-important public relations war with Moscow. But if it knuckled under to Soviet demands for German neutralization, they would be ceding "whatever control mechanisms" Moscow wanted, which was anathema to the ideal of a free Germany established through free elections.

Here was the critical issue. The United States must lead yet not be belligerent to either its allies or the Soviets, a high-wire act that would be difficult even in the best of times. But in a world only eight years removed from total war, the odds seemed overwhelming that the United States could square this circle. The Working Group argued that the loss of Germany "would gravely endanger our national security." The Soviets had concentrated on detaching Germany from the West but would not resort to force to achieve this goal. Instead, it would appeal "to the German desire for unity and fear of war and to exploit Western differences." The IWG worried that the United States would then be blamed for maintaining the division of Germany, thereby "repairing Soviet prestige in world eyes" as well as jeopardizing the cohesion of the NATO alliance. Most glaringly obvious from this report, however, is that the IWG did not put forward any concrete recommendations for how the administration could reconcile all of these competing factors.[25]

In a top-secret September 11, 1953, address to 230 officers from the U.S. Army War College, Bowie noted the close "interrelation between the military aspects and the political and economic and opinion aspects" of U.S. foreign policy in the face of the threat from the Soviet Union. One "of the main weapons of the Soviets," he argued, "is the cold war technique, the tactics of division and diversion." Without strong and principled U.S. leadership of the Western alliance, Bowie warned, "they will triumph by friction and dissents in the free world." The United States needed to build its military strength yet also "try to provide the cement and ties to maintain the cohesion of the free world as the leader of the principle coalitions," in particular the Western European coalition.

Bowie warned that this would be a difficult feat to achieve. Because "we do not have the broad kind of authority" in Western Europe "which we have at home," the United States had to depend "much more on persuasion and leadership and the attitudes of others abroad toward us." He lamented that the United States "cannot coerce allies over any substantial period of time into a common policy." The United States must therefore convince the Europeans that "their interests and our own are the same." The Western alliance must stand united or face defeat by the Soviets. This speech typifies Bowie's keen sensitivity to Europe's needs that is reflected in the IWG reports on European integration and the German question and were lacking in Dulles's public speeches.[26]

Later that week, Bowie again tasked the IWG to come up with a scenario for dealing with the Soviet Union's demand for a German settlement. This time, the IWG wondered if Washington should not only dispense with its ideological struggle with Moscow but also offer "security guarantees" to the Soviets similar to the ones it had already proposed to France. The West, the IWG argued, must convince the Soviets that the Germans would be allowed to assume only a "defensive" role in the EDC—something that they could not even convince the French to accept.

The United States must accept Soviet unease of a German remilitarization at face value. In reality, the IWG posited, the Soviet "peace offensive" did not really extend to Germany. Instead of beating the drum of reunification on Western terms, NATO should accept the status quo in the short term and ensure that public recognition of this artificial and unfair division "might possibly have some long-term effect on Soviet intentions" in Western Europe.

Using IWG recommendations, Bowie advised Dulles to accept the plan proposed by Belgian Prime Minister Paul van Zeeland. His plan called for U.S. troop withdrawal from Germany and Soviet troop withdrawal from "one or more of the satellites. Only EDC troops would be stationed in a united Germany" and the establishment of neutral zones free of any troops on the Polish-Eastern German border. American support for this "European initiative" epitomized the policy of U.S.–European interdependence that Bowie had been advocating since he joined the State Department. While the IWG predicted the Soviets would reject the proposal, it would serve two purposes: it would buttress cohesion of the alliance in the long term, and it would serve as a useful and inexpensive propaganda vehicle. The Soviets would not be able to play to German neutralist opinion if it had just rejected a European plan that established just such neutrality. Dulles, however, spurned Bowie's advice, rejected the Van Zeeland plan, and pressed forward with his vision of the EDC.[27]

While the PPS grappled with the German problem, the secretary met with West German Foreign Secretary Walter Hallstein in Washington to discuss German participation in the EDC. Adenauer, Hallstein told Dulles, considered ratification by the Parliament "essential" to his "continued political life." Dulles replied that the administration had also studied the problem and had also rejected any alternatives. Dulles said he felt "encouraged" by his most recent discussions with Bidault, and Hallstein noted that Adenauer hoped that when he next met with Bidault that the two countries could work out "certain principles" that would "make it impossible for the French to delay consideration of the EDC indefinitely." Adenauer also believed that "strong intervention by the United States" might be needed in order to "bring about Franco-German agreement."

Hallstein also stated that Van Zeeland had once again presented his plan to Adenauer, but the chancellor was "concerned" that Van Zeeland's plan would merely substitute U.S. forces for Soviet forces, which to him meant another form of occupation and was "entirely unacceptable." He also worried that the plan would strengthen anti-EDC forces within France which would use the presence of U.S. troops to "stall" French participation in the EDC. Dulles replied that he and the other NATO foreign ministers "had agreed politely to discourage the idea."[28]

While Dulles dealt with the Germans, Bowie decided to try to convince the French to ratify the EDC. While there is no evidence that Bowie consulted with Dulles before he approached the French, it is doubtful that he acted on his own. In all likelihood, he notified the secretary before he met with France's ambassador, Henri Bonnet, on October 23. Bonnet, however, beat Bowie to the punch. In what was characteristic of French diplomacy during this period, Bonnet launched into a pointed criticism of the administration's perceived new defense strategy. The administration's "New Look," Bonnet argued, "would play into the hands of the neutralists in Europe and might hurt the prospects for the EDC." A withdrawal of U.S. troops from Europe, Bonnet warned, would force even the most pro-EDC Frenchman to vote against it because he would believe that the United States would abandon Western Europe to both the Soviets and a rearmed Germany. Clearly caught on his heels, Bowie said little in response and then quickly called Dulles with this unwelcome news.[29]

The administration, however, did not share Hallstein's sanguine mood of late September. All sectors of the administration recognized that the Soviets dreaded a unified Germany. Even as the JCS argued for German reunification, they warned that the United States would not be able to sway the Soviet

Union to agree to "a satisfactory basis for the unification of Germany and for the conclusion of a peace treaty." The CIA also forecast that the Soviets "will seek by *political* warfare to prevent or at least retard" the rearmament of West Germany and concluded that the Soviets would accept only a reunified, neutral Germany. Dulles stated that the Soviets "would not consent to the unification of Germany under any circumstances" since that would threaten their hegemony over Eastern Europe. The president agreed.[30]

Meanwhile, Conant reported that quick ratification of the EDC in the German parliament looked unlikely. "There can be no doubt," Conant wrote Dulles, "that the Chancellor has run into resurgent German nationalism in connection with the formation of his Cabinet." Hallstein had also underestimated the degree of "political ambitions and party ambitions" among Adenauer's coalition. The upshot was that these developments would delay Adenauer's upcoming meeting with Bidault.

Instead of admitting problems within his own government, Adenauer, Conant reported, "has probably convinced himself that the French and not the Germans are responsible for the delaying tactics." Adenauer seemed to be willing to play a game of chicken with the French, believing that the Eisenhower administration would compel the French to ratify the EDC without settling the Saar. There even existed a "remote possibility," Conant believed, that German nationalists could "influence" Adenauer to create a German army under NATO auspices. This, of course, would undermine the entire raison d'être of the EDC and would represent a complete reversal of Adenauer's position. Conant also confessed to a "deep concern" about "any possibility of a national German army." Such a national army could swing toward the East and align against NATO.[31]

Two weeks later, Conant wrote with even more bad news. Recalling his prediction that Adenauer might "flirt" with the creation of a national army, Conant reported that "it seems clear that the Chancellor is interested in exploring an alternative to EDC. Adenauer, Conant, wondered, might be "anxious to test out the United States position in order to demonstrate to some of his colleagues that there is no real alternative to EDC."[32]

Meanwhile, Bowie provided what he called "a lawyer's analysis" of the EDC treaty for the secretary that once again highlighted some unwanted but necessary critiques. The treaty, Bowie said, did not truly provide the supranational powers to a new European community that its creators had promised. For example,

> no grant of power which is subject to subsequent unanimous agreement by the member States is a true grant of power to the Community. When it speaks of exercise of a power by the Community, the memorandum means

exercise of such power by the Community's executive, subject to no more than a majority or two-thirds weighted vote in the Council of Ministers.

Therefore, any unified action contemplated by the EDC nations would have to jump through two hoops rather than one simple vote. While Bowie noted that this would not do too much harm in the short run—assuming the treaty's ratification—he cautioned that this could hurt the EDC in the long run if integration were not achieved. If an individual signatory asked the EDC to help defend it against Soviet aggression, it might not be able to get the other signatories to fulfill their obligations if integration consisted only of words in a treaty.

The United States, Bowie warned, must remain engaged in Western Europe and work together with its allies for the common defense, or the EDC would collapse like a house of cards. While the French in particular feared a U.S. withdrawal from Europe, French nationalists also feared placing the French army under U.S. control. The United States, therefore, had to tread lightly and make the necessary sacrifices, including the permanent deployment of U.S. troops in Europe. This would also require a nimble political hand that, Bowie implied, the administration had not heretofore played with the NATO allies.[33]

Just before Dulles and Eisenhower left for Bermuda to discuss the status of the EDC with British Prime Minister Winston Churchill and French Prime Minister Joseph Laniel, Bowie and the PPS completed a list of possible alternatives to the EDC. While the PPS believed that this was not an immediate issue, "formidable obstacles" to ratification still existed, the most important being French that a rearmed Germany would "overbalance France and reduce her European and world role." Any substitute, however, must achieve the same ends, including European integration and a common defense against the Soviet Union. Alternatives must also establish "a new status of equality and independence" for West Germany that ensured against the revival of "German nationalist excesses" and avoided "any undue provocation of the Soviets."

No magic bullet existed, however. Only the EDC as presently conceived offered the best way to accomplish all these goals. The PPS thus decided that if the EDC failed, each goal had to be ranked in order of importance. First, West Germany's independence must be the "*sine qua non* of any arrangement," followed closely by a new spirit of Franco-German cooperation. "German rearmament," it warned, could "scarcely be sacrificed to the purely non-military objective because the right of self-defense is a corollary of German independence" and, everyone agreed, "indispensable" to any defense of the Continent. Last on the list was any settlement on the German question, given

"Soviet attitudes" toward not only the EDC but also any measure "seeking to accomplish essentially the same ends." The United States, Bowie argued, should pursue "the positive ends of our European policy" and not worry about the Soviets.

The PPS recommended five alternatives: German membership in NATO, unilateral German rearmament, the "modification" of the EDC, German neutralization, and a peripheral defense of Europe, each of which had pluses and minuses. Not surprisingly, the biggest stumbling block to any of the alternatives remained placating the French while achieving both real political integration and the necessary German defense component. The PPS reflected the frustration of the rest of the administration and had to guard against the temptation to throw up its hands, let the Europeans figure out their own future, and return the United States to its pre–World War II isolationist sentiment. The Europeans had feared a return to isolationism until Eisenhower decided to run for president in the spring of 1952 but seemed to fear the New Look almost as much because of the strategy's emphasis on nuclear weapons, smaller defense budgets, and decreased U.S. troop levels. That the EDC had originally been a French idea galled even more. Given these alternatives, Bowie advised Dulles to immediately push for French and British support for the EDC in Bermuda.[34]

Eisenhower, Dulles, Churchill, Laniel, and Bidault met in Bermuda in early December 1953 to discuss the status of the EDC. Again, Bowie attended all the meetings but did not speak. Eisenhower privately reassured the allies that the administration would not "redeploy" U.S. ground forces, or "our new weapons," from Europe. Unfortunately, these pledges did not ease Churchill's concerns about a U. S. withdrawal from Europe. Eisenhower then criticized French intransigence over the EDC. The president noted that Bidault continued to complain that "France alone among the great Western powers" had made the "great sacrifice of integrating its forces with those of another nation which had long been its enemy.'"[35] Eisenhower explained that all the allies had fought against Germany and had made great sacrifices. Now the alliance faced a new enemy, the Soviet Union. Churchill reluctantly backed Eisenhower and made it clear that Western Europe could not be defended without the Germans. Despite Eisenhower's and Churchill's personal appeals for European unity in the face of the Soviet threat, Bidault refused to commit his government to the ratification of the EDC.[36]

While he publicly highlighted the "unity of the Big Three" at Bermuda in order to avoid giving the Soviets a golden propaganda opening, privately the president vented his anger over France's attitude. France "prefers to shut its eyes to the dangers represented by the extremes," he wrote a close friend, even though Laniel had admitted that the Soviet Union, not Germany, threatened France's national security. French national pride seemed to trump European unity and the security of the Western alliance.[37]

Even as the French drove him crazy, Secretary Dulles took the time to write Bowie to thank him for all the work he had done over the past seven months. Bowie had made a "tremendous contribution" to the State Department "in the vital area of planning." Furthermore, Dulles said, "I had expected you to be good. However, the reality has greatly exceeded even that expectation. I greatly admire the clarity of your reasoning" and, in recognition of Bowie's unique position as the devil's advocate, "your steady support of your conviction—a steadiness which, however, is very different from inflexibility to meet the adjustments in arriving at agreed national policy."[38]

Bowie, typically, was engaged in vital work when he received Dulles's letter. He was in the processing of writing what ultimately became four drafts of the foreign policy section of Eisenhower's 1954 State of the Union Address. In particular, he grappled with how to put the best public face on the bleak outlook for the alliance that the Bermuda Conference engendered. On the one hand, he wrote in the third draft on December 30, 1953, "the past year has been a momentous one" with "growing strength and unity of the free peoples" against the Soviet threat. On the other hand, he cautioned that this strength and unity "are a vital element in our security" and, as the devil's advocate, changed the language from the second draft, where he highlighted the EDC, to the "European *Political* Community," which reflected his skepticism about U.S. reliance on the treaty in the wake of Bermuda. Dulles, however, struck the latter phrase and included the EDC in his final draft to the president. Eisenhower agreed, and in the address he stated "the building of a united European community, including France and Germany, is vital to a free and self-reliant Europe. This will be promoted by the European Defense Community which offers assurance of European security."[39]

After the Bermuda Conference, the administration had to turn on a dime and prepare for the Four-Power Conference in Berlin on the German question. Not only would the United States have France to contend with, but they would also have to tangle with Dulles's bête noire, Soviet foreign minister Vyacheslav Molotov. The day after the State of the Union Address, Fuller submitted a summary of the final report of the Paris Tripartite Working Group to Bowie. The study repeated the administration's objectives—the reunification of Germany through free elections, Western European integration through the EDC, and the avoidance of an "impasse as a result of Soviet delaying tactics"— as well as a plan to explain how "our proposals assure security requirements of Europe and USSR and serve peaceful relations of USSR to West." The three Western powers should also repeatedly remind the Soviets that the EDC "precluded any individual armed action by members," that is, Germany.[40]

Admittedly, it seems surprising that the IWG's report did not warn about French unreliability on both issues, given that the PPS had repeatedly advised Dulles of this. Fortunately, the embassy in Paris notified the secretary that the French (and other Europeans) considered the Berlin Conference a sham because the administration believed that "no basis for agreement with Soviet Union can be reached, rather than in order to explore meticulously and objectively all possibilities for reaching agreement." The administration should therefore adopt a more "flexible tactical course on either of these two issues." Otherwise, it looked as if the United States held a "big stick over France" that would result in the continuance of the mutual distrust between East and West.[41]

Meanwhile, Bowie directed another staff member, Jacob Beam, to prepare a study of the prospects for the Berlin Conference and Fuller to examine the long-term prospects for U.S. German policy. Both remained pessimistic. Beam predicted that the Soviets would "play two gambits—the French and the German, with stress probably on the first." They would try to peel Paris away from the West by dangling a comprehensive European security system that concluded with a Franco-Soviet alliance that would render NATO moot. Then it would dangle German reunification based on neutrality. Fuller, meanwhile, argued that Germany remained "of prime importance to the US" because of "the basic facts of its geographic position, power potential, and key situation in the broad European position." But he cautioned that while NATO members suspected any German revival, "elements of instability and danger" existed within Germany that had been "artificial[ly]" restrained by the postwar occupation and its unresolved status as both a divided area and a political entity. Bowie forwarded both studies to Dulles and advised that the United States maintain its position that the EDC would protect both Paris and Moscow from a revived Germany and abandon its call for German reunification.[42]

Clearly influenced by Fuller's paper, Dulles told the NSC that the Berlin Conference "would be more important in its negative than in its positive aspects" because the Soviets would try to "disrupt the Western alliance and to destroy the security of Western Europe." He also said "the prospects for unification" were "very poor. Soviet agreement to German unification would, in effect, represent an invasion of freedom deep into the Iron Curtain." The Soviets would allow reunification only with neutralization *and* if France abandoned the EDC.[43]

The Berlin Conference lasted from January 25 to February 18, 1954, and fulfilled all of Bowie's predictions. Dulles tangled with Molotov, who plotted to torpedo the EDC by emphasizing the German threat to Western Europe. Dulles tried to hold the alliance together when Molotov "went out of his way to woo" Bidault in an attempt to play on "French fears of a revived Germany and French anxiety to settle the Indochina conflict." Seeing the way the wind was blowing, Dulles wondered if NATO should grant France a "partner's share in world leadership" with the United States and Britain in order to gain France's commitment to the EDC. If this carrot did not succeed, then NATO could use the stick and cut France out of the leadership of the Western alliance.[44]

Molotov in turn proposed the establishment of "a system of European collective security, premised on the elimination of the US from European councils." In a private dinner, Dulles and Molotov fenced over the EDC and repeated their conflicting views on German reunification. Dulles argued that the EDC remained the best way to bring Germany into the Western European community. Molotov simply did not accept this view, and the Berlin Conference ended without any tangible achievements.[45]

Meanwhile, a German public opinion poll found that 47 percent of West Germans agreed with the Soviet idea of neutrality as the price for reunification. Even a quarter of West Berliners would accept such a deal. Clearly, the administration had failed to convince *the Germans* themselves, much less the other NATO allies, about the Soviet threat.[46]

During the next four months, Bowie and his staff examined the state of U.S.–European relations and the odds that the French would ratify the EDC. In May, Bowie informed the secretary that relations with Europe "are rapidly approaching a critical stage. If present trends continue, the U.S. may be forced to revise radically its policies regarding Europe." The Europeans, thanks to successful Soviet propaganda, "no longer consider a Soviet attack as an imminent danger as it did in 1950–51" and "seem to think the U.S. is more likely to provoke war than the Soviet Union." They also distrusted the United States and criticized Washington for its "impetuous and impatient" manner that undermined its stated goal of providing European security. He also again warned that both France and Germany were still internally weak. The former would likely fail to ratify the EDC, while Germany would respond by turning more nationalistic. Either way, the Soviets would continue to exploit the situation and work to weaken the alliance.[47]

Fuller, meanwhile, detailed the possibility of a German–Soviet "rapprochement" in the wake of "German impatience with the status quo" after the "failure" of the Berlin Conference and the administration's apparent inability to pressure France to end its "evasive tactics" over the EDC. But new evidence of French "stalling . . . for the deliberate purpose of having a context for non-action on EDC" had angered Adenauer, who wondered now if his own governing coalition could hold together given his many promises that the EDC proposals would establish German security. Conant, Fuller explained, blamed the "prolonged delay in ratification of EDC" for the rumors swirling in Bonn about an overture to Moscow. Even Adenauer had floated the possibility of an exploratory trip to Moscow to see if something could shake up the status quo. While Fuller dismissed the opening of official diplomatic relations between Germany and the Soviet Union, he warned that such talk would simmer under the surface if Bonn continued to feel "ignored" by the West.[48]

In June, Bowie asked Fuller to again check on the European situation. Fuller responded with an even drearier forecast. He first questioned whether the United States could rely on Western Europe for its own security, given the fundamental problems of mutual suspicion, the hesitation to even unite economically let alone militarily, and Moscow's adept exploitation of European fear of another war. He then admitted that European integration could not serve as a panacea "for the deep-seated ills that affect some of the European countries." Not surprisingly, France and Germany had been traumatized by the shattering experience of World War II, and the United States should lower its expectations appropriately. "Integration," he contended, was a "useful device, but a means rather than an end." The proponents of unity had seriously underestimated the opposition in both countries to the idea of integration. Fuller also warned that unless the United States and Britain permanently committed their own forces to the Continent, France and Germany would never reconcile let alone cooperate militarily no matter how severe the Soviet threat.[49]

On July 13, Dulles warned France's new prime minister, Pierre Mendes-France, that the delay in ratifying the EDC played directly into Russia's hands. The Soviets, Dulles argued, wanted to split the alliance and then neutralize Germany. He further warned the French that if German rearmament had to be arranged without the EDC, Congress "would not appropriate a dollar for European military aid connected with NATO." Mendes-France agreed that the failure of the EDC would mean a victory for the Soviet Union but could not promise the ratification of a treaty that allowed Germany to rearm regardless of the safeguards. Fuller noted this conversation and predicted that the French National Assembly would reject the EDC. He assured Bowie that the United States and Britain were looking for alternatives to the EDC, including the "transplant to NATO" of "as many of the EDC safeguard as possible, and admit the Federal Republic to membership." This, of course, ultimately occurred in 1955.[50]

Robert Bowie and the PPS accurately predicted that France would not ratify the EDC treaty and argued that the United States should not push for the reunification of Germany. He also identified a number of problems inherent in the Eisenhower administration's conception of European integration, the defense of the European continent, and the administration's own strategy to achieve U.S. national security. This analysis shows how Bowie's ability to work on Dulles "from below" led to the exposure of some uncomfortable truths about U.S. national security policy and diplomacy during the 1950s but did not basically change Dulles's views. That Dulles left him in that position illustrates the importance of his sometimes contrary views to the secretary of state as he fought a losing battle with the European allies.

NOTES

1. See "Substance of Discussions of State-DMS-JCS Meeting," January 28, 1953, Miscellaneous Lot Files, Department of State, Meeting Summaries and Project Files, 1951–1959, Box 51, Vol. V, Folder 1, National Archives II (hereafter cited as MLF, NA); Robert J. Watson, *The History of the Joint Chiefs of Staff: Vol. V. The Joint Chiefs of Staff and National Policy, 1952–1954* (Washington, D.C.: Historical Division, Joint Chiefs of Staff, 1986), 6–7; Thomas A. Schwartz, "Eisenhower and the Germans," in *Eisenhower: A Centenary Assessment*, ed. Günter Bischof and Stephen Ambrose (Baton Rouge: Louisiana State University Press, 1995), 212–15; and William I. Hitchcock, *France Restored: Cold War Diplomacy and the Quest for Leadership in Europe, 1944–1954*. (Chapel Hill: University of North Carolina Press, 1998).

2. The EDC had originally been proposed by French Premier René Pleven in 1950. Two years later, as a result of the Bonn Convention and the Treaty of Paris, "the NATO allies made the ratification of the EDC a condition for the restoration of German sovereignty." See Brian R. Duchin, "The 'Agonizing Reappraisal': Eisenhower, Dulles, and the European Defense Community," *Diplomatic History* 16 (March 1992): 201. For the formal goals of the EDC within NATO, see also "Draft Declaration by the Members of the North Atlantic Council," February 25, 1952, Department of State, Record Component Offices of the Bureau of European Affairs, 1944–1962, RG 59, Lot File 56 D38, Box 31, EDC-NATO Documents, National Archives (hereafter cited as Bureau of European Affairs, NA). For the Bowie and Fuller exchange, see "Note from Fuller to Bowie," September 7, 1954, which mentions Bowie's September 1 request for the study, and "Post-EDC European Reactions," September 3, 1954, RG 59, General Records of the Department of State, RG 59, Records of the Policy Planning Staff, 1954, Lot 65 D 101, Subject Files, Country and Area Files, Box 87, Germany 1954, National Archives (hereafter cited as PPS Records, NA).

3. See "Telegram from the Ambassador in the Netherlands [Chapin] to the Department of State," October 17, 1951, *Foreign Relations of the United States 1951: Vol. III. European Security and the German Question, Part 1* (Washington, D.C.: U.S. Government Printing Office, 1981), 888 (hereafter cited as *FRUS*). The Dutch also warned the United States to be wary of French motives in proposing the EDC (889). Bowie has argued, however, that Eisenhower represented a sharp break from Truman's national security strategy, which he disparaged as reactive "to crises" such as the Korean War. This approach "produced a confused legacy of objectives, policies, and programs

in disarray" that Eisenhower systematically fixed. See Robert R. Bowie and Richard H. Immerman, *Waging Peace: How Eisenhower Shaped an Enduring Cold War Legacy* (New York: Oxford University Press, 1998), 3. For a general description of then General Eisenhower's view on European integration in his prepresidential years, see Bowie and Immerman, *Waging Peace*, 50–51.

4. "Telegram from the United States High Commissioner for Germany (McCloy) to the Department of State," January 3, 1952, in *FRUS 1952–1954: Vol. V. Western European Security, Part 1* (Washington, D.C.: U.S. Government Printing Office, 1983), 576–78. As HICOG, McCloy worked to convince both the Germans and the French to accept the EDC, mainly because he believed that German participation in a European army would prevent Germany from becoming neutralized either by its own actions or through a Soviet–Western settlement. See Kai Bird, *The Chairman: John J. McCloy: The Making of the American Establishment* (New York: Simon & Schuster, 1992), 378, and Thomas Alan Schwartz, *America's Germany: John J. McCloy and the Federal Republic of Germany* (Cambridge, Mass.: Harvard University Press, 1999), 219–21.

5. Jean Monnet, France's leading proponent of European unity and the EDC, had argued that the Schuman Plan, which established the European Coal and Steel Community (ECSC) in 1951, would create a basis of trust between the French and the Germans. The successful implementation of the ECSC would in turn convince his countrymen to ratify the EDC and further the cause of European unity. Monnet lamented the fact that at the present time France could not "lose her fear of German industrial domination" let alone allow Germany to participate in the armed defense of Western Europe. At the same time, Adenauer warned that if the French persisted in establishing the coal-rich Saar region as an independent nation, then he could not "possibly bring Germany into a European coalition to maintain security against Russia." For a detailed analysis of the Saar and Ruhr Valley controversies, see John Gillingham, *Coal, Steel, and the Rebirth of Europe, 1945–1955: The Germans and the French from the Ruhr Conflict to Economic Community* (New York: Columbia University Press, 1991), and Fredric J. Fransen, *The Supranational Politics of Jean Monnet: Ideas and Origins of the European Community* (Westport, Conn.: Greenwood Press, 1996), 94–105. For Monnet's quote, see his *Memoirs* (Garden City, N.Y.: Doubleday, 1978), 286–92.

6. For Conant and the CPD, see James G. Hershberg, *James B. Conant: Harvard to Hiroshima and the Making of the Nuclear Age* (New York: Knopf, 1993), 493–94, 516–22.

7. "Memorandum from Roderick L. O'Connor to Dulles," March 27, 1953, The John Foster Dulles Papers from the Eisenhower Library, Telephone Conversation Series, January 1953–October 31, 1953, Box 1, Folder 1, Seeley G. Mudd Manuscript Library, Princeton University, and "Letter from Dulles to Erwin N. Griswold," April 7, 1953, Papers of John Foster Dulles, Correspondence, Box 67, Bowie, Robert R., Seeley G. Mudd Manuscript Library, Princeton University (hereafter cited as Dulles Papers).

8. Townsend Hoopes, *The Devil and John Foster Dulles* (Boston: Atlantic Little Brown, 1973), 147, and Andrew McFadzean, "The Bigger Picture: Biography and/or

History? Robert Bowie," *Australasian Journal of American Studies* 22, no. 1 (2003): 42–43, 45, 53.

9. "Oral Interview with Dillon Anderson," OH-165, Interview 1, Columbia University Oral History Project, Dwight D. Eisenhower Library and Richard H. Immerman, *John Foster Dulles: Piety, Pragmatism, and Power in U.S. Diplomacy* (Wilmington, Del.: Scholarly Resources, 1999), 49.

10. "Annual Message to the Congress on the State of the Union," February 2, 1953, *Eisenhower Papers 1953*, 5–7; "Substance of Discussions of State-DMS-JCS Meeting," January 28, 1953, RG 59, MLF, Box 51, Vol. V, Folder 1, NA; "Oral Interview with Robert Bowie," OH-102, Columbia University Oral History Project, Dwight D. Eisenhower Library; "Interview with Robert Bowie by the National Security Archive," 1998, http://www.gwu.edu/~nsarchiv/coldwar/interviews/episode-7/bowie21.html. See also Thomas A. Schwartz, "Eisenhower and the Germans," in Bischof and Ambrose, *Eisenhower*, 212–15.

11. "Memorandum from Lewis Fuller to Bowie," May 13, 1953, RG 59, PPS, 1947–53, Lot 64 D 563, Subject Files, Country and Area Files, Box 29, Europe 1952-53, Folder 4, NA. McFadzean argues that Bowie especially "supported economic interdependence rather than military containment" as the best means to support Western Europe against the Soviet threat. See "The Bigger Picture," 46.

12. National Security Adviser Robert Cutler and Secretary of Defense Charles Wilson, respectively, assigned representatives to the IWG.

13. "Memorandum from Fuller to Bowie," June 25, 1953, under cover of "Memorandum from Bowie to Dulles," June 27, 1953, PPS, Country and Area Files, Box 16, Germany 1950–53, Folder 2, NA.

14. "Report to the National Security Council by the Executive Secretary (Lay), with Enclosure: Statement of Policy by the National Security Council, NSC 153/1," June 10, 1953, *FRUS 1952–1954: Vol II. National Security Affairs, Part 1* (Washington, D.C.: U.S. Government Printing Office, 1984), 378–85. Bowie briefed Bowie about NSC 153 in "Memorandum by the Director of the Policy Planning Staff to the Secretary of State," June 8, 1953, *FRUS 1952–1954*, 370–71. A Basic National Security Strategy Paper was written every year during the Eisenhower administration as conditions changed.

15. The quotes about the specifics of Project Solarium are from Bowie, *Waging Peace*, 123–27. Bowie passed on a précis of Solarium's Task Force Reports to Dulles. See "Memorandum by the Executive Secretary of the Policy Planning Staff," August 12, 1953, *FRUS 1952–1954: Vol. II, Part 1*, 441–42. For more on Solarium, see H. W. Brands, "The Age of Vulnerability: Eisenhower and the National Insecurity State," *American Historical Review* 94 (October 1989): 963–89; Meena Bose, *Shaping and Signaling Presidential Policy: The National Security Decision Making of Eisenhower and Kennedy* (College Station: Texas A&M University Press, 1998), 29–41; and Frank Schumacher, *Kalter Krieg und Propaganda: Die USA, der Kampf um die Weltmeinung und die Ideele Westbindung der Bundesrepublik Deutschland, 1945–1955* (Trier: Wissenschaftlicher Verlag, 2000), 104–5.

16. Historians of Soviet diplomacy have argued that the peace offensive was designed to strengthen Soviet control over Eastern Europe, maintain the division of

Germany, and destroy the EDC. As David Holloway has pointed out, Khrushchev in particular believed that "peaceful coexistence" did not "mean *ideological* coexistence . . . nor did it entail renunciation of the struggle with imperialism." William Taubman argues that Khrushchev chose to "woo the West" with peaceful overtures "while at the same time undermining it" in the long term. Meanwhile, the Soviet Union would pursue strategic, political, and diplomatic parity with the United States. John W. Young has also noted that the new leadership used the peace offensive "as a weapon of the Cold War" in order to fight "a determined enemy in a struggle where lies and deception were the norm." See David Holloway, *Stalin and the Bomb: The Soviet Union and Atomic Energy 1939–1956* (New Haven, Conn.: Yale University Press, 1994), 336, and William Taubman, *Khrushchev: The Man and His Era* (New York: Norton, 2003), 348–52.

17. "Memorandum from Bohlen to Dulles," March 6, 1953, PPS Working Papers, Eisenhower 1953 Folder 1, Box 72, NA; OCB Paper, "Effects of Stalin's Death," March 6, 1953, RG 59; Records Relating to Department of State Participation in the Office of Coordinating Board and the National Security Council, 1947–1963: OCB Series, Box 125, NA; "Memorandum of Discussion at the 136th Meeting of the National Security Council, March 11, 1953," *FRUS 1952–1954: Vol. VIII* (Washington D.C.: U.S. Government Printing Office, 1988), 1120; and "Press Conference, April 3, 1953," Dulles Papers, Articles, Papers, Reports, Box 312. Kenneth Osgood shows that Eisenhower agreed that the Soviet "peace offensive" was "a psychological threat of the first magnitude" because it reflected only a tactical change, not an evolution, in Soviet policy. See his "Form before Substance: Eisenhower's Commitment to Psychological Warfare and Negotiations with the Enemy," *Diplomatic History* 24 (summer 2000): 410–11. Christian Ostermann argues that the United States rejected the psychological offensive because the Soviet call for talks on Germany threatened the stability of West German Chancellor Konrad Adenauer's government, which was preparing for elections and would be challenged by the Socialists to meet with the Soviets. See his "Keeping the Pot Simmering: The United States and the East German Uprising of 1953," *German Studies Review* 21, no. 1 (February 1996): 61–89. Eisenhower also feared that this tactical change could jeopardize Western European security, especially the EDC. See M. Steven Fish, "After Stalin's Death: The Anglo-American Debate over a New Cold War," *Diplomatic History* 10 (fall 1986): 334. Indeed, Adenauer agreed that Stalin's death could jeopardize the EDC. He also argued that the FRG's "hopes and salvation itself rest in American policies maintaining a constant course." Adenauer subsequently backed the administration's rejection of the peace offensive. Quoted in Hans-Peter Schwarz, *Konrad Adenauer: German Politician and Statesman in a Period of War, Revolution, and Reconstruction: Vol II. The Statesman, 1952–1967* (Providence, R.I.: Berghahn Books, 1997), 35 (originally published in Germany in 1991).

18. "Memorandum from Fuller to Bowie," June 30, 1953. For more on the East Berlin uprising, see Christian F. Ostermann, "The United States, the East German Uprising of 1953, and the Limits of Rollback," *Cold War International History Project Working Paper 11* (Washington, D.C.: Cold War International History Project, 1994), and "Keeping the Pot Simmering"; Valur Ingimundarson, "The Eisenhower Administration, the Adenauer Government, and the Political Uses of the East German Up-

rising," *Diplomatic History* 20 (summer 1996): 381–400; Mark Kramer, "The Early Post-Stalin Succession Struggle and Upheavals in East-Central Europe: Internal-External Linkages in Soviet Policy Making (Part 1)," *Journal of Cold War Studies* 1, no. 1 (1999): 3–25; David G. Coleman, "Eisenhower and the Berlin Problem, 1953–1954," *Journal of Cold War Studies* 2, no. 1 (winter 2000): 3–34; and Hope M. Harrison, *Driving the Soviets up the Wall: Soviet-East German Relations, 1953–1961* (Princeton, N.J.: Princeton University Press, 2003).

19. "Memorandum from Jacob Beam to Bowie," June 30, 1953, PPS, Country and Area Files, Box 16, Germany 1950-53, Folder 2, NA.

20. "Telegram from the Secretary of State to the Office of the High Commissioner for Germany," June 30, 1953, *FRUS 1952–1954: Vol. V. Western European Security, Part 2*, 1585–87.

21. "Telegram from the Secretary of State to the Office of the High Commissioner for Germany." For the text of Stalin's 1952 offer, see "Note from the Soviet Ministry of Foreign Affairs to the American Embassy in Moscow," March 10, 1952, *FRUS, Vol. VII, Part 1* (Washington, D.C.: U.S. Government Printing Office, 1984), 169–72; Rolf Steininger, *The German Question: The Stalin Note of 1952 and the Problem of Reunification* (New York: Columbia University Press, 1990), 24–29; Ruud Van Djik, "The 1952 Stalin Note Debate: Myth or Missed Opportunity for German Unification?," *Cold War International History Project Working Paper* 14 (May 1996): 26–30; John W. Young, *Winston Churchill's Last Campaign: Britain and the Cold War 1951–55* (Oxford: Clarendon Press, 1996), 135–36; Hannes Adomeit, *Imperial Overstretch: Germany in Soviet Policy from Stalin to Gorbachev* (Baden-Baden: Nomos Verlagsgesellchaft, 1998), 88–89; Schumacher, *Kalter Krieg und Propaganda*, esp. 240–54; and Ronald J. Granieri, *The Ambivalent Alliance: Konrad Adenauer, the CDU/CSU, and the West, 1949–1966* (New York: Berghahn Books, 2003), 7, 49–52.

22. Telegram from the German High Commissioner and Bruce to the Secretary of State, July 2 and 9, 1953, *FRUS 1952–1954, Vol. V, Part. 1*, 1587–90.

23. "Draft of Memorandum by the Assistant Secretary of State for European Affairs to the Secretary of State," July 7, 1953, RG 59, The Secretary's and the Undersecretary's Memoranda of Conversation, 1953–1964, Box 1, January–December 1953, NA. Ironically, before he left the NAC, Draper had warned Eisenhower that the United States must "decentralize" its policy positions because it looked as if the United States were publicly dictating terms to the allies. In addition, Draper argued that the "downgrading" of representatives to the NAC gave the impression that the administration would only pay lip service to the idea of globalism. See "Telegram from Draper to Eisenhower," June 5, 1953, Administrative Series, Papers of Dwight D. Eisenhower as President of the United States (Ann Whitman File), 1953–1961, Box 13, William Draper, Folder 1.

24. "Memorandum from Bowie to Dulles, with attached Talking Points for Washington Foreign Ministers Conference," July 8, 1953, Dulles-Herter Series from the Eisenhower Library, Box 1, Bermuda Conference, Folder 2, Dulles Papers, and "Meetings of the Foreign Ministers," July 10–13, 1953, *FRUS, Vol. V, Part 2*, 1607–96. These pages included Memoranda of Conversation of all four meetings. The Dulles, Bidault, and Salisbury opening statements are at 1609–13.

25. "United States Position with Respect to Germany: General Considerations," July 31, 1953, RG 59, PPS, Subject Files, Country and Area Files, Box 16, Germany 1950–53, Folder 1, NA.

26. "Transcript of Proceedings: Address by Robert Bowie at Public Liaison Meeting," September 11, 1953, PPS, PPS Members, Chronological File, Box 44, Bowie, Robert R., NA. Bowie appeared before a receptive audience, for members of the military had been very supportive of the idea of close military and political coordination with Western Europe for years. See "Memorandum from the Joint Chiefs of Staff to the Secretary of Defense," August 30, 1959, in RG 59, Records of the Bureau of European Affairs, Lot 55 D 258, Subject Files Relating to European Defense 1948–1954, Box 1, European Defense Force, NA. I have explored the relationship between Dulles's and Eisenhower's confidential policies, which endorsed cooperation with Europe and the division of Germany, with their public, more belligerent pronouncements that threatened withdrawal from Europe if the EDC were not ratified and the reunification of Germany that I have called "rhetorical diplomacy." See Chris Tudda, *The Truth Is Our Weapon: The Rhetorical Diplomacy of Dwight D. Eisenhower and John Foster Dulles* (Baton Rouge: Louisiana State University Press, 2006), 48–73.

27. "Memorandum from Beam to Bowie," September 22, 1953, PPS, Subject Files, Country and Area Files, Box 16, Germany 1950–53, Folder 2, NA.

28. "Memorandum of Conversation between Dulles and Hallstein," September 22, 1953, PPS, Subject Files, Country and Area Files, Box 16, Germany 1950–53, Folder 2, NA.

29. "Memorandum of Conversation between Bowie and Bonnet," October 23, 1953, PPS, Subject Files, Country and Area Files, Box 29, Europe 1952–53, Folder 3, NA, and "Telephone Call from Bowie to Dulles," October 23, 1953, John Foster Dulles Papers from the Eisenhower Library, Telephone Conversation Series, Box 1, Folder 7. The administration's New Look relied on an increase of the nation's nuclear stockpiles and a corresponding reduction in the number of forces as well as collective security alliances like NATO and the EDC because Eisenhower and Dulles believed that the United States would bankrupt itself if it spent too much on the military. While it seemed to make fiscal sense and strategically Western Europe needed to contribute to its own defense, it seemed to confirm the fears of many Europeans that the United States could not be trusted to help defend Western Europe against a Soviet attack. For more on the New Look, see Gaddis, *Strategies of Containment* (New York: Oxford University Press, 1982), 164–97; Marc Trachtenberg, *History and Strategy* (Princeton, N.J.: Princeton University Press, 1991), 132–40; and Robert A. Wampler, "Eisenhower, NATO, and Nuclear Weapons: The Strategy and Political Economy of Alliance Security," in Bischof and Ambrose, *Eisenhower*, 167–71.

30. "Statement of Policy by the National Security Council, August 17, 1953," *FRUS, Vol. VII. Germany and Austria, Part 1*, 511–17; "Paper Presented by the Joint Chiefs of Staff, undated, attached to a JCS Note," August 31, 1953, *FRUS, Vol. VII, Part 1*, 521. For the CIA report, see "NIE No. 81," May 22, 1953, *On the Front Lines of the Cold War: Documents on the Intelligence War in Berlin, 1946–1961* (Washington, D.C.: Center for the Study of Intelligence, Central Intelligence Agency, 1999), http://www.odci.gov/csi. For Dulles's comments, see "Memorandum of Discussion at

the 164th Meeting of the National Security Council," October 1, 1953, Papers of Dwight D. Eisenhower as President of the United States (Ann Whitman File), 1953–1961, NSC Series, Box 4, AWF (hereafter cited as Series, AWF).

31. "Letter from Conant to Dulles," October 28, 1953, *FRUS, Vol. VII, Part 1*. Conant also reported that his French counterpart "is very disturbed about the growing impatience of the United States" over the EDC. See "Telegram from Conant to Dulles," October 27, 1953, JFD Chronological Series, October 1953, Box 5, Folder 2, John Foster Dulles Papers, Eisenhower Library.

32. "Letter from Conant to Dulles," November 13, 1953, *FRUS, Vol. VII, Part 1*. and "Memorandum from Bowie to Fuller," November 14, 1953, PPS, Subject Files, Country and Area Files, Box 29, Europe 1952–53, Folder 3, NA.

33. "Memorandum from Bowie to Dulles," November 21, 1953, PPS, Subject Files, Country and Area Files, Box 29, Europe 1952-53, Folder 5, NA. Three days later, the embassy in Paris reported that Bidault feared that the United States would substitute German forces for its own and withdraw from Europe. See "Telegram from Theodore Achilles in Paris to Dulles," November 24, 1953, Bermuda Papers, Office of the Department of Defense, Assistant Secretaries of Defense, International Security Affairs, State Department Papers, 1952–54, Box 18, NA.

34. "Paper: Alternatives to the EDC, attached to Memorandum from Bowie to Dulles," December 1, 1953, PPS, Subject Files, Country and Area Files, Box 29, Europe 1952–53, Folder 5, NA. Beam also informed Bowie that DOD had also written an alternatives paper similar to the PPS paper, which repeated the military's position that German military participation in the EDC was critical and that any "limitation" of those forces "would be unacceptable." See "Memorandum from Beam to Bowie," December 9, 1953, PPS, Subject Files, Country and Area Files, Box 29, Europe 1952–53, Folder 2, NA.

35. "Notes on the Bermuda Conference, December 4–8, 1953, by President Eisenhower," December 10, 1953, Box 3, Folder 2, International Series, AWF. Eisenhower, Dulles, and Churchill all agreed that the alliance should not "single out Germany." They did not want a repeat of the 1920s, when Germany's isolation led to the rise of Hitler. However, the administration refused Churchill's call for a summit with the Soviets and his idea of "infiltrating" the Soviet bloc through trade and commerce. See "Telegram from Dulles to the State Department," December 8, 1953, Bermuda Papers, Defense Department, ISA, Box 18, NA, and Klaus Larres, *Churchill's Cold War: The Politics of Personal Diplomacy* (New Haven, Conn.: Yale University Press, 2002), 308–11.

36. "Personal Notes by Livingston T. Merchant," December 1953, Papers of Livingston T. Merchant, Correspondence and Related Materials 1944–1968, Box 1, Bermuda Conference 1953, Seeley G. Mudd Manuscript Library, Princeton University Libraries (hereafter cited as Merchant Papers, Princeton). For more on Churchill's ambivalence over the EDC, see John W. Young, *Winston Churchill's Last Campaign: Britain and the Cold War 1951–55* (Oxford: Clarendon Press, 1996), 58–61; Larres, *Churchill's Cold War*, 175–80; and Hubert Zimmerman, *Money and Security: Troops, Monetary Policy, and West Germany's Relations with the United States and Britain, 1950–1971* (New York: Cambridge University Press, 2002). Zimmerman

notes that the British especially feared that they would have to pay through the nose in terms of both troops and costs on the Continent because West Germany would not be able to afford to contribute its own forces to the EDC (19–22).

37. See "Memorandum on Bermuda Meeting Follow-Up," December 11, 1953, Paris Embassy France, Policy Guidance USIA CA Series, Box 40, NA, and "Letter from Eisenhower to Swede Hazlett," December 24, 1953, Swede Hazlett Papers, Box 3, Eisenhower Library.

38. "Letter from Dulles to Bowie," December 28, 1953, Dulles Papers, Correspondence, Box 67, Bowie, Robert R.

39. "Memorandum from Bowie to Bryce Harlow," December 30, 1953; "Insert by Bowie: Suggested Changes to the State of the Union," December 31, 1953; and "Memorandum from Dulles to Harlow," with attached "State of the Union Message: Foreign Affairs Section," January 2, 1954, all in PPS 1954, Box 81, State of the Union, NA, and "Annual Message to the Congress on the State of the Union," January 7, 1954, *The Public Papers of the Presidents of the United States: Dwight D. Eisenhower 1954* (Washington, D.C.: U.S. Government Printing Office, 1953), 7–9.

40. "Memorandum from Fuller to Bowie," January 5, 1954, PPS, Paris Tripartite Conversations, NA.

41. "Telegram from the Chargé in France to the Department of State," January 7, 1954, and "Telegram from the United States High Commissioner to the Department of State," January 13, 1954, both in *FRUS, Vol. VII, Part 1*, 747–50.

42. "Memorandum from Beam to Bowie with attached Paper: Briefing Paper on Prospects for Berlin Conference," January 20, 1954; "Memorandum from Fuller to Bowie with attached Paper: Long-Range Considerations in US German Policy," January 14, 1954, PPS 1954, Box 87, Germany; and "Memorandum from Bowie to Dulles with attachments," January 20, 1954, Dulles-Herter Series from the Eisenhower Library, Box 1, Berlin Conference, Folder 1, Dulles Papers.

43. "Memorandum of Discussion at the 181st Meeting of the National Security Council," January 21, 1954, NSC Series, Box 5, AWF.

44. "Telegram from Dulles to Eisenhower," January 26, 1954; "Telegram from Dulles to Eisenhower," January 30, 1954; "Telegram from Dulles to Acting Secretary of State Smith," February 16, 1954, all in Dulles-Herter Series, Box 2, January 1954, Folder 2, AWF.

45. "Memorandum of Conversation between Dulles and Molotov," February 6, 1954, Dulles-Herter Series, Box 2, Folder 1, AWF. Merchant recalled "the attack of the Russians on the rearmament of the Germans was directed you might say in a very real sense against the EDC." "Oral Interview with Livingston Merchant," Interview #2, OH-117, Columbia Oral History Project, Dwight D. Eisenhower Library. See also "Substance of Discussions of State-JCS Meeting," February 26, 1954, Box 51, Vol. VI, Folder 1, Meetings and Summaries, NA. Douglas MacArthur II noted that the Soviets' "objective was to divide and confuse allied opinion and present the posture of being willing to negotiate anything and everything. The main U.S. objective was to expose publicly what the U.S.S.R. stood for."

46. "Intelligence Report No. 5550.142," February 1, 1954, RG 59, Department of State, Bureau of Intelligence and Research, Coordinator for Psychological Intelligence, Intelligence Reports: Developments Significant for Propaganda, Box 3, NA.

47. "Memorandum from Bowie to Dulles," with attached Paper: "Reappraisal," May 16, 1954, PPS 1954, Box 86, Alliances, NA.

48. "Memorandum from Fuller to Bowie," May 11, 1954, and "Memorandum from Fuller to Bowie," May 27, 1954, PPS 1954, Box 87, Germany, NA.

49. "Memorandum from Fuller to Bowie," June 10, 1954, PPS 1954, Box 88, Europe, NA. Another member of the PPS, Louis Halle, meanwhile warned Bowie that the United States should take a long look in the mirror and recognize its own responsibility for the situation. Domestic pressure to turn inward, the "spectacle" of the McCarthy hearings, and the administration's continued discussion of the need to trim the defense budget had led to, as Merchant and Draper had advised the year before, "an increasing loss of confidence in our leadership." This had, Halle argued, "increased the cussedness in our allies of which we complain." The "present course," he argued, only helped the Kremlin. "Memorandum from Halle to Bowie," June 25, 1954, PPS 1954, Box 86, Alliances.

50. "Memorandum of Conversation between Dulles and Mendes-France," July 13, 1954, *FRUS 1952–1954, Vol. V*, 1020–21, and ""Memorandum from Fuller to Bowie," July 30, 1954, Box 87, Germany, NA. On July 24, the Soviets renewed their call for a European collective security without U.S. participation that they had first broached at the Berlin Conference in the winter.

• *3* •

Walt Whitman Rostow: Hawkeyed Optimist

Lloyd Gardner

*M*any years ago looking back on Vietnam, Walt Whitman Rostow discussed the historic reasons for involvement in Southeast Asia with a group of students and faculty attending a conference at the University of Texas. We were in Vietnam, he said, to give peoples in those countries a chance to choose their future unimpeded by great power interference and ideological dogmatism. To illustrate, he chose an autobiographical example from his youth in New Haven, Connecticut. His father, a baker and a Jewish immigrant with strong and active socialist leanings, named his sons after famous Americans Walt Whitman, Eugene Victor Debs, and Ralph Waldo Emerson. On Sunday mornings, he sent his boys out on bicycles to deliver bread across the city and into New Haven's black ghetto. The experience shaped Walt's outlook ever afterward. It was during those bicycle rounds, Rostow told his listeners, that he determined to spend his life dedicated to providing such people with a real chance for a better life.[1]

The fall of Saigon in the spring of 1975 had hit Rostow especially hard. It was the darkest day for American foreign policy, he told a television interviewer, since the failure to respond to the Japanese invasion of Manchuria in 1931. In other conversations, he declared that it was the end of the heroic postwar era that had begun with the Truman Doctrine and the Marshall Plan. By that time, most Americans had already gone past the point of no return in thinking about saving Vietnam, and Congress had passed the War Powers Act to prevent any more "Vietnams." But so much of Walt Rostow's career and personality became associated with the struggle in Southeast Asia—America's "longest war"—that he could hardly give it up. Up until the very end, he had been President Lyndon Johnson's loyalist supporter. And even after Richard Nixon tried and failed to save either Vietnam or his presidency,

Rostow urged a last-ditch effort. The United States, he said in a CBS television interview on April 4, 1975, should "land two Marine divisions in North Vietnam and keep them there" to make sure Hanoi abides by the 1973 Paris Peace Accords. President Gerald Ford should do this "as a matter of conscience."[2]

The missionary zeal that Rostow brought to the White House office of the national security adviser was not unique except perhaps in his insistence that America's obligations were indivisible; that is, the nation's duty to its less advantaged citizens could not be performed unless it was also engaged in promoting and sustaining the democratic revolution globally. This conviction separated him from Cold War "realists," who, when it was clear that Vietnam was a lost cause, urged Johnson to halt the bombing and negotiate a "decent interval" retreat from folly. True, choosing that path was not easy for "realists" either, and they backed out of the saloon, as one wit put it, with guns blazing. But not even Nixon was ready to send more troops once "Vietnamization" had begun. Walt Rostow was. What Presidents Nixon and Gerald Ford had done, he said, had undermined American alliances and the American cause worldwide.

Rostow's thoughts about the inseparability of manifest destiny and mission began in public schools in New Haven and matured into conviction at Yale and while he studied at Oxford from 1936 to 1938 on a Rhodes scholarship. He watched very apprehensively as British leaders debated policy at the height of the appeasement era in England or, as he would see it, the *depth* of the appeasement era. His contemporaries at Oxford included Edward Heath, Denis Healey, and Roy Jenkins, men who would make their marks as outstanding political leaders in the Cold War and like him were determined not to make new mistakes of the magnitude of Neville Chamberlain's Munich humiliation. Before Pearl Harbor, he had finished a doctorate at Yale and taught economics at Columbia. During the war, he worked in the Office of Strategic Services, the precursor of the Central Intelligence Agency (CIA) and a nursery of American Cold War intellectuals. He also saw duty as a target planner for the American and British air forces in the war against Germany. Describing his experience as target planner for American and British air forces in the war against Germany later, he emphasized that his team had to contend with German fighters, weather, and flak. "Essays on grand strategy," he told an interviewer "wouldn't have been worth a nickel to General [Carl] Spaatz." While he was correct that target selectors were not asked to be theoreticians, they were still at quite a remove from actual fighting and somewhat detached from the realities of combat on the ground. Given his famous role as the grand strategist of the Johnson years, when the president carefully selected *his* targets at Tuesday lunches each week with close advisers

in an effort to keep the Vietnam War from exploding into a general confla-
gration across Asia, his career seems all of a piece and part of the historic
American romance with technological solutions to political problems.[3]

After various academic positions at Ivy League schools, Rostow settled
in at the Massachusetts Institute of Technology (MIT), where he and another
economist, Max Millikan, were instrumental in the early 1950s in founding
the Center for International Studies (CIS). The CIS was an early example of
the think tanks that later came to play such a role in formulating policy positions, such as the more famous American Enterprise Institute in Washington.
The CIS never left Cambridge, but Millikan and Rostow dedicated the center's work to promoting successful Cold War policies and were anxious to link
up with government agencies as well as to improve the prospects of the social
sciences at MIT. The center's main website still features a tantalizing brief introduction to the hush-hush Project Troy, "a report, some of which remains
classified a half-century later":

> Project Troy resulted in the establishment of a research center at MIT
> funded by the CIA and located in a warehouse on Albany Street. Its first
> study, "Soviet Vulnerability," was conducted by Walt Rostow, the MIT
> economic historian who later served as national security advisor to presi-
> dents Kennedy and Johnson.[4]

An early 1953 memorandum from Project Troy's study of Soviet vulnerability emphasized that a key psychological moment would arrive with Stalin's
death. At such a moment, the Soviet Union would be particularly vulnerable
to a presidential initiative. Rostow's interest in psychological warfare com-
mended him to President Eisenhower's "psywar" specialist, C. D. Jackson,
who lobbied for just such a speech offering the Soviets "a chance for peace."
Ike delivered the speech in mid-April, but there was no real follow-up, as policy makers feared initiating anything that might weaken resolve at a time
when questions of German rearmament in a unified Western Europe were at
stake.[5]

Jackson and Rostow worked together on a series of speeches, nevertheless, not always appreciated by the dour secretary of state, John Foster Dulles,
who had a different take on psychological warfare. Writing to Jackson on August 20, 1953, the forty-year-old academic suggested that Jackson should say
in explaining the importance of big ideas, "I strongly feel that the basic
strength of the United States lies in the fact that our interests, properly formulated and properly explained, do coincide with the interests of people
everywhere. This includes the people of Russia and China."[6]

Indeed, if from a different angle than Dulles, Rostow was always more
of a "liberationist" thinker than a "containment" Cold War realist, an identi-

fication that became fully evident during the Vietnam War. Meanwhile, he was the unacknowledged author of Eisenhower's famous "Open Skies" proposal to the Soviet Union, which Ike threw out at the 1955 Geneva summit conference. It was a proposition sure to put the Russians on the defensive. The idea appealed to Americans and the mythical figure of Uncle Sam's honest Yankee traditions summoning the world back to common sense. It got a terrific press. But no one really expected the Soviet leaders to agree to American overflights. The United States kept pressing the plan anyway until the end of the Eisenhower years, calling the proposal a major step toward ending the threat of nuclear war. Russian efforts to point out that the American proposal excluded foreign bases seemed nitpickish to the Western press.

In 1958, the MIT economic historian and think-tank originator came to the attention of Massachusetts Senator John F. Kennedy, already eyeing a run for the presidency. Once they met, Rostow became a devoted supporter, supplying position papers on a vast range of subjects. "Of all the Cambridge crowd," said a Kennedy associate, "he was the most accessible, most versatile, and most for Kennedy." Returning from a year's sabbatical in England, Rostow undertook a nationwide speaking tour taking political temperatures along the way. He had discovered a general sense of uneasiness and worry about a lack of direction, he told the senator. Kennedy needed a winning campaign slogan, and Rostow had one to offer: "This country is ready to get moving again—and I'm prepared to lead it." Kennedy was slow to warm up to the phrase, but once he did, it became the campaign battle cry: "Let's get this country moving again." Rostow was also the source of the phrase "The New Frontier." Some even said the professor had become a one-man "brains trust." Kennedy's New Frontiersmen were generally leery, however, of casting themselves as heirs to the New Dealers, now thought to be too ideological for Kennedy's efforts to convey a postideological and technocratic approach to the nation's problems and the burgeoning crises bubbling up in the nonindustrial world. Rostow fit well with that temperament. He made an intriguing comment in 1962 on that very point. He was too young to have been an original New Dealer, he said, and his experience was different. "Many of us who now work in Washington were too young to be caught up in the New Deal, but we're products of the second World War, junior officer class." The statement implied that Americans had said good-bye to all that talk by President Franklin Roosevelt about malefactors of great wealth and his image as an anticapitalist scourge. The new liberalism's task instead was to shape America's role as world leader. No one, indeed, contributed more ideas for that role than Rostow. Kennedy quipped about Rostow's twelve books, "Walt is the only man I know who can write faster than I can read."[7]

The most famous of these, published in 1960, was *The Stages of Economic Growth*, aptly subtitled *A Non-Communist Manifesto*. It brought him instant attention in political circles as well as among his contemporaries in the academic world. The review-catching formulation in the book was his picture of the so-called takeoff stage, the point where traditional societies suddenly begin to leave their centuries-old fatalism behind and grasp at the possibilities of modernization. What forces trigger such a process? asked Rostow Sometimes they may boil up from inside the traditional society, he wrote, but mostly they occur from the outside: "The more general case in modern history . . . saw the stage of preconditions arise not endogenously but from some external intrusion by more advanced societies. These invasions—literal or figurative—shocked the traditional society and began or hastened its undoing; but they also set in motion ideas and sentiments which initiated the process by which a modern alternative to the traditional society was constructed out of the old culture."

Communism and capitalism were cast as opposing external forces in this Pilgrim's Progress drama of world development. Capitalism was the pilgrim doing the heavy lifting and suffering the taunts of ideology bound, while communism was an opportunistic "scavenger" in the transition period to modernization. In this centuries-old drama going back to the French Revolution, romantic revolutionaries (Rostow would call them) often surged to the top briefly—wreaking havoc and bringing in their wake years of tyranny and human suffering. The last of these, he would say, was Mao Tse-tung, the Chinese communist ruler. To thwart such deceivers and anticipate crises was the task of the National Security Council. In a 1961 speech at the U.S. Army Special Warfare School in Fort Bragg, North Carolina, for example, he declared that "Communism is best understood as a disease of the transition to modernization." "I decided when I was 18," Rostow told a congressional committee, "that when I learned enough I was going to do an alternative to Marxism because I knew a lot of people in the world were taken in by this theory, and I finally took my shot at it." The underlying assumption of *Stages of Economic Growth* was that the American Revolution was the *only* revolution the world needed or could live with in safety. Outside the Kennedy administration, Rostow's efforts did not meet universal acclaim. His theories were anglocentric, complained critics, tracing all modernization to Great Britain in the eighteenth century and to the United States as its only heir. "Rostow conceded so many non-typical cases," observed Godfrey Hodgson at the time of his death in 2003, "that it is hard to identify a case that exemplified his theory."[8]

Whatever these critics might say, his views commanded attention on the watchtowers of the New Frontier. *The Stages of Economic Growth* held such a strong appeal for the Kennedy team because Rostow offered a grand theory for encouraging dynamic change in the underdeveloped world, where Americans perceived malign influences feeding off the inevitable difficulties of modernization. On taking office, Kennedy had distributed to his advisers a speech by Soviet Premier Nikita Khrushchev that praised wars of "national liberation" and posed the question to them, "What is our answer?"

Not in a vain effort to find security in a "garrison state," Max Millikan and Rostow had long argued. To do so would undermine democracy at home. "With modern communications it is difficult to envisage the survival of a democratic American society as an island in a totalitarian sea."[9] The image of a powerful communist movement generated in Moscow and sweeping across Asia and Africa was an incredibly simplistic reading of world events and fatefully shaped the proposed remedies to meet the challenge, but the president's advisers responded to Kennedy's call with a range of answers, from the Peace Corps to the Green Berets and a race to the moon. Counterinsurgency became the buzzword with military libraries around the country buying huge numbers of books by communist and precommunist theoreticians so that no officer might be illiterate on the subjects being discussed at the Pentagon and in the National Security Council.

Rostow had originally been tabbed by the new president to head the Policy Planning Council in the Department of State, but when his secretary of state designate, Dean Rusk, objected, he wound up in National Security Adviser McGeorge Bundy's office as deputy with special responsibility for Southeast Asia. But in either place, he ranked high among Bundy's celebrated "action intellectuals," described in deftly ambiguous terms by David Halberstam as *The Best and Brightest*. Another writer, Stanley Karnow, commented that Rostow was best understood as an armchair tactician trying to prove "that a short bespectacled intellectual could be tough."[10]

After the embarrassing flop at the Bay of Pigs in mid-April 1961, Rostow did have some "tough" advice. The problem, as he saw it, was where to pick the place to start afresh. There was no time to lose because delay would give the impression "that we are up against a game we can't handle." "A clean-cut success in Viet-Nam would do much to hold the line in Asia while permitting us—and the world—to learn how to deal with indirect aggression." His job, as he would say, was to anticipate where such alien forces sought openings and to devise the means to thwart their purposes with whatever methods necessary. In Vietnam, he decided, that meant military forces, not just diplomacy.[11]

Vietnam was the newest Cold War battlefield, where outside intervention was playing havoc with the traditional societies that made up the new states of the former French Indochina: Cambodia, Laos, and Vietnam. In political terms, of course, an Asian success would repair the damage to Kennedy's bruised post–Bay of Pigs image in the American press. In mid-1961, Kennedy sent Rostow and General Maxwell Taylor to Vietnam to survey firsthand the worsening situation. For Rostow, Vietnam became a test case for *Stages*. When he arrived in Saigon, the president of the Republic of Vietnam, Ngo Dinh Diem, asked him for advice as an expert on such wars as the Vietcong had initiated against his government. Alas, Rostow had to conclude, Diem did not have the right temperament to encourage the new generation of technocrats, men who could be instrumental in saving his country from the communists. He was locked in Oriental ways, not trusting anyone he could not confront face-to-face. Perhaps his resistance to modern ways of dealing with subordinates could be overcome. The key problem, however, was not of his making. Diem faced an "open frontier" situation, and no nation since Napoleonic times had won a guerrilla war where an open frontier allowed the insurgents to cross back and forth with impunity. From this first real encounter with Vietnam, Rostow zeroed in on the hard decision to send troops to close that "open frontier." He was still pushing the idea as the final days of the war approached nearly fifteen years later.

On their return, Taylor and Rostow recommended sending troops, not just military advisers. They shared a firm belief that they had not been sent to Vietnam to accept defeat. As Taylor put it, "The question was how to change a losing game and begin to win, not how to call it off."[12] There was only one way to do that. "We wanted some American troops to be flown in," he said in one of many postwar interviews. "Uh, Kennedy, who was much influenced by [General Douglas] MacArthur and generally took the view that he didn't want to put troops in unless he was forced to[,] made a compromise and had a . . . battalion of marines put offshore. In . . . in other words he missed the point that was. . . that Taylor and [he had] made it, that without putting men . . . additional men—aside from the trainers and the advisers, military advisers—uh, he didn't put any regular troops in at that time."[13]

At the time, their report set off a battle royal. Several key members of the administration lined up behind the idea of sending troops—regardless of previous international agreements on arms and manpower limitations on outside aid, such as the 1954 Geneva Agreement, which ended the first Indochina War. Geneva had ended with an agreement on all-Vietnamese elections to be held in 1956, although the United States had refused to sign the final declaration. Elections were never held because the United States had replaced the French as the power behind the throne in Saigon and said no, ostensibly because elections could not be free in the north but in reality because Eisenhower knew that the communist leader, Ho Chi Minh, would win all-Vietnamese elections. A guerrilla war began in the countryside. With typical hyperbole, Rostow proclaimed that the conflict in Southeast Asia "might be the last great confrontation" with communist wars of national liberation and, indeed, with communism itself. That was justification enough for ignoring Geneva.[14]

As the Rostow–Taylor report circulated in the White House, Kennedy's old friend, John Kenneth Galbraith, then ambassador to India, arrived in town with Prime Minister Pandit Nehru in tow. Hearing what was afoot, Galbraith went to Rostow's office and asked to see the report. Galbraith had known Rostow for twenty years and did not trust his opinions. Rostow refused. "Ken, this is eyes-only for the President of the United States, top secret, you can't take a look at this report." Galbraith retorted, "That's nonsense Walt, I have the same security clearance as a senior US Ambassador that you have as a National Security Advisor. I want to see the report." When Rostow turned to answer the phone, Galbraith snatched it up and walked out of his office. It was a dramatic beginning to a two-week-long campaign by the ambassador to dissuade Kennedy from sending troops.[15]

This time the skeptics won. But the Galbraith–Rostow debate was only the first of many subsequent intra-administration wrestling matches to come in both the Kennedy and the Johnson years. Rostow lost on this one, whether it was Galbraith's influence or Kennedy's own doubts. But the struggle for the president's heart and mind had barely begun.[16] It lasted until Kennedy's assassination in 1963, when Lyndon Johnson assumed the burden and was terrified of both accusations that he had "lost" Vietnam or of getting bogged down in a new Korea. Rostow rightly called this a period of deep anxiety. Kennedy's "will" on Vietnam has been the subject of endless debate both inside the academy and among policy makers. It has been read by supporters to justify escalation and by opponents of the war to anticipate withdrawal. The argument is ongoing even today, with moments of great passion, because it goes far beyond the academic community into the spinning vortex of later policy debates over Middle Eastern policies. Those who see Kennedy pulling back from a fateful commitment at the last moment find in his doubts a useful past for their own fears about staying the course in another deteriorating war.

Not for Rostow, however, such black thoughts. He never backed off from his effort to solve the problem of closing Vietnam's "open frontiers" by attacking north of the Geneva-imposed barrier originally designed to facilitate all Vietnamese elections and to last only until the nation was reunited. He spoke often of his regret that neither Kennedy nor Johnson were willing to take that step for fear of widening the war and bringing on a Chinese ground intervention—or even possibly a nuclear exchange. Had Kennedy acted in 1961 or 1962, he insisted, the whole history of the war might well have ended in a victory for the noncommunist revolution. Bombing North Vietnam would never in itself be the final answer to guerrilla warfare. "No . . . let me get it straight. Uh, it [the bombing] was successful in that it imposed a certain tax. It could've been much more effective I think. But I took the view from the beginning that given the nature of the Ho Chi Minh trails . . . that we could only block them, not from the air but by sending, say, 2 American divisions into Laos, and that would've been a splendid place to fight because no civilians lived there. We could block those trails on the ground but we couldn't block them from the air."

Why didn't the presidents take his advice, asked his interviewers? "Well, the reason. . . I've often wondered about that and I think that [General William] Westmoreland and I have very much the same view. LBJ undertook this war with a very heavy heart, as I say, but with a great responsibility that it not lead to a nuclear war. He thought he was facing two—the nuclear powers, Russia and China—and he was very careful. . . . He had plenty of nuclear weapons but he saw that it was not in the American interest—and above all, it was not in the global interest—and that was a very deep thing. . . . After all, he was elected president, I wasn't elected . . . I wasn't elected by anybody. I was an adviser, I gave him my best advice. I thought the situation was that say you could . . . put ground forces across the trails in Laos. But he was elected, not I, to make the decision. I stayed with it to the last day."[17]

Rostow's rambling postwar critique of Kennedy and Johnson for not sealing the "open frontier" by moving into the Laos "corridor" early on was a variant of the missed opportunities thesis of why the war was lost, although he never agreed with later Vietnam revisionists that it was lost because of failure to carry out a much more ruthless bombing campaign than Rolling Thunder. He also dodged the question of whether it was a mistake (morally or practically) to begin serious American involvement by removing Diem from power at the end of October 1963, a point of no return that made the war an American enterprise once and for all. All he would say on that point was to enlarge a bit on his concern that Diem did not work out a relationship with those "young technocrats" as he had urged in 1961. Diem was, Rostow said, a difficult man—and left it at that.

Rostow insisted that he really was out of the loop on most of the discussions about Vietnam until he became national security adviser midway in the Johnson years. That might be so, but his voice was heard frequently in the Kennedy administration alongside the most hawkish of the president's advisers. In May 1964, Rostow, now back at the State Department, was asked to write a major policy recommendation for Vietnam. The continuing turmoil after Diem's removal and assassination at the end of October 1963 had raised questions about Washington's willingness to go on tolerating a messy situation and might be willing to consider French President Charles deGaulle's suggestion of pursuing an interim "neutralist" solution, which, everyone knew, meant accepting a communist Vietnam. The French leader had earlier warned Kennedy that Vietnam was a rotten place to attempt a stand against what John Foster Dulles had habitually called the menace of "international communism," a terminology that unfortunately reduced international politics to a flat-earth east–west axis and made raising such questions un-American.

Kennedy's ambiguity had not resolved itself by the time of his assassination, and Johnson was left with the feeling that he would be blamed for "losing" Indochina or, as eventually happened, winding up with a new Korea on his hands—a battlefield stalemate at higher and higher troop levels. Rostow's draft memorandum, according to British historian Godfrey Hodgson, became the basis for Johnson's August 4, 1964, speech announcing that he had sent planes to bomb North Vietnamese PT-boat bases in retaliation for the attacks on American ships in the Gulf of Tonkin. There was scant evidence at the time that the second, more provocative attack had even taken place. At the time, Johnson envisaged the Gulf of Tonkin Resolution he secured with scarcely a demur from both Houses of Congress as an antidote to anticipated Republican attacks for running away from a fight—or so, at least, he said to supporters. He wanted no wider war, he insisted, as he took each fateful step up the ladder. Yet it was true that his primary goal in 1964 was to achieve a huge margin of victory to get on with his Great Society domestic program. But Rostow clearly saw it as a different sort of opportunity. The primary purpose of the retaliation and securing in advance congressional support for other steps as they became necessary was to put an end to the period of anxiety. Tit-for-tat responses would never do the job. As he saw it, the Tonkin Resolution opened a new page in war planning, beginning with a diplomatic offensive but also a willingness to cause pain on the Chinese "mainland" to halt a drift toward a much bigger war—inevitable unless the communists backed off. "They [Hanoi and Beijing] should now feel they confront an LBJ who has made up his mind. Contrary to the anxiety expressed at an earlier stage, I believe it quite possible to communicate the limits as well as the seriousness of our intentions," he wrote to Secretary of Defense Robert McNamara, thereby avoiding stirring up fears that the United States intended to land troops in China itself.[18]

No troops to China, then, but Rostow eagerly anticipated using two divisions in Laos to close the frontier. Neither he nor anyone else expected a war in which 500,000 men would be sent to Southeast Asia. He would argue vehemently that troops to Laos would cut short the war without bringing on a Chinese reaction. But the consensus held that the North Vietnamese would rather preserve their hard-earned gains since 1954 rather than face an American assault from the air. Rostow had considerably less faith in that assumption than did others, such as General Taylor, but he did not deny that the threat to destroy North Vietnam's infrastructure would give Hanoi pause. He had written to President Johnson on June 6, 1964, boldly speculating that closing off the open frontiers could bring about a fragmentation of the communist movement in South Vietnam like what happened in Greece in the early Cold War after Stalin closed the Yugoslav frontier as a result of his rift with Tito. The Greek analogy was a favorite one as the war went on, used often by Secretary of State Dean Rusk to suggest that insurgencies could be defeated. Whatever it was, Vietnam was not something new under the sun, Rostow argued. It was simply inaccurate historically to contend that Mao or Ho Chi Minh or Che Guevara had invented insurgency. There had been successful insurgencies long before they came along, such as those led by the American revolutionary hero Francis Marion, the "Swamp Fox," or T. E. Lawrence, known to all the world as "Lawrence of Arabia," who led the Arabs against the Ottoman Empire. There had been unsuccessful insurgencies as well but only when one understood the need to close frontiers. Rostow's creed accepted the Cold War premise that the Kremlin could turn revolutions on and off depending on circumstances and, further, that closing an open frontier would produce discouragement, leading insurgents to abandon the field. Sealing off South Vietnam by invading Laos was a foolish temptation because it rested on the false premise that the insurgency had been "exported" and therefore could be shut off in a few easy steps, like shutting a water tap.[19]

Johnson sent the first 100,000 troops to South Vietnam in July 1965. A few months later, Secretary of Defense Robert McNamara gave the president a Rostovian argument for why American policy had reached this point where massive intervention had become necessary as a result of China's efforts to build an anti-American coalition across Asia:

> This understanding of a straightforward security threat is interwoven with another perception—namely, that we have our view of the way the U.S. should be moving and of the need for the majority of the rest of the world to be moving in the same direction if we to are achieve our national objectives . . . . Our ends cannot be achieved and our leadership role cannot be played if some powerful and virulent nation—whether Germany, Japan, Russia or China—is allowed to organize their part of the world according to a philosophy contrary to ours.[20]

These were also Rostow's sentiments. He moved into Bundy's office in 1966 long after the basic decisions had been made to start the bombing campaign known as Rolling Thunder and the seemingly never-ending process of troop escalation. Just before assuming these duties, on April 21,

1966, he sent President Johnson a memorandum, "Vietnam—the Critical Issues," that argued for stepped-up military action to close the infiltration trails and cause greater enemy casualties. Time was running short. "They are playing us as they did the French in 1953." "Our task is to convince them at the earliest possible moment that they are wrong; and that time is their enemy, not their friend." War weariness, he feared, could cause a breakdown in both Saigon and Washington if the struggle appeared endless. He hoped the president could gain enough time by explaining to the nation what the stakes were by saying something like, "We are all being tested by this crisis." In words that might have come right out of *The Stages of Economic Growth*, Rostow urged the president to educate the people "to understand the nature of the war; to understand the confusing but essentially constructive struggle of a democratic nation to bloom; and, above all, by the fact that the Communists are counting on us to despair and give up." "If our people really understand, I believe they would be quite tolerant of the birth pangs."[21]

Rostow had followed another self-confident national security adviser, McGeorge Bundy, the Harvard dean whom John Kennedy brought to the White House. Bundy's dominant personality largely defined the nation's idea of a national security adviser even down to the present. He remains the yardstick for measuring others.[22] Even so, Kennedy never relied on his predecessor in the same way Johnson used Walt Rostow. Kennedy felt more at home dealing with foreign policy questions, and the relationship Bundy would have with Johnson was quite different and on a different order completely than Rostow's closeness to Johnson. Presidential chronicler Hugh Sidey put it this way about Johnson and Rostow: "The value of being physically close to the President was fully realized in those years. L.B.J. was profoundly influenced by the fact that Rostow was always close by. Visitors being harangued by Johnson in the dead of night were often astounded when L.B.J. would mash one of his numerous signal buttons and Rostow would materialize out of the darkened corridors."[23]

From the moment Rostow took up his duties, the president faced an increasingly restive Congress, not willing to break with Johnson on the war or with the Cold War assumptions behind it yet uneasy about the direction things were heading. Walt Rostow had been named national security adviser when Bundy resigned to head the Ford Foundation. Not a few regarded Bundy's departure as a telling sign of Kennedyite disapproval of the direction Johnson had taken in Southeast Asia, but others pointed out that Kennedy had also picked out Rostow to be Bundy's deputy and then, a few months later, to head the State Department's Policy Planning Council. Rostow was ready to take up the challenge.

Senator Fulbright's reconsideration of the Vietnam War, meanwhile, had begun with a sharply worded speech criticizing the administration's intervention in the Dominican Republic. During hearings on the war in January 1966 that he called as chairman of the Senate Foreign Relations Committee under the guise of considering a special appropriation for funding of the war, Fulbright captured the nation's attention with his old-South drawl. Rostow was not called to testify. Defending the war against Fulbright's skepticism, Dean Rusk carried the burden of the administration's case. Asked if the United States believed it could avert all revolutions in the underdeveloped world, the secretary of state responded with a quietly self-assured definition of good and bad revolutions that left several committee members agog at his implications. "Not necessarily avert all of them," began Rusk, "but I do believe there is a fundamental difference between the kind of revolution which the Communists call their wars of national liberation, and the kind of revolution that is congenial to our own experience, and fits into the aspirations of ordinary men and women right around the world."[24]

Johnson and Rostow had been stung recently by a letter from Fulbright, who now bitterly regretted having guided the Gulf of Tonkin Resolution through the Senate in such confident fashion. It had become a vehicle for unlimited expansion of the war. The White House, he charged, was using the war in Vietnam to build a client-state "U.S. Empire" in an attempt to prevent China from dominating Asia, as its size and potential made seem inevitable. Rostow drafted a response that argued that American policy had to sustain equilibrium of forces in Asia. But first, given China's new armies and emerging nuclear power, the war in Vietnam had to be won to allow for an "irreducible interdependence" with the West for all states bordering on the mainland power, an interesting way of defining containment under a different rubric. Johnson also relied on Rostow's ideas in a July 12, 1966, speech on the theme of U.S. desire to build a "truly world civilization in the Pacific." Fulbright responded with a speech saying he had discussed this subject of the U.S. role in Asia with Rostow and come away with the troubling impression that the national security adviser believed it was proper for the United States to become the major power in the area. "I am not saying this policy is necessarily wrong," but it "comes as a great shock to think that this concept of our role could be contemplated without consideration by the Senate." Fulbright put his doubts into a book titled *The Arrogance of Power* (1966), making him even less popular in the White House.[25]

Johnson turned back all congressional challenges by waving a creased and crinkled piece of paper under the noses of every group of legislators who came to the White House. Rescind it, he said, holding out the Gulf of Tonkin Resolution; go ahead, stop supporting the war with our boys over there in the jungle counting on the home front to hold steady. It would take almost another decade for Congress to do anything like that and then only when a president had already begun the process of withdrawing ground forces and, even more important, struggling to keep above the tides of the Watergate investigation swirling into the Oval Office.

Rostow's personal experiences back in New Haven when he was growing up began to take on a new relevance for him as the war situation worsened in 1967 and the sense of crisis compounded by summer riots in several American cities, mostly involving the black ghettos. Johnson felt particularly aggrieved at this untoward development, as he felt he could rightly claim to have done more for black Americans than any American president since Abraham Lincoln. Rostow looked at the situation and concluded that it meant—more than ever—that the fate of American society depended on victory in Vietnam. He even invoked a Republican Party theme, law and order, to make his point. "It is a fact that we cannot play our part on the world scene unless we do so from a base of order and progress at home; and, equally, we cannot build order and progress at home in a world where U.S. withdrawal from its responsibilities result in an international environment of chaos and violence. . . . Therefore, we must—and we can—find the energy, talent, and resources to work for order and progress at home and abroad."[26]

In another message to the president, Rostow argued the odd position that Hanoi might be willing to negotiate an acceptable deal now, midsummer 1967, out of fear that if the Republicans won the White House in a year, they would face an even tougher prospect. One wonders how Johnson received that piece of advice. What had to be done, said the national security adviser, was to add to the building pressure on the Vietcong, whose morale, he said that he knew from intelligence reports, was getting lower as the enemy had a difficult time recruiting new troops and even foraging for food. Now was the time to press the issue with every possible means in the north and the south. Once again, also, the idea of sending troops to Laos emerged—as it always would in Rostow's manifestos. He gave Johnson the impression that his conclusions were based on the reading of "literally hundreds" of intelligence reports in several provinces. What was Johnson to make of all this as Rostow told him the one thing to do was not to discourage the view that the Republicans "may even be tougher"? The implications were hardly flattering to a president who had wagered so much, for they suggested that so far he had not fought the war to win and that the Republicans would, thereby destroying his heritage as the man who had outdone Roosevelt in war and peace. And they would do so even at the risk of bringing on a war with China, always Johnson's worst fear.[27]

Rostow, like other presidential advisers during both the Kennedy and the Johnson administrations, did not believe it at all likely that China would intervene even if, as he had argued from the beginning, the United States sought to close the "open frontier" or attacked above the eighteenth parallel, the 1954 truce line. In February 1967, he traveled to Leeds University in England to deliver the Sir Montague Burton Lecture. He chose as his title, "The Great Transition: Tasks of the First and Second Postwar Generation." His theme, as usual, was that Vietnam now stood as the center of the great transition and that the concept of wars of national liberation was "old-fashioned." "It is being overtaken not merely by the resistance of the seven nations fighting there, but also by history and by increasingly pervasive attitudes of pragmatism and moderation." Place by place, the Chinese communist offensive in the developing world had fallen apart, "leaving the war in Viet Nam perhaps the last major stand of Mao's doctrine of guerrilla warfare." Even so, a failure in Vietnam would have terrible implications and "could destroy the emerging foundation for confidence and regional cooperation in Asia, with further adverse consequences on every continent."[28]

Communist ideology was all but moribund, he argued, but losing Vietnam would destroy the chances for progress. It sounded contradictory. But he continued spooning out megadoses of an elixir of optimism even as the situation grew worse and the nation's patience grew thin. Rostow soon became the target of satirical jibes. In 1967, a departing White House Asia expert, James C. Thomson, circulated an imaginary account of a National Security Council (NSC) meeting held on the morning after the fall of Saigon. It was chaired by the "Hon. Herman Melville Breslau." Mr. Breslau was unfazed by this temporary setback. "In general, he felt, the events of the previous day were a wholesome and not unexpected phase in South Vietnam's growth toward political maturity and economic viability. The fall of Saigon to the Viet Cong meant that the enemy was now confronted with a challenge of unprecedented proportions for which it was totally unprepared: the administration of a major city." What had to be done now was to drop supplies to the anticommunist Vietnamese in other regions, and soon Saigon could be back in the hands of America's allies.[29]

Thomson's account of Breslau's ability to spin silver linings from dark clouds mirrored real events. At one NSC meeting, recalled CIA analyst George Allen, Rostow cited the defection of a supposed Vietcong leader as proof of low morale among the enemy. Let the Saigon press corps deal with that evidence, Rostow said. Allen interrupted to say that this particular defector had come in from the jungle at least twice before, whenever he wished to stock up on some needed commodity. Rostow shot back, "Get on the team." The national security adviser would simply not hear the rising tumult of dissenting voices. In the summer of 1967, Rostow assembled a group from White House staffs, the Department of State, the Department of Defense, and the U.S. Information Agency along with a CIA representative to develop a campaign to persuade Congress and the public that real progress was being made in pacification of the countryside. Allen refused to go along with any report that "cooked the books." Infuriated, Rostow scraped together optimistic bits and pieces culled from several CIA reports. Included with the summary, however, was a qualifying page the agency insisted on adding, detailing recent setbacks and adverse trends. Rostow stripped the page off before giving it to the president with a covering note, "At last, Mr. President, a useful assessment from the CIA."[30]

Resentful of Rostow's handling of the report, Allen protested the implication that the CIA was a chronic naysayer. CIA Director Richard Helms sent Johnson in September 1967 a much more heretical memorandum prepared by the agency that even challenged the premise of the war, the near sacrosanct "domino thesis" that Eisenhower had announced almost casually at a 1954 press conference. Helms closed his covering letter with an ambivalent nod to Oval Office convictions about the war. "It has no bearing on whether the present political-military outlook within Vietnam makes acceptance of such an outcome advisable or inadvisable."[31] It was not an argument for or against getting out: "We are not defeatist out here" (at Langley). But the memorandum's author argued that gradual withdrawal could be managed to minimize damage to the nation's position abroad and lessen the domestic political fallout. And it ended, "If the analysis here advances the discussion at all, it is in the direction of suggesting that the risks [of an unfavorable outcome] are probably more limited and controllable than most previous argument has indicated."[32]

Comments Johnson made to Australian journalists about the domino thesis, with the assistance of National Security Adviser Walt Rostow, standing close by might be seen as his response to the memo. Turning to the national security adviser, the president asked him to summarize the consequences of pulling out of Vietnam. Rostow gave the domino thesis a new spin by suggesting the first reaction would be "an immediate and profound political crisis" not in Vietnam but in the United States. Out of this turmoil, he argued, the forces behind a "powerful isolationism" would emerge triumphant. Johnson then led him on to a further conclusion: "They would say our character had worn out?" Rostow replied, "Yes." And while we were divided and preoccupied by the debilitating debate, the Soviet Union and China would seize dangerous initiatives. The North Atlantic Treaty Organization "could never hold up" as America searched in vain for its lost self-confidence. On and on he continued this litany of disasters, countering any and all arguments advanced in the Helms memo.[33]

Rostow seized on the capture and death of Fidel Castro's comrade in arms, Ernesto Che Guevara, as indicative of world trends away from wars of national liberation. He had been taken alive, he wrote the president, by Bolivian armed forces, who then ordered him shot. "I regard this as stupid, but understandable from a Bolivian viewpoint." There were significant positives from his death that extended beyond the removal of an irritant presence in Latin America. It marked the passing of another of the "aggressive, romantic revolutionaries like Sukarno, Nkrumah, Ben Bella—and reinforces this trend." Second, it would discourage other would-be guerrillas throughout Latin America. Finally, "it shows the soundness of our 'preventive medicine' assistance to countries facing incipient insurgency—it was the Bolivian 2nd Ranger Battalion, trained by our Green Berets from June-September of this year, that cornered him and got him." He was making sure that all these points were being made to several news reporters.[34]

For the national security adviser, all the world had become Vietnam, and Vietnam had become all the world. Rostow presented President Johnson with a chart he had devised demonstrating that the "crossover point" was approaching—the moment when American troop reinforcements surpassed North Vietnamese and Vietcong ability to replace their losses. According to a chart of the sort Rostow treasured, infiltration had fallen off dramatically in the first eight months of 1967 from a monthly average the previous year of between 7,000 and 8,000 to between 4,000 and 5,000. From such statistics, it was possible to glimpse the crossover point just beyond the next rice paddy. But Johnson never got there. The president even brought his commander, General William Westmoreland, back to Washington at the end of 1967 to assure Congress and the public. The general made speeches, gave television interviews, and was guided along by Johnson at a congressional briefing. "We feel that we are somewhat like the boxer in the ring," Westmoreland told congressional leaders, "where we have got our opponent almost on the ropes. And we hear murmurs to our rear as we look over the shoulder that the second wants to throw in the towel."[35]

Johnson then urged the general to talk about what bad shape the enemy was in. "Tell them the story about the company that came down the other day and [most] over 38 years of age and 20 of them didn't make it." Westmoreland was eager to oblige. "I talked to the President today about this, and made the point that North Vietnam is having manpower problems." The general then related how *his* intelligence—not those sitting 12,000 miles away from the scene—had learned from a captured prisoner about a company of 120 men who left North Vietnam to head south to battle. Twenty men fell out sick or deserted. Of the rest, forty were over thirty-eight years old. "And 38 for a Vietnamese is an old man, I can assure you. . . . So, they are having to go now to the young group and to the old group."[36]

Westmoreland returned to Saigon leaving a trail of "bring 'em on" statements behind to aid Rostow in rallying Democratic troops behind Johnson. They came. And they came in such numbers that the immediate fate of President Thieu's government was in doubt for several days. Afterward, the enemy's 1968 Tet Offensive was labeled a great failure by those who continued to believe that the war could be won with a different strategy and a different president. The point can be argued until one is blue in the face, but it remains true that the Saigon government after Diem's ouster was little more than an army without a state. At some point, moreover, the Americans would have to come home, as the war was now causing major disruptions to the world economic system and posing a direct challenge to the dwindling supply of gold that had backed the dollar, the world's reserve currency since the end of World War II.

The eldest of the Cold War elders, former Secretary of State Dean Acheson, who had been, as he wrote, *Present at the Creation*, now intervened in an effort to save Johnson from Walt Rostow's blindness to political realities. Acheson, after meeting with the so-called Council of Wisemen, wrote Johnson about the urgent need to begin withdrawing from Vietnam. He was worried about the danger that withdrawal would signal that the United States had lost its stomach for managing other commitments, but he insisted that disengagement could be carried out over "a period of time" to lessen the impact. Rostow interceded yet again, this time to argue that the Acheson approach represented an extremist alternative:

> We are at a most important moment in postwar history. Both the Communist world and the non-Communist world are in considerable disarray. The outcome—whether in Vietnam or in the gold crisis—depends on how free men behave in the days and weeks ahead.[37]

Two weeks later, Johnson announced a partial bombing halt and his decision not to run for reelection. Leaks had become newspaper headlines about Westmoreland's supposed request for an additional 200,000 troops to pursue the Tet "victory." Questions about the origins of the troop request remain unanswered, but it appears to have been an effort to force mobilization of the reserves to fight the war at a different level politically as much as militarily. The debates inside the president's tightest circle had become centered on what kind of speech Johnson should give to announce his new decisions on the war. Some drafts had him hunkering down, as he liked to say, like a jackrabbit in a dust storm. But over a period of days, Johnson began moving in the direction of a "peace" speech. Rostow at one point passed a note to CIA Director Richard Helms:

Dick:
About the only hope we've got, I conclude, is that:
— the North Vietnamese *do* mount a big offensive (B-3, Hue, Quang Tri, Khe Sanh);
— the 101, Airmobile, and the marines clobber them between now and May 15.
— Just like Lincoln in 1864.
Walt[38]

The infuriating thing about the war had always been the asymmetrical challenge. Rostow ached for the enemy to "mount a big offensive" that could be met by conventional forces. But after Tet, that was unlikely. The North Vietnamese/Vietcong forces had suffered great losses, and the battle had been, in strictly military terms, a "defeat." The hope that the enemy would provoke such action before May 15 seemed an unlikely prospect. What Rostow meant by the deadline was not entirely clear, but it appeared to have to do mostly with the political calendar in the United States. At this point, Rostow did not know that Johnson would be a lame-duck president. He had not confided in his national security adviser about this decision, but Rostow put in May 15 as a likely last-ditch moment to show that the war could be won by military means before politics trumped strategy.

Mac Bundy had one last lap around the policy circle when he was summoned to Washington to sit with the Wise Men. It fell to him to give the president the news that the Wise Men had decided against the war. "There is a very significant shift in our position." At an earlier meeting of these Cold War knights of the roundtable, there had been some hope. Not now. Acheson chimed in, saying that it was not possible to build "an independent South Vietnam." This shaft was aimed directly at Rostow's belief that with a little more time and a little help from Saigon's friends, it could all turn out right in the end. General Earle "Buzz" Wheeler, back from consultations in Saigon, protested that the United States was not trying to win a military victory in the ordinary sense. Acheson found that a fatuous statement. "Then what in the name of God are five hundred thousand men out there doing—chasing girls? This is not a semantic game, General; if the deployment of all those men is not an effort to gain a military solution, then words have lost all meaning."[39]

Upset by this evidence that everything had come apart, Johnson appealed to Rostow for help. "What the hell do they want me to do? What *can* we do that we're not doing?" The national security adviser saw his opening, perhaps his last chance. "Well, Mr. President, you know, as we've talked about before," and launched into the case for invading North Vietnam and Laos. An aide, Harry McPherson was present and reported on Johnson's reaction.

"Johnson just *flinched*, just *jumped*." He did not even want McPherson to hear such things. "No, no, no, I don't want to talk about that," he said. The president did not want somebody going public with the idea of a surge into North Vietnam, saying, "Oh, my God, we're going to invade North Vietnam."[40]

After Johnson gave his speech taking himself out of the presidential campaign, at least as a candidate, and ordering a partial suspension of the bombing, the internal struggle in the administration shifted to the instructions to be given to the American representatives at peace talks. Hanoi accepted Johnson's invitation, and the talks were set to take place in Paris. Rostow suggested that it was unrealistic (to say the least) to assume that all the communists would be converted or go north after the fighting ended. He still believed, apparently, that the war had been won and that Hanoi, in accepting the Paris meeting, was actually suing for peace. But then he added, Saigon should give consideration to allowing the National Liberation Front (Vietcong) to participate as a political party "after a period of delay." "The President's formulation is a one-man-one-vote solution." It was not, he insisted, a coalition solution. Secretary of State Dean Rusk had repeated umpteen times during the war that the communists would never be allowed to shoot their way into the South Vietnamese government. Now here Rostow was, suggesting that Saigon allow the National Front for the Liberation of South Vietnam (NLF) a role—but, of course, only on a one-man-one-vote basis. This idea of saving face "after a period of delay," to allow time to elapse so that it would not appear to be anything like a coalition or, worse, deGaulle's "neutralization," was scarcely different from his successor Henry Kissinger's appeal for a "decent interval" before the fall.[41]

The long summer of 1968 saw the Paris talks stalemated on what shape the conference table should be: round, or square, or some odd contour. While it was symbolic, the issue was serious as it forced the American delegation to consider what role the NLF would have not after a period of delay but immediately. Meanwhile, Johnson wrestled with demands that the partial bombing halt be made a complete cessation. In the very last days of the presidential campaign, Johnson bit the bullet and ordered the bombing stopped. But he could not deliver the Saigon regime to the table in time to save Vice President Hubert Humphrey's bid for the White House. Former Vice President Richard Nixon won, having said only that he had a "secret plan" for ending the war. Johnson's procrastination down to the final days may have assured Nixon's win and the five more years of war that ensued.

However that may be, Rostow's parting words in an interview with *New York Times* reporters cruised along familiar lines from his theoretical works that China was the bad outside influence in Vietnam, so it was up to China to cease its historically backward-looking activities and take up the challenge of creating a modern state. When it did so, he said, the Chinese would find Nixon, as they would have found Johnson, eager to work out "decent and normal relations." On this occasion, however, there were tough questions in the follow-up. He had spoken of what Russia must do and what China must do. "Is there no unfinished business on our side? Are there no further steps that we are to take to make our policy conform to realities of the seventies?" Rostow denied that Washington had been unimaginative in dealing with China. Until they wanted to move in a different direction, there was little to do except wait.[42]

But even after Nixon had walked on the Great Wall of China and toasted Chou En-lai in the Great Banquet Hall while a Chinese orchestra struggled with "Home, Home on the Range," Rostow was not ready to concede Vietnam's history to the Vietnamese. The supposed China menace had dissipated, but Rostow, still close to Johnson physically as a professor of the University of Texas, told CBS television even as Saigon's forces melted away that the United States should send two marine divisions to invade North Vietnam. The United States had "a very direct burden" morally to supply such military aid because Washington had pressured Saigon to accept the Paris accords. He did not mention that the accords permitted North Vietnam and the NLF to hold their positions at the time of cease-fire. He was right, certainly, in expecting that without a new influx of military support, the end was near. Nixon had gotten American prisoners of war back, which was what he wanted, and while there were later accusations that Watergate had crippled efforts to create a Korea-like situation in Vietnam, such charges were good only for domestic political purposes.[43]

Twenty years later, Rostow had some final words to say on "The Case for the Vietnam War." The occasion for his essay in the *War College Quarterly*, *Parameters* was the publication of Robert McNamara's first volume of memoirs, *In Retrospect: The Tragedy and Lessons of Vietnam*. Rostow listed McNamara's arguments about why the war was unwinnable and added, "To a degree impossible to determine, his conclusion, by his own account, was influenced also by the anti-war sentiment in the country which extended to his immediate family." However couched in praise for McNamara, this was an accusatory statement—one that Rostow would repeat at the end of a lengthy effort to refute the arguments presented by Johnson's secretary of defense.

After defending the nation-building exercise and contending that the Tet Offensive had been launched by the enemy as an almost desperate effort to halt the erosion of its position in the South (as in his 1967 assurances that the Vietcong had recruitment problems and the crossover point was near), Rostow doubled back on his arguments to the position he had held since the 1961 exploratory mission ordered by Kennedy had taken him to Saigon for his first close-up encounter with a war of national liberation. His conclusion thirty-five years later was the same. "Another weakness of McNamara's book is his failure to discuss systematically the gift of sanctuary which rendered the war inevitably 'long and inconclusive.' There have been no examples in which a guerrilla war (or a war dependent on external supply) has been won in which one side was granted sanctuary by the other." Updating his examples of success for the guerrillas, Rostow talked about American supply to the Afghan defenders against the Russians through Pakistan. Rostow then spent considerable time in the article citing authorities on how the United States missed its opportunity to close the frontier. "Those who advocated blocking the trails on the ground [he does not mention here his persistent advocacy] believed that action would force a concentration of North Vietnamese troops to keep the trails open, and two or three reinforced U.S. divisions together with air supremacy could deal with them."

His essay ends where it began, with a sharp thrust at the antiwar movement through the screen of McNamara's supposed inner turmoil. "One returns to the wild card in this story: the manner in which the United States, including McNamara's own family, was driven into painful controversy over the war. And that is part of the equation that all Americans must weigh for themselves. In fact, only McNamara can weigh all the factors that have driven him into the position that, whatever the cost, the United States should have withdrawn its troops from Vietnam."[44]

Such confidence in the rightness of his course foreshadowed statements in America's "new" longest war four decades later when President George W. Bush asserted in Hanoi (without any sense of irony) that Americans were too impatient. A reporter had asked if there were any "lessons" for the debate over the Iraq War? "One lesson is," he replied, "is that we tend to want there to be instant success in the world, and the task in Iraq is going to take a while. . . . We'll succeed unless we quit."[45]

NOTES

1. The author was present for this conversation in Austin, Texas.

2. *New York Times*, April 5, 1975. It is not too much to say, however, that the neoconservative movement was born in the wreckage of the Vietnam War. Rostow's assertions that the nation had lost its nerve in Vietnam—a more serious problem than military defeat from the perspective of foreign policy theorists than military defeat—was a staple of the Reagan years and came into full fruition in the "Rise of the Vulcans," as detailed in James Mann's deservedly famous book *Rise of the Vulcans: The History of the Bush War Cabinet* (New York: Penguin Books, 2004).

3. Peter Lisagor, "Mr. Rostow Presents a Paper," *New York Times*, July 8, 1962.

4. http://mit.edu/cis/pdf/panel_ORIGINS.pdf. The blurb lists Rostow as national security adviser to both Kennedy and Johnson. In fact, Kennedy named him a deputy assistant to the national security adviser, McGeorge Bundy, and he then became later in 1961, chairman of the State Department's Policy Planning Council.

5. See Lloyd Gardner, "Poisoned Apples: John Foster Dulles and the 'Peace Offensive,'" in *The Cold War after Stalin's Death: A Missed Opportunity for Peace?*, ed. Klaus Larres and Kenneth Osgood (New York: Rowman & Littlefield, 2006), 73–94.

6. Rostow to Jackson, August 20, 1953, *The Papers of C. D. Jackson*, Dwight D. Eisenhower Library, Abilene, Kansas, Box 6.

7. Lisagor, "Mr Rostow Presents a Paper"; "The Hawk-Eyed Optimist," *Time*, July 15, 1966, http://www.time.com/time/printout/0,8816,835995,00.html.

8. Godfrey Hodgson, "Walt Rostow," *The Guardian*, February 17, 2003.

9. Lloyd C. Gardner, *Pay Any Price: Lyndon Johnson and the Wars for Vietnam* (Chicago: Ivan R. Dee, 1995), p. 28.

10. David Halberstam, *The Best and Brightest* (New York: Fawcett Crest, 1972); Stanley Karnow, *Vietnam: A History, the First Complete Account of Vietnam at War* (New York: Viking, 1983), 358.

11. Rostow to Secretary of State et al., April 24, 1961, Box 115, President's Official File, *The John F. Kennedy Papers*, John F. Kennedy Library, Cambridge, Massachusetts.

12. Karnow, *Vietnam*, p. 251.

13. "Interview with Walt Rostow," undated, http://www.gwu.edu/~nsarchiv/cold-war/interviews/episode-9/rostowI.html.

14. "Interview with Walt Rostow," 358.

15. Richard Parker, "J. K. Galbraith," ABC Radio, National Briefing, July 31, 2005, http://www.abc.net.au/rn/talks/bbing/stories/s1423535.htm.

16. See Gareth Porter, *Perils of Dominance: Imbalance of Power and the Road to Vietnam* (Berkeley: University of California Press, 2005), 148–52.

17. "Interview with Walt Rostow."

18. Rostow to McNamara, November 16, 1964, Department of State, *Foreign Relations of the United States, 1964–1968: Vietnam 1964*, vol. I (Washington, D.C.: U.S. Government Printing Office, 1992), 906–8.

19. Rostow to Dean Rusk, November 23, 1964, Gravel Edition, *The Pentagon Papers*, vol. 3 (Boston: Beacon Press, 1971), 645–47; Lisagor, "Mr. Rostow Presents a Paper."

20. Memorandum, November 3, 1965, quoted in, Lloyd Gardner, "Hall of Mirrors," in *Why the North Won the Vietnam War*, ed. Marc Jason Gilbert (New York: Palgrave, 2002), 233–40.

21. William Conrad Gibbons, *The U.S. Government and the Vietnam War: Executive and Legislative Roles and Relationships*, pt. 4 (Washington, D.C.: U.S. Government Printing Office, 1994), 297–98.

22. See Lloyd Gardner, "Harry Hopkins with Hand Grenades? McGeorge Bundy in the Kennedy and Johnson Years," in *Behind the Throne: Servants to Power to Imperial Presidents, 1898–1968*, ed. Thomas J. McCormick and Walter LaFeber (Madison: University of Wisconsin Press, 1993), 204–31.

23. Hugh Sidey, "The Value of Proximity," *Time*, May 12, 1980, 1.

24. Cited in Gardner, *Pay Any Price*, 286.

25. Gibbons, *The U.S. Government and the Vietnam War*, 415–17.

26. Rostow to Johnson, July 28, 1967, White House Aides, McPherson, Box 53, *Johnson Papers*, Lyndon Baines Johnson Library.

27. Rostow to Johnson, July 22, 1967, Box 19, Rostow Memos, National Security Files, *Johnson Papers*, (hereafter LBJL).

28. Gravel Edition, *The Pentagon Papers*, vol. 4 (Boston: Beacon Press, 1971), 666–67.

29. Gardner, *Pay Any Price*, 362. The memo was later reprinted in the May 1967, *Atlantic Monthly*. Rostow wrote Johnson that the only response would be to point out "that people have differing ideas about what is 'funny.'" Gardner, *Pay Any Price*, 363.

30. George W. Allen, *None So Blind: A Personal Account of the Intelligence Failure in Vietnam* (Chicago: Ivan R. Dee, 2001), 234–37.

31. Helms to Johnson, September 12, 1967, cited in Lloyd Gardner, "Introduction," National Intelligence Council, *Estimative Products on Vietnam, 1948–1975* (Washington, D.C.: U.S. Government Printing Office, 2005), xxvi.

32. Memorandum, *Implications of an Unfavorable Outcome in Vietnam*, September 11, 1967, cited in Gardner, "Introduction."

33. "Notes of the President's Meeting with Australian Broadcast Group," September 20, 1967, Box 3, Meeting Notes File, *Johnson Papers*, LBJL.

34. Rostow to Johnson, October 11, 1967, http://www.gwu.edu/~nsarchiv/NSAEBB/NSAEBB5/che7_1.htm.

35. Congressional Briefing by General Westmoreland, President Johnson, and Mr. Rostow, November 16, 1967, Box 1, Congressional Briefings, *Johnson Papers*, LBJL.

36. Congressional Briefing by General Westmoreland, President Johnson, and Mr. Rostow. (I have reversed the order of the last two sentences quoted from the minutes of the briefing.)

37. Rostow to Johnson, March 14, 1968, Box 127, Vietnam, National Security File, *Johnson Papers*, LBJL.

38. Note dated "3/25/68," Box 6, Files of Walt Rostow, *Johnson Papers*, LBJL.

39. Gardner, *Pay Any Price*, 454.

40. Gardner, *Pay Any Price*, 454.

41. Gardner, *Pay Any Price*, 466.

42. "Excerpts from Interview with Rostow at the White House," *New York Times*, January 5, 1969.

43. "Send the Marines, Rostow Proposes," *New York Times*, April 5, 1975.

44. W. W. Rostow, "The Case for the Vietnam War," *Parameters*, winter 1996–1997, 39–50.

45. Office of the Press Secretary, "Remarks by President Bush and Prime Minister Howard of Australia, Hanoi, Vietnam, November 17, 2006, http://fpc.state.gov/fpc/76236.htm. Like Rostow, also, officials in the second Bush administration had pressured the CIA and other intelligence agencies to extract estimates needed to justify the Iraq War.

4

Senator Henry Jackson and the Demise of Détente

Anna Kasten Nelson

handwritten note (top left): need personality to realise position & held in congress to wield it to his agenda

handwritten note (right): personality as a spark

Nineteen seventy-two was a banner year for President Richard Nixon and his national security adviser, Henry Kissinger. On February 21, after extensive secret planning on the part of Kissinger, Nixon arrived in Beijing, China, bringing an official American presence to China for the first time in twenty-five years. A well-photographed meeting with the aged chairman, Mao Ze-dong, lent official support to the working meetings that ensued between Nixon, Kissinger, and Premier Zhou Enlai as well as meetings between the Chinese foreign minister and Secretary of State William Rogers. While no new diplomatic initiatives resulted, Nixon's trip finally gave de facto U.S. recognition to the People's Republic of China.

The following May found the president in Moscow, consulting with Leonid Brezhnev. Nixon returned from this Moscow summit with an Anti-Ballistic Missile (ABM) treaty and an interim Strategic Arms Limitation Treaty (SALT). After three years of lengthy and exhausting negotiations, Nixon and Brezhnev ceremoniously and symbolically signed the first treaty of the Cold War that limited armaments. Nixon returned home with a solid diplomatic achievement.

Once home, however, Nixon and Kissinger found themselves facing another set of difficult negotiations. This one was with members of the U.S. Senate. Chief among their adversaries was Senator Henry "Scoop" Jackson, a Democrat from the state of Washington. In spite of the Senate's ability to "advise and consent," it is rare for a senator to have a major impact on foreign policy. But as William Bundy noted, Jackson's "effect on events and attitudes must rank him among the top American public figures concerned with foreign policy in the 1970s."[1]

handwritten note (bottom): he got what he wanted demise of détente (mentee of Reagan first term behaviour)

Henry Jackson was born in Everett, Washington, in 1912, the son of Norwegian immigrants. As a boy, he picked up the nickname "Scoop," and it followed him the rest of his life. His political career began when he was elected prosecuting attorney of Snohomish County, Washington, in 1938, three years after his graduation from the University of Washington Law School. In 1941, he entered the U.S. House of Representatives as its youngest member and spent the rest of his life in the U.S. Congress.

Jackson entered Congress soon after the United States instituted the draft and went to war, but unlike some of his fellow representatives, he accepted President Franklin D. Roosevelt's offer to aid the war effort by staying in the Congress. As a result, in contrast to most of his generation, Jackson never had military experience.

Although the United States was being transformed into a global power, Jackson spent his early years in Congress on the domestic policies important to his constituency, flood control, rivers and harbors, and the generation of public power. As a New Deal Democrat, he strongly supported labor unions, including the powerful maritime unions important to the Seattle area.

He emerged from the war years as an even stronger supporter of the tenets of the New Deal, repackaged by President Harry Truman as the "Fair Deal." He believed that a strong federal government was necessary to support economic growth while simultaneously providing a social net for Americans. He supported national health insurance, aid to education, and federal support for public housing. Throughout his life he remained a champion of organized labor.

Just as his constituents begin to turn their attention to internationalism, so did Jackson. But Jackson also became a strong supporter of President Harry Truman's foreign policy. He vigorously supported military containment as expressed in the 1950 document, NSC 68; approved of the decision to develop the hydrogen bomb; and supported Truman's decision to go to the aid of South Korea.[2]

His early years in both Washington State and in the House of Representatives had a lasting influence on his political ideas and actions. For example, Jackson emerged in the postwar years as very pro-Chinese, which may have reflected the disdain of his fellow Washingtonians for the Japanese.[3] During the years of World War II, the people of Washington State felt particularly threatened by the possibility of a Japanese fifth column, and Jackson supported the internment of Japanese Americans. He was further influenced by the brutality the Japanese practiced against the Chinese. Only much later, as a senator, did he see Japan as a counterbalance to the Soviet Union.

Jackson also maintained that he was deeply affected by a visit he made to Buchenwald, one of Hitler's death camps, as a young congressman. He contended that the sights there turned him into an ardent supporter of the state of Israel and the plight of Jews in other anti-Semitic countries.

By the time Jackson moved into the Senate in 1953, he had morphed into a Cold Warrior. He was not alone, joining many of his fellow New Dealers in supporting military containment and the concomitant large military budgets requested for "mutual security." These Cold War liberals who dominated the Democratic Party until it split over the Vietnam war continued to support progressive domestic programs while fully embracing a foreign policy dominated by fear of Soviet military might and its alleged control of worldwide communist parties.

In a 1956 Senate speech, Jackson declared, "The basic aim of the Kremlin remains unchanged—a Moscow dominated world. The Soviet rulers stand ready and able to employ every last weapon in the Communist arsenal of conquest."[4] Meanwhile, he warned, the Soviets are catching up with the United States on technologically sophisticated weapons. Hence, he argued in this and other speeches, the Senate must continue to approve new weapons. Until his sudden death in 1983, Jackson never wavered from this view of the Soviet Union, even though the Soviet–Chinese split was evidence that the Soviet Union did not have control over world communism, and Soviet and American leaders began meeting in each other's countries. Jackson was never convinced that the entire nature of the Cold War changed. In his final press conference, he was just as adamant about the "malevolence" of the Soviet Union and the need to preserve American strength.[5]

Jackson remained actively involved in the concerns of his constituents and continued to be an outspoken member of the Senate Interior Committee, ultimately becoming chairman. But he also became increasingly involved in national security issues. For example, before the end of his first six-year term, he spoke out in opposition to President Dwight D. Eisenhower's effort to cut the defense budget and supported the development of ballistic missiles, including an ocean-based force.[6]

When Democrats took control of the Senate after the 1954 election, Jackson was assigned to the Armed Services Committee and the Interior Committee while retaining his seat on the Government Operations Committee. Although he later chaired the Interior Committee, he used his other assignments to further his growing interest in foreign policy, including his Armed Services Subcommittee on Arms Control, which provided a platform for his strong, negative views on arms limitation and disarmament.

In spite of his interest in foreign policy, Jackson never became a member of the Senate Foreign Relations Committee, largely because of the opposition of Senator J. William Fulbright (D-Ark.), who was ranking Democrat and then chairman of the committee until his defeat in 1974. Part of the bad blood between the two men was the product of personal rivalry, especially as Jackson became more involved in national security policy. Rivalry was only the more visible reason, however. Fulbright scorned Jackson, the hawk, who, he assumed, promoted armaments and airpower because of his cozy relationship to his home industry, the Boeing Company. Jackson, a western liberal, saw Senator Fulbright as an apologist for racists, standing firm with other southerners against civil rights legislation. Even more important, the two men had radically different views about the nature of American national security. When Fulbright was defeated in 1974, Jackson's staff reportedly celebrated with champagne.[7]

Jackson's determined interest in foreign policy was not to be thwarted in spite of the fact that he was on the "wrong" committee. The Government Operations Committee, which had no jurisdiction over foreign policy, did have oversight over government processes. In 1959, in spite of opposition from the White House and Fulbright, Jackson made imaginative use of this jurisdiction by forming a Subcommittee on National Policy Machinery, which was ostensibly only about the process of making foreign policy rather than policy itself. The premise behind the hearings was that good process makes good policy, a questionable assumption. After extensive staff work and interviews with former officials, academics, and other foreign policy specialists, Senator Jackson launched a series of public hearings on the National Security Council, State Department, and Defense Department just in time for the 1960 elections. For the most part, the hearings discredited Eisenhower's policymaking process and indirectly his policies. They also served to encourage the new president, John F. Kennedy, to jettison the process of his predecessor. Kennedy had other advisers suggesting the need for a new foreign policy structure, but Jackson's subcommittee was credited with that decision and was heralded for its work, especially since Kennedy publicly stated that he was "much impressed with the constructive criticism" contained in the subcommittee's report.[8] It was the work of this subcommittee that made Jackson an actor in the national security world. It also helped Jackson's growing influence that he was a friend of the new president, whom he had first met shortly after his election to Congress.

The transformation of U.S. foreign policy during the Cold War also was responsible for Jackson's ascent. The State Department was no longer the only player on the field. National security policy now included policies made in both the Defense Department and the intelligence agencies. This change easily empowered the Armed Services Committee and the chairman of the Subcommittee on Arms Control.

Unlike many senators, who gain influence as chairmen of committees, Jackson gained influence though his dedication to detail, his understanding of the Senate's rules and procedures, the force of his personality, and his able and devoted staff.

Jackson met his chief foreign policy adviser, Dorothy Fosdick, at a dinner party in 1954 and hired her in 1956. For his remaining twenty-eight years as a senator, Fosdick was at his side. Before joining Jackson, she had earned her PhD at Columbia and spent ten years in the State Department, where she worked as a member of the policy planning staff under George Kennan and Paul Nitze. By the time she joined Jackson, she had became a committed supporter of military containment.[9] It is to Jackson's credit that he overcame the gender bias of his generation and hired a woman to advise him on foreign policy at a time when the only woman working for senators were their secretaries.

Jackson appointed Dorothy Fosdick as staff director of the Subcommittee on National Policy Machinery. The subcommittee survived for fifteen years, but it never again had such an important influence on policy. It was important to Jackson, however, because it provided the necessary home for his foreign policy staff, which after 1969 included Richard Perle, who would become a pivotal figure during the Nixon and Ford administrations. Perle came to Washington at the suggestion of his former teacher, Albert Wohlstetter, and was a consistent proponent of a defense posture that would always surpass the Soviets.[10] Perle remained on Jackson's staff until 1981 when President Reagan appointed him assistant secretary of state for international security affairs.

look how Reagan acted

In 1969, when Nixon and Kissinger assumed the responsibility for American national security, they regarded Jackson as among the ranks of their supporters. Nixon even offered Jackson the position of secretary of defense, which the Washington Democrat quickly declined. Instead, by 1972, his long tenure on the Senate Armed Services Committee plus his knowledgeable staff gave Jackson the expertise and authority to challenge the policies promoted by the president and his national security adviser.

Richard Nixon came to office with the promise to end the war in Vietnam, which had essentially driven his predecessor from office. Both China and the Soviet Union were supporting and supplying the North Vietnamese. Hence, removing that support would force negotiations. Nixon and Kissinger had a grand plan that would achieve this goal while restructuring the Cold War. Taking advantage of the tensions on the Soviet–Chinese border and an apparent rift between the Soviet Union and China, Nixon decided to exploit the unease and suspicions of the Soviets by reaching out to China. Meanwhile, he also moved to create a détente with the Soviet Union. In the end, he and Kissinger hoped to persuade both the Soviets and the Chinese to abandon their support of North Vietnam and encourage their perceived client to negotiate for peace.[11]

The policy of détente was central to the foreign policy of Nixon and Kissinger. Détente is a diplomatic term signifying the relaxation of tension between two former or present adversaries. Both men believed that international disagreements were linked and that a policy of détente would resonate in curbing Soviet activities elsewhere in the world.

Nixon and Kissinger chose several specific paths to pursue détente. First, they began with reviving the stalled negotiations over arms control. Second, Kissinger promised the Soviets a trade treaty with a most-favored-nation (MFN) clause. In addition, the United States agreed to provide grain shipments to compensate for a Soviet agricultural shortfall.

As noted previously, although driven by many concerns, Nixon and Kissinger went to Beijing and held summit meetings in Moscow as part of their diplomatic effort to end the war in Vietnam. Ultimately, détente did not lead to the end of the Vietnam War, although it did serve to reduce tensions and considerably warm the Cold War.

One of the first moves toward détente was the decision to negotiate an Anti-Ballistic Missile (ABM) treaty and a Strategic Arms Limitation (SALT) agreement.

After the Cuban missile crisis of 1962, the Soviets began a crash program to achieve some kind of parity with the United States so that they would never again have to back down because of the threat of American force. By 1969, they had achieved their goal and therefore, in their view, were able to discuss limiting armaments from a position of strength. Both countries also realized that they were on the cusp of new technology that would drain budgets and once again destabilize parity. The time was ripe for negotiations.

The Soviets expressed an interest in negotiations to limit armaments as early as the Johnson administration, but it was only in 1969 that talks began in earnest. Even then, it took until 1972 before the ABM treaty and the SALT I agreement were completed.

Antiballistic missiles are defensive weapons designed to destroy incoming missiles before they reach their target. But as critics of the agreement pointed out, ABMs were potentially destabilizing because they could undermine their adversary's deterrent capability. Neither side had developed a completely workable system, so the ABM was more amenable to negotiations. The two countries basically agreed not to have enough ABMs scattered across their extensive terrain to protect every one of their citizens. Instead, only two ABM sites would be allowed: one to protect the capitals, Moscow and Washington, and the other a missile site. In 1974, the limit was dropped to one site for each.

The interim SALT agreement, which concerned offensive intercontinental ballistic missiles (ICBMs) and submarine-launched ballistic missiles (SLBMs), was a different matter. It became largely a numbers game. After months of negotiation, the agreement froze the number of ICBMs to those already deployed or under construction. This gave the Soviets 1,607, a leading edge over the American's 1,054; SLBMs were also frozen at 740 for the Soviet Union and 656 for the United States.

Neither the negotiators nor Nixon regarded the imbalance as unfair. Aside from the fact that the United States had 450 long-range bombers to the Soviet Union's 200, the United States had 5,700 warheads on its missiles compared to the Soviet number of 2,500. In addition, the United States was already deploying multiple independently targetable reentry vehicles (MIRVs) in 1970 and so needed fewer missiles.

MIRVs were devices able to send out many nuclear warheads on a single missile to widely scattered areas. Unfortunately, MIRVs were deliberately not subject to the SALT treaty. The United States regarded them as a trump card. The Soviet Union was still testing MIRVs, although they quickly caught up with the United States in 1975. In the long run, ignoring the number of MIRVs in the arms control agreement was a significant failure.

When Nixon signed the SALT agreement at the 1972 summit meeting in Moscow, he and Kissinger judged it a success, as much because of what it said as what it left out. New weapons could be developed, new submarines built, and a new bomber built to replace the B-52. Given the totality of the American arsenal, Russian superiority in numbers of ICBMs and SLBMs posed no threat to American national security, they reasoned. To Kissinger, the arms permitted by the agreements were "sufficient" to accomplish their purpose, preventing the Soviets from a first strike.[12]

As a gesture of goodwill, Brezhnev also offered for joint signature an agreement establishing "Basic Principles of Relations" between the two nations. Both countries agreed that since, in the nuclear age, there was no substitute for peaceful coexistence, they would work to prevent situations from emerging that might cause military confrontations leading to a nuclear war. The document advocated the expansion of economic and commercial ties, which would serve to the advantage of both since the Soviet Union needed grain and the United States needed to sell it. They also pledged not to interfere in other countries in order to avoid confrontation, a provision both sides ignored. While cynics did not expect these lofty provisions to prevail very long, the treaties and agreements signed in May 1972 did provide a momentary break in the Cold War. The Moscow summit was the high point of détente.[13]

Senator Jackson strongly supported Nixon's defense budgets and, unlike so many of his fellow Democrats, did not part with Nixon over his Vietnam policy. An enthusiastic proponent of Nixon's ABM-building program, he was partly responsible for its passage through the Senate by a one-vote margin.

Nixon and Kissinger therefore assumed that Jackson would support a treaty favorable to the United States that had taken three years to negotiate. Both men, however, seriously misjudged the senator's strong commitment to the Cold War and his suspicion of détente with the Soviet Union. Improbably, given his past support of Nixon's defense program, Jackson opposed both the ABM treaty and the SALT agreement. To Jackson, sufficiency was not good enough, and to the discomfort of Nixon and Kissinger, he turned his attention to opposing the agreements.[14]

Jackson firmly held to his belief that more missile launchers were necessary to defend the United States against a first strike from the Soviets. When the president signed the treaty in Moscow severely limiting the number of ABMs allowed in each country, Jackson argued that American capacity had been bargained away. Nevertheless, he ultimately voted for the ABM treaty and turned his attention to the interim SALT agreement (or SALT I). Jackson objected vociferously to its unequal provisions. It did not establish parity, he argued, but gave the Soviets a considerable nuclear advantage. He held Nixon and Kissinger responsible for sinking a strong defense on the shoals of détente.

Senate Hearings on SALT I were held by both the Senate Foreign Relations Committee under Chairman Fulbright and the Senate Armed Services Committee in the summer of 1972. Fulbright insisted that the Pentagon was inflating the estimates of Soviet capability. Jackson, on the other hand, was concerned that the lack of data proved that the American estimates were too low. He wanted an agreed database from which to start counting ICBMs.[15]

When Secretary of Defense Melvin Laird came before the Armed Services Committee to present the president's budget proposal for the following year, Jackson took advantage of the opportunity to air his dissenting views. Unlike those of his fellow Democrats on the committee who were eager to probe the defense budget figures on Vietnam, all of Jackson's questions in the hearings indirectly concerned SALT since they pertained to comparisons between Soviet and U.S. capability. Jackson asked one question of Laird, but he asked it many times and in many forms. He wanted to know if Laird would support SALT if the budget requests for the strategic weapons systems were not forthcoming. Laird refused to say no but repeated that the ABM treaty, SALT, and new equipment were all of a piece.

Jackson then turned toward the SALT agreement signed in Moscow. He presented a chart to Laird that he and his staff had compiled on the provisions of the SALT agreements. His chart illustrated what he saw as a clear advantage for the Soviets. But Laird also had a chart. His told quite a different story. In fact, as Laird pointed out, the figures were subject to interpretation, and no figures had been agreed on.

Jackson exploited that very fact and noted that he hoped to gain from the hearing just what the U.S. government thought it had agreed to regarding the land-based strategic forces. He remarked on the lack of detail in the agreement and the deleterious effect of ambiguity. He illustrated his own capacity for detail, for example, by pointing out that that there was no effort to distinguish between "heavy" ICBMs and "light" ICBMs or the size of the silos. Without a clear understanding as to the number of land-based missiles, the Soviets could interpret the treaty in quite a different way. These were missing details that, in his view, could cause trouble in the future.

Jackson continued to harp on what he insisted were critical details as he questioned Laird. Finally, Laird turned to his assistant secretary, Paul Nitze, who had been on the negotiating team. Even Nitze, who often met with Jackson and was a mentor to his staff and a strong proponent of military preparedness, seemed to lose patience when Jackson began to question terms such as "starting construction." Jackson was unpersuaded and continued to harp on ambiguity.[16]

Jackson may have been correct in his assumptions that the ICBM agreement simply stopped the Soviets from building new ones without an exact count of what they already had in place. But that was not really a relevant issue to the negotiators, the president, Kissinger, or Laird. They had an estimate, and they knew that under the terms of the agreement, the Soviets could not start construction of any more ICBMs. Meanwhile, the United States had a "sufficient" number.

It is hard to know if that particular issue troubled Jackson as much as he indicated. He publicly continued to discredit the agreement because it did not offer parity. In his view, parity could be achieved only if the Soviets were forthcoming in giving the United States accurate numbers.

While Kissinger and Nixon had turned to peaceful coexistence predicated on the view that the alternative of mutual destruction was untenable and hence unlikely, Jackson remained unconvinced. His arguments centered on the possibility—almost inevitability—of a serious Soviet attack. He derided détente, pointing out that it lacked definition even as the administration "has revolved, like a tether ball, around the pole of that détente." We have been left, he continued, "without a clear sense of where we are going or, for that matter, a common understanding of where we have been."[17] To Jackson, the SALT agreements were examples of the dangerous direction of policy in the name of détente. Compromise exhibited weakness in the face of the Soviet strength. Therefore, in the Armed Services Hearings called to examine the SALT agreement, he argued that under that agreement, the United States would be inadequately prepared given the imbalance in offensive weapons between the Soviet Union and the United States. He noted several times the brief window of time once an attack began.

Summing up his views in a speech on the floor of the Senate on August 11, 1972, Jackson pointed out that since the agreement went to the "heart of American security—the capacity to deter nuclear war," precision was essential.[18] Once again, he noted that the interim agreement did not indicate how many ICBMs the Soviets actually had. Hence, there was no way of knowing whether the numbers would "add up to stable parity or unstable inferiority." When he added up the numbers that were known, Jackson concluded, the Soviets could deploy the number of weapons that exceeded those of the United States "by a 50 percent margin." He dismissed out of hand the idea that numbers do not matter when there is sufficiency. As far as he was concerned, the agreement would not slow the buildup of Soviet offensive forces, which he continued to see as threatening to the United States.

On the other hand, Jackson did not totally dismiss the interim agreement. Instead, returning to form, his goal was to amend the agreement in order to influence the upcoming negotiations on SALT II treaty, which would replace the interim agreement. He quite clearly stated in his Senate speech of August 11, 1972, that he offered his amendment to the agreement so that the United States would never again sign an arms limitation treaty that did not "assure equality between the parties on offensive intercontinental strategic arms."[19]

Richard Perle wrote in a posthumous publication devoted to the senator that Jackson never voted *against* arms control. While this is true, he also never voted *for* an arms control treaty without instituting major changes, beginning with the Limited Nuclear Test Ban Treaty of 1963, President John F. Kennedy also assumed that Jackson would support the treaty, and, indeed, the senator ultimately voted for it. But after expressing his opposition in lengthy hearings and on the floor of the Senate, he negotiated with the administration for the "safeguards" that he regarded as crucial. He insisted that underground testing continue, that the nuclear laboratories be maintained, that the United States remain ready to test aboveground, and that the United States improve its ability to verify the conduct of the enemy. These "safeguards" ensured that testing would continue, if only underground, and that nuclear research would continue. Because of Jackson, the treaty that emerged from the Senate was not quite the same peace pipe that Kennedy planned to pass to the world.[20]

The interim SALT I agreement was to last for five years followed by a SALT II treaty. Jackson determined that Nixon's prestige was too high for SALT I to be defeated, so he proposed an amendment to modify the interim agreement and in so doing had an effect on every subsequent arms agreement.

The Jackson amendment declared that any future arms negotiations must not limit the United States to levels of intercontinental strategic forces inferior to those of the Soviet Union. The legislative history behind the amendment indicated that equality did not mean equity but absolute equality of numbers. Jackson drafted the amendment in an extremely clever way. A senator could either vote for the amendment or vote for American inferiority vis-à-vis the Soviets. Consequently, it was approved by the Senate on September 14, 1972. When the negotiators returned to Geneva in 1975 to work on SALT II, the amendment requiring a database and equality became a major American objective immediately resisted by the Soviets.

Nixon was worried about a "massive right-wing revolt" in the Senate as early as May 1972, when the treaty was signed. He instructed Kissinger to develop a team to meet with recalcitrant senators, including Jackson, and to assure them that he was moving ahead in the development of other weapon systems not covered by the agreement.[21]

Throughout the discussion on arms control and in spite of his public attack on SALT, Jackson never lost touch with either Kissinger or Nixon. Nixon, for his part, realized that Jackson was too powerful a senator to ignore. The senator respected Nixon's strong political backing in 1972. Certainly, Jackson was not planning to vote against the agreement, even as he successfully amended it and irrevocably changed the playing field.

Nixon probably acquiesced to Jackson's amendment for two reasons: first, he wanted Congress to enact the SALT I treaty to enhance his own stature in the months before the 1972 election and, second, he was not concerned with solving problems for agreements that would not be negotiated until after he left office.[22]

Jackson's amendment would prove to be an enormous stumbling block in future negotiations, but that would by no means be his only impact on future arms control policy. Soon after the treaty was signed on September 30, 1972, Jackson met with Nixon and Kissinger in the Oval Office of the White House. He came to warn them about the mood in Congress that he thought was on the verge of cutting U.S. conventional forces and bringing U.S. forces home from Europe. Jackson was vocal in his complaints about his fellow senators. They did not understand SALT or equality, warheads, or other important military components protecting the country. Education was badly needed, he told them. Kissinger agreed, noting that they (congressmen) are "dumb."

The SALT negotiators and the Arms Control and Disarmament Agency (ACDA) were the subjects on Jackson's mind, however, and here he found a ready audience for his views. Kissinger provided the opening for this discussion by raising the question of ACDA officials. In a voice full of scorn, Jackson immediately noted that those who negotiated arms control and led

ACDA were totally disloyal to the president and to the country. He singled out Raymond Garthoff, who had been on the negotiating team, as especially guilty.[23] "Transfer the assholes," was Nixon's response. Kissinger joined in with a story of how the Russian-speaking Garthoff independently conversed with his counterparts during the negotiations, intimating the very disloyalty Jackson had raised.

Senator Jackson had come with an agenda. When he left the Oval Office, it had been fulfilled. New negotiations for SALT II would soon be under way. He provided the name of a new negotiator, Ed Rowny, and encouraged Nixon to appoint people in ACDA who were not for arms control. As the meeting wound to a close, Nixon asked for the names of all those "people in ACDA who were bastards" and took Jackson's advice.[24]

Jackson was not the only critic of SALT. He had support from other hard-liners in the State and Defense departments and even the White House. But Jackson had leverage they lacked. Nixon needed his support and vote on important defense decisions such as the one to build two Trident submarines. Jackson was a leader of an important group in the Senate who were supportive but often critical of aspects of Nixon's defense budget. The president seemed to see no contradiction between his international move to détente and his encouragement of Senator "Scoop" Jackson.

Immediately after the treaty was signed in the White House on September 30, Nixon and Jackson took a forty-five-minute walk in the Rose Garden. The subjects of their conversation are unknown. It has been assumed that it was during this walk that Jackson expressed his views about the personnel running ACDA. But Nixon's taped conversations suggest otherwise. While ACDA might have been discussed, their disagreement over other aspects of détente may have been uppermost on their minds.[25]

Both ACDA and the SALT negotiating team were "purged," and ACDA's budget was cut by a third. In January 1973, the head of the SALT delegation (and ACDA), Gerard Smith, resigned and was replaced by U. Alexis Johnson, a more cautious career diplomat. Of seventeen top positions in ACDA, only three occupants remained in place. Among the negotiating team, only two remained for the opening of talks on SALT II. The new appointees were hard-line negotiators whom Jackson knew and could influence. Prominent among the new group was Lieutenant General Ed Rowny representing the Defense Department.

The long-run effect of these changes was to weaken support for arms control. As one author notes, whereas Kissinger had been able to negotiate between "hard-liners and soft-liners," with the new team he no longer had that luxury. The views of ACDA were also so "hard line" that there was no longer any debate within the administration.[26]

At the conclusion of their Oval Office conversation on September 30, Nixon and Jackson also briefly mentioned trade negotiations between the United States and the Soviet Union. But the brevity of that discussion and the amiable agreement of the participants that day in no way reflected the reality of their profound disagreement.

As noted, Nixon had promised the voters in 1968 that he would end the war in Vietnam. Whatever else they accomplished, he and Kissinger knew that Vietnam would remain an albatross hovering over the administration and coloring its history. The road to end the war, they thought, ran through the Soviet Union, the country that primarily supplied the North Vietnamese. Moves toward détente were thus influenced by the desire to extend enough carrots to the Soviets to accomplish that goal.

The agreements at the Moscow summit were an important carrot. Another concerned trade between the two countries. A new trade agreement that the administration was proposing to Congress contained a provision to give the Soviet Union MFN status. Almost every nation that traded with the United States had achieved that status. Kissinger knew how much Brezhnev wanted this provision and assured him that it would be forthcoming. Inclusion of the Soviets would further indicate U.S. support of détente and serve to reward Soviet efforts to move the North Vietnamese toward negotiations. The trade agreement and the MFN provision, therefore, were crucial to Kissinger's policy.

Looking abroad, the president and his adviser neglected to spot the beginning of a domestic grassroots movement that would ultimately undermine both MFN and their vision of détente. Once again, Jackson chose to impose an amendment that in this instance ultimately destroyed the legislation and contributed to the end of détente. The Jackson-Vanik amendment stipulated that the Soviets could achieve MFN status only if they allowed their citizens to freely emigrate. Most of those who sought to emigrate were Jews who were escaping what they regarded as second-class citizenship.

Although Jackson is generally credited with the idea to tie emigration to trade, he was almost at the back of the band. The movement began with agitation on the part of a few concerned Jewish individuals who worried about the anti-Semitism in the Soviet Union and the inability of the Jews to emigrate. Forming an organization, they drew up legislation that tied emigration to the Export Administration Act since it gave the president authority to withhold exports under certain conditions. The group did not even try to contact Jackson because in their view he was on the wrong committee.

The American Jews unexpectedly got a boost from the Soviet Union itself. Congress suddenly paid attention when the Soviets imposed a tax on all potential émigrés. The Soviets pointed out that many of those seeking visas had completed many years of professional education. The government, they argued, was merely seeking to be paid back for their investment in the individuals who were now leaving the country to work elsewhere.

With the encouragement of their senators, Richard Perle of Jackson's staff, and Morris Amitay from the staff of Senator Abraham Ribicoff (D-Conn.) began meeting with other staffs and representatives of Jewish organizations. Perle and Amitay dominated the group, which first conceived of the idea to link Soviet emigration policy to MFN. Encouraged by Perle, Jackson began assembling a bipartisan group of senators and in September 1972 offered his amendment to the East-West Trade Relations Act in the waning days of the 92nd Congress.

Jackson did not offer new legislation. Instead, he again offered an amendment that completely changed the character of the original act. "Under this amendment," he told the Senate, "no country would be eligible to receive most-favored-nation treatment or to participate in U.S. credit and investment guarantee programs unless that country permits its citizens the opportunity to emigrate to the country of their choice." The amendment even required the president to report to Congress on compliance of countries gaining MFN status.

Jackson's speech announcing his amendment stated views that he would emphasize over and over during the two years it took to pass his amendment. He quoted the Russian dissident Alexander Solzhenitsyn, a man he greatly admired; pointed out state repression in the Soviet Union; and denounced the emigration tax, which he regarded as "ransom from Jews" who wished to leave. He reminded his listeners that Himmler also sold exit permits for Jews wishing to leave Nazi Germany, stretching his argument to note a parallel with the Holocaust.[27] He was joined in his effort by Ohio Congressman Charles Vanik, whose family fled Czechoslovakia and whose district included many Jewish residents.

Jackson did not represent a city with a large Jewish population, yet he took up the fight for Jewish emigration even before it attracted the attention of most American Jewish organizations. Furthermore, it was his leadership and persistence for two years that finally led to the passage of the Jackson-Vanik amendment. Several explanations have been offered for Jackson's persistence in helping the Soviet Jews. One explanation looks at his two attempts to run for president and concludes that he wanted his share of the money that American Jews contribute to Democratic political campaigns as well as votes. If so, his efforts proved futile, for his campaigns in 1972 and 1976 were aborted and money did not flow into his campaign in great amounts.

Richard Perle, who discounted any devious intentions on the part of the senator, repeated Jackson's own explanation that his visit to Hitler's ovens deeply affected him and was at the root of his efforts to help the Soviet Jews escape harsh anti-Semitism. Jackson's parents were Norwegian immigrants, and he was proud of his heritage. He bitterly resented the Nazi occupation of the country. Perle also thought that between observing the Nazis and Soviets, the senator just became a consistent foe of totalitarianism.[28]

Another of Jackson's former staff members later maintained that Jackson also saw the right to emigrate as a human rights issue.[29] He pointed to the senator's support for the growing dissent in the Soviet Union. When Brezhnev invited Jackson to Moscow, for example, the senator replied that if he accepted, he would want to arrange a visit with Alexander Solzhenitsyn. The invitation was withdrawn.[30] Without disputing the senator's support for human rights, it should be noted that support for the dissidents was also one more blow to détente.

Nixon and Kissinger paid little attention to the amendment when it was introduced in 1972 since, as even Jackson pointed out, the bill was not "going anywhere." Senator Jackson raised the amendment in his September 30 conversation with Nixon and Kissinger because he was gathering cosponsors and wanted the administration to unleash the Senate Republicans so that they could add their names.[31] The conversation was very brief, no more than a passing comment. The Senate would be adjourned long before it could even be considered.

There were other reasons for the lackadaisical reaction. An election year was not a propitious time to wrangle with the problems of Soviet Jews. In addition, Jackson was regarded as a friend of the administration, not as an adversary. Although he had imposed restrictions on future arms control agreements, he had voted for the legislation, and that was what counted. Their assumption must have been that he would ultimately go along with the administration bill.

Kissinger would come to regret his failure to understand Jackson's tenacity. The amendment did not go away in 1973 but, instead, gained momentum. Jackson found an eager supporter in Congressman Charles Vanik, who lined up many cosponsors in the House of Representatives. Jackson contacted more Jewish organizations and other groups, such as labor, that had its own drum to beat. By including the MFN restrictions in the general Trade Reform Act, Jackson was assured of the support of George Meany, the president of the AFL-CIO, who was traditionally opposed to all the provisions included in the entire Trade Reform Act, which he deemed threatening to American workers.

Jewish groups in the United States quickly joined Jackson's crusade. Israeli leaders were torn between loyalty to Nixon and support for emigration. Without his administration's willingness to resupply Israel with military equipment, the Jewish state could easily have lost the Yom Kippur War of that year. Ultimately, Israel began leaning toward Jackson-Vanik. It is noteworthy that almost all the organized Jewish groups followed behind Jackson rather than in front of him. Jackson-Vanik was not the product of either organized American Jewish groups or American supporters of Israel. But once the amendment was offered, both groups became powerful forces that Jackson could use to further his own goals.

By early 1973, the administration was fully awake to the danger posed by Jackson. By rallying around the emigration issue and reframing it as a human rights issue, Jackson publicly obscured his strong opposition to détente. Nevertheless, both the White House and Jackson saw the MFN as symbolic of the recent moves toward détente, and they were soon locked into battle. Kissinger, who turned to the Soviets for help in reaching a compromise, found it easier to negotiate with Dobrynin than with Jackson.

Recognizing their mistake, the Soviets first failed to implement their education tax and then withdrew it altogether. But it was too late to mollify Jackson, who increasingly began to see emigration as just one of the human rights denied by the Soviets.[32] The Soviets, evidently for internal political reasons, played right into his hand as they began to crack down once again on dissidents, including the physicist Andrei Sakarov and Solzhenitsyn.

To the chagrin of both Dobrynin and Kissinger, who became secretary of state in 1973, Jackson continued to refuse to compromise. By the end of 1973, the House of Representatives had voted for a trade bill that fully encompassed the Jackson amendment, including Vanik's restrictions on the extension of credit to the Soviets.

The amendment moved to the Senate in January 1974. Kissinger began a flurry of activity. He met with representatives of Jewish organizations, eager to convince them that quiet diplomacy would be more effective than Jackson's amendment.[33] He met with Jackson and talked to other senators, such as Alan Cranston (D-Calif.), who suggested seeking a compromise from Jackson through Jewish supporters on the one hand and the Senate leaders on the other. Kissinger agreed with Cranston that the Jewish leaders were willing to compromise, but Jackson was standing firm. Both men disparaged the influence of Richard Perle, with Kissinger referring to him as a "bloody fanatic" and Cranston as a "wild man." Finally, Kissinger told Cranston that he had come to believe that Jackson really wanted to scuttle the entire trade bill.[34]

He repeated that view in a conversation with Peter Flanigan, who was the assistant to the president for international economic policy. Flanigan reflected a more sinister view of Jackson's intransigence. He thought that Jackson was worried about losing the support of those senators who did not want to "kill the trade bill." Nor did Flanigan see the principled man described by

Jackson's staff. The senator, he thought, was just holding firm to keep labor support for his presidential bid.[35]

Curiously, compromises proposed by members of the Senate Finance Committee were never pursued by Kissinger perhaps because in his private conversations with Jackson the latter made clear his opposition to any compromise that did not include actual numbers of émigrés.

As the Watergate scandal unfolded and President Nixon was replaced by President Gerald Ford, both Ambassador Dobrynin and Secretary of State Kissinger evidently concluded that since there was no way to defeat Jackson, it was time to negotiate. At Kissinger's suggestion, an extraordinary, even unique, three-way negotiation was initiated between the senator, secretary of state, and foreign ambassador. Kissinger was the middleman.

Kissinger had promised the Soviets the MFN treaty as well as the extension of credits and now could no longer deliver. Needless to say, Brezhnev and his foreign minister, Andrei A. Gromyko, were unhappy with both the new secretary of state and Ambassador Dobrynin as it became clear that there would be no trade concessions passed by the 93rd Congress as long as Jackson would not compromise.

The Soviet leadership regarded the matter of emigration as a domestic concern and resented the effort to interfere with Soviet internal policy. Nevertheless, to Kissinger's surprise, they expressed the willingness to negotiate for a compromise.

Kissinger moved with alacrity, meeting first with Soviet Foreign Minister Andrei Gromyko and then, on April 26, 1974, with Jackson and his strongest supporters, Senators Abraham Ribicoff (D-Conn.) and Jacob Javits (D-N.Y.). The Soviets' position was that they would quietly continue to release émigrés at the 1973 level of 35,000. The senators, especially Jackson, found that number completely inadequate. They wanted the number at least doubled and wanted assurance that there would be no official harassment suffered by those who tried to leave.

Meanwhile, Senator Jackson and his staff were working to solidify their position in the Senate. Several of the more moderate leaders of the two leading Jewish organizations concerned with Soviet Jewry left their positions and were replaced by men much more willing to put their trust in Jackson's leadership.

As Peter Flanigan had correctly noted, danger lay in efforts of a number of senators to offer compromise legislation. Jackson had to watch carefully, or the coalition of sponsors of his amendment would fade away. His amendment originally had seventy-eight cosponsors, but after two years of jockeying, several of those were now more than willing to seek a compromise in an effort to pass a Trade Reform Bill. Fortunately for Jackson, several, including New

York Senator Jacob Javits, were up for reelection in 1974, while others were considering a run for the presidency. Jackson's staff actively sought out Jewish leaders in home states and on the national scene so that they would apply pressure. He and his staff, especially Richard Perle, moved aggressively, shamelessly using every Jewish supporter they knew to influence the senators from their home states. Javits was particularly vulnerable to this pressure since New York had the largest Jewish population in the country. These moves continued to strengthen Jackson's position, and in May 1974, Jackson's staff succeeded in preventing a compromise from emerging from the Senate Finance Committee.

The Nixon administration and the Soviets were also interested in the extension of credit to allow for more trade between the two countries. Nixon planned to use the Export-Import Bank for that purpose but needed a new congressional authorization of money to continue to operate the bank. It was obvious to everyone concerned that since the authorization would include the Soviets, it was closely connected to the Trade Reform Act. The bank authorization bill went to the Senate Banking Committee and Subcommittee chair, Adlai Stevenson III. Stevenson also did not want to give the administration *carte blanche* in their efforts to promote trade. Joining with Jackson, the subcommittee offered two changes in particular: Congress would review all transactions of more than $50 million, and a ceiling of $300 million was placed on credits that could be extended to the Soviet Union. Although the committee ultimately removed the ceiling, it would reappear when the bill was being considered on the House floor.[36]

Kissinger returned from an early summer meeting with Gromyko and announced that some progress had been made in their discussions. The newspapers reported that Gromyko had agreed to 45,000 exit visas a year. This number was unsatisfactory to the senator, given that none of the Soviet dissidents, whom Jackson thought he represented, were guaranteed one of these visas.

Nixon headed back to Moscow in July but returned empty-handed. No doubt his motives for taking the trip were mixed. He wanted to distract the country from the burgeoning Watergate scandal and needed another international success. He hoped that the definitive date for the summit would help bring closure on the trade bill. The Soviets were annoyed by the very premise of Jackson's amendment—that trade would have to be accompanied by "American supervision over freedom of emigration of Soviet citizens from the USSR. That is how détente, Jackson-style looks." Brezhnev in his public toast also made mention of "those who oppose international detente."[37]

On August 9, 1974, only weeks after the last Moscow summit meeting, Richard Nixon left the White House, and his appointed vice president took charge. President Gerald Ford met with Jackson, Javits, Ribicoff, and Kissinger within a week of taking office. Kissinger followed up with a meeting with Gromyko and subsequently reported that the Soviets would be willing to negotiate but only if they were not subject to public embarrassment, that is, if they could come to unofficial agreements that need not be announced. Jackson was not averse to this approach as long as the Soviets agreed to a steady flow of departures and the end of harassment of members of the intelligentsia.

Finally, Kissinger proposed a possible solution. He would arrange an exchange of letters that would reflect his discussions with Gromyko. Three letters were planned. First, with Gromyko's agreement, Kissinger would write a letter to Jackson outlining the Soviet position. The second letter would be a reply from Jackson, presumably agreeing to the Soviet position. The third, a Kissinger letter, would confirm Jackson's understanding of the Soviets' position.

Jackson and Kissinger exchanged letters on October 18, 1974. The first letter to Jackson presumably reflected Kissinger's discussions with Foreign Minister Gromyko. He wrote that he had received the following assurances: no punitive actions, no unreasonable impediments, and applications to be processed in the order that they were received. The emigration tax would remain suspended, and the rate of emigration would begin to rise. It is noteworthy that Kissinger, in his letter to Jackson, offered no numbers but left Jackson with the impression that the Soviets had accepted Jackson's numbers.

Jackson's response was much more specific and included specific actions the Soviets had to take, such as "no denial of exit visas to those who had access to sensitive secret information for more than three years beyond their last exposure to such secrets." Finally, Jackson specified that visas had to be issued at a rate of 60,000 per year. The Soviets would not agree to any numbers.

There was to be no third letter. Dorothy Fosdick reported that Helmut Sonnefeld, Kissinger's deputy, had "sent up a completely *watered down, useless* revision of our third letter . . . Richard [Perle] told Hal it was completely unacceptable; it reduces our second letter to unilateral statements only!"[38] A furious Jackson assumed that Kissinger had deliberately misled him. But Kissinger knew that the Soviets had not agreed to 60,000 emigrants a year. He could not send Jackson a third letter confirming Jackson's demands.[39]

Meanwhile, Richard Perle released to the public the letters exchanged between Kissinger and Jackson. Gromyko, assuming that the entire correspondence would remain secret, sent Kissinger an angry letter accusing him of distorting the Soviet position in the letter to Jackson. Kissinger quietly secreted the letter from Gromyko for two months without telling anyone he had received it. But in December, the Soviets released their letter to Kissinger, confirming that they had given no promises in order to get a trade agreement.[40]

Ultimately, Jackson agreed to a waiver that allowed the president to waive the provisions of his amendment so that the Soviets could have MFN status for eighteen months. After that, Congress would have to approve an extension that Jackson clearly would oppose unless the Soviets allowed at least 60,000 people to emigrate each year. In December, the Senate passed the trade bill with no dissenting votes. The House of Representatives followed five days later.

The story of the trade bill does not end here even though Jackson visibly celebrated the passage of his amendment in a press conference. In January 1975, the Soviets rejected the entire MFN clause of the American trade bill and simultaneously rejected a joint American–Soviet effort to develop some gas fields in Soviet Asia. Kissinger blamed Jackson, and he was not alone in his accusations. Editorials around the country condemned his actions. Jackson's efforts did not even help the Soviets wishing to emigrate. Total Jewish emigration in 1973 was 34,734. In 1975, it was only 13,221.

In some ways, Jackson's lengthy fight over the trade bill was inexplicable. Jackson got on well with both Nixon and Kissinger, even inviting the latter to dinner at his home.[41] He continued to support Nixon's moves in Southeast Asia long after most Democrats had abandoned support for the Vietnam War, even reminding Nixon that he had supported his moves in Cambodia. If his motive was to promote his presidential bid, after his initial defense of the Soviet Jews, he could easily have maintained the support of American Jews.

His staff and supporters point out that his deep concern over human rights gave him the tenacity to fight to the finish. But Jackson's battle was also about détente. The Soviets wanted to be treated like other countries and given the status of almost every other nation that traded with the United States. Kissinger promised that the trade bill would include the MFN provision, and in return the Soviets would intercede with the North Vietnamese and refrain from meddling in other small countries. Jackson could not support this policy because he did not think of the Soviet Union as a normal nation. It was a totalitarian state with a massive number of weapons waiting to attack the United States the minute it let down its guard. It was in this context that Jackson waged his fight against arms control and for the emigration of Soviet citizens.

To his staff, Jackson was a warmhearted man who cared about them, his constituents, and oppressed people around the world. When constituents called with a problem, important issues had to wait until the telephone conversation was completed. When he learned that the husband of an American woman married by an American rabbi in the Soviet Union was arrested at the airport in Moscow, Jackson called Kissinger to ask for his intervention. Kissinger promised to talk to Dobrynin if the matter was private and out of the public eye.[42]

Jackson's staff and supporters also saw him as a principled man devoted to the human rights of those unfortunate enough to live under totalitarianism. He was a consistent advocate of defense spending, they note, because he was genuinely concerned about his country.

His colleagues saw in Jackson a disciplined, principled, and articulate man with an especially intelligent and loyal staff. There was almost a symbiotic relationship between Jackson, Fosdick, Perle, and others on his staff. If there was a weakness in the relationship between Jackson and his staff, it was that no one seemed to disagree with him.

His detractors in and out of the Senate were suspicious of his motives. Boeing Aircraft was one of the biggest employers in the state of Washington. Jackson's ardent support of high defense budgets and new technology prompted the epithet "the senator from Boeing," and certainly the hometown business profited greatly from Jackson's votes.

The ambitious Jackson ran for the presidency twice, in 1972 and 1976, but Jackson did not have the necessary persona for a politician and abandoned the battle for nomination in the early stages of campaigning. Nevertheless, suspicious opponents saw a man who befriended American Jews because he needed campaign funds.

William Bundy, who held positions in the State and Defense departments during the 1960s, described Jackson as a "man of principle but also of consuming personal ambition." Bundy continued by noting that he was "exceptionally sure of where he stood, he was courageous and forthright" but considered his opponents as "foolish, lazy or even malevolent."[43]

Jackson was a formidable opponent, knowledgeable in parliamentary and legislative procedures, incisive in his questioning, and a master at gaining support. Crafting his amendments, he managed to gain an impressive number of cosponsors, often because of the clever use of words. As noted previously, his amendment to SALT I meant that opponents who voted no would have voted for American inferiority in relation to the Soviet Union.

But Jackson never moved beyond the Cold War fears that motivated him in the 1950s. He could not come to terms with a stodgy Soviet Union in charge of men who were no longer Stalin's direct heirs.

Jackson was not the only senator who opposed détente, nor did he defeat it single-handedly. But he was undeniably one of its most formidable and effective opponents and played a crucial role in its demise. To Jackson, the Soviet Union remained an aggressive nation bent on the destruction of the

United States. But by 1974, the Soviet Union was much more interested in trading with the United States than in blowing it up. In spite of the changing Cold War, Jackson continued to rally his troops to support the high military budgets and new technology he thought necessary to contain the Soviet Union. Even those who disagreed found it hard not to admire his principled stance and the consistency of his views throughout his public life.

Jackson's views on military superiority and his suspicion of détente with the Soviets found new adherents after his death. With Richard Perle in the vanguard, he became a hero to the neoconservatives who entered the government after Ronald Reagan became president. They admired his standing firm against both Henry Kissinger's policy of détente and his own political party's "left wing." Jackson soon became one of the "fathers" of neoconservatism.

Jackson was not a neoconservative. He was a Cold War liberal like so many of his fellow Democrats. Big government did not worry him. Unlike many neoconservatives, he believed in the federal government's obligation to intervene on behalf of its citizens. Ultimately, the Cold War would divide him from the leadership of his party, but Jackson remained a Democrat by party and a democrat by persuasion.

NOTES

1. William Bundy, *Tangled Web: The Making of Foreign Policy in the Nixon Presidency* (New York: Hill and Wang, 1998), 342.

2. Robert G. Kaufman, *Henry M. Jackson: A Life in Politics* (Seattle: University of Washington Press, 2000), 9–52.

3. Kaufman, *Henry M. Jackson*, 35–36.

4. Dorothy Fosdick, ed., *Henry M. Jackson and World Affairs: Selected Speeches, 1953–1983* (Seattle: University of Washington Press, 1990), 38.

5. Kaufman, *Henry M. Jackson*, 430.

6. Fosdick, *Henry M. Jackson and World Affairs*, 36–60.

7. Randall Woods, note to the author. Richard Perle remembered the celebration but not the champagne. Interview, Richard Perle with the author, March 5, 2007.

8. Kaufman, *Henry M. Jackson*, 105.

9. Susan Ware, ed., *Notable American Women* (Cambridge, Mass.: Harvard University Press, 2004).

10. *Notable American Women*; Robert David Johnson, *Congress and the Cold War* (New York: Cambridge University Press, 2006), 81–82.

11. Raymond L. Garthoff, *Détente and Confrontation: American-Soviet Relations from Nixon to Reagan* (Washington, D.C.: Brookings Institution, 1994), 325–486.

12. Seyom Brown, *The Crisis of Power* (New York: Columbia University Press, 1979), 21; Garthoff, *Détente and Confrontation*, 146–223.

13. Memorandum of Conversation, Moscow, May 22, 1972, *Foreign Relations of the United States (FRUS), 1969–1976*, vol. XIV (Washington, D.C.: U.S. Government Printing Office, 2006), 982–91.

14. The ABM treaty like other treaties required a two-thirds vote in the Senate. The interim agreement on SALT I required a simple majority.

15. Thomas Graham Jr., *Disarmament Sketches Three Decades of Arms Control and International Law* (Seattle: University of Washington Press, 2002). "Military Implications of the Treaty on the Limitations of Anti-Ballistic Missile Systems and the Interim Agreement on Limitation of Strategic Offensive Arms," Hearing, Committee on Armed Services, United States Senate, 92nd Cong., 2nd sess., June 6, 1972, 63–66.

16. "Military Implications of the Treaty on the Limitations of Anti-Ballistic Missile Systems and the Interim Agreement on Limitation of Strategic Offensive Arms," Hearing, Committee on Armed Services, United States Senate, 92nd Cong., 2nd sess., June 20, 1972, 161–68.

17. "Detente and SALT," speech by Senator Henry Jackson before the Overseas Press Club, April 22, 1974, reprinted in Fosdick, *Henry M. Jackson and World Affairs*, 15.

18. "The Senate and the Interim SALT I Agreement, United States Senate, August 11, 1972," reprinted in Fosdick, *Henry M. Jackson and World Affairs*, 137.

19. "The Senate and the Interim SALT I Agreement, United States Senate, August 11, 1972," reprinted in Fosdick, *Henry M. Jackson and World Affairs*, quotations from pp. 129 and 146.

20. Dorothy Fosdick, *Staying the Course: Henry M. Jackson and National Security* (Seattle: University of Washington Press, 1987), 87–107.

21. Memorandum, Nixon to Deputy Assistant for National Security Affairs, Alexander Haig, May 20, 1972, Department of State, *FRUS, 1969–1976*, vol. XIV, 965.

22. Jussi Hanhimaki, *The Flawed Architect* (New York: Oxford University Press), 221–22.

23. Raymond Garthoff was a highly respected negotiator who had a long career as a foreign service officer. Among his several books is one about the SALT I negotiations.

24. Tape 789-4, conversation between Jackson, Nixon, and Kissinger, September 30, 1972, Oval Office, Nixon Material, National Archives and Records Agency.

25. See Bundy, *Tangled Web*, 346–47.

26. Raymond L. Garthoff, *A Journey through the Cold War: A Memoir of Containment and Coexistence* (Washington, D.C.: Brookings Institution, 2001), 273–75; Bundy, *Tangled Web*, 345–47.

27. Remarks, United States Senate, September 1972, reprinted in Fosdick, *Henry M. Jackson and World Affairs*, 180–84.

28. Richard Perle, interview with author, March 5, 2007, Washington, D.C.

29. Charles Horner, "Human Rights and the Jackson Amendment," in Fosdick, *Staying the Course*, 111–28. Horner was on Jackson's staff from 1972 to 1977, encompassing the period of the Jackson-Vanik amendment.

30. Horner, "Human Rights and the Jackson Amendment," in Fosdick, *Staying the Course*, 111–28.

31. Nixon, tape 789-4, September 30, 1972. Nixon Materials, National Archives. Unless otherwise noted, the discussion of Jackson-Vanik is based on Paula Stern, *Water's Edge: Domestic Politics and the Making of American Foreign Policy* (Westport, Conn.: Greenwood Press, 1979).

32. Horner, "Human Rights and the Jackson Amendment," in Fosdick, *Staying the Course*, 111–28.

33. Henry Kissinger, telephone conversation with Max Fisher, March 9, 1974, F-March 5–9, Box 25, Nixon Material, National Archives (hereafter cited as TelCon).

34. TelCon, Kissinger and Senator Jackson, March 6, 1974. TelCon, Kissinger and Senator Alan Cranston (D-Calif.), April 27, 1974, F-April 25–27, Box 25.

35. TelCon, Kissinger and Peter Flanigan, April 20, 1974, F-April 25–27, Box 25.

36. TelCon, Kissinger and Bill Casey, April 27, 1974, F-April 25–27, Box 25.

37. Stern, *Water's Edge*, 130.

38. Box 1, Folder 1a, Papers of Henry Jackson, University of Washington Library, Seattle, Washington.

39. Joseph Albright, "The Pact of Two Henrys," *New York Times Magazine*, January 5, 1975.

40. Kaufman, *Henry M. Jackson*, 279

41. TelCon, Senator Jackson/Mr. Kissinger, March 8, 1973, F-March 6–9, Box 19.

42. TelCon, Senator Jackson/Mr. Kissinger, June 26, 1972, F-June 15–15, Box 14; Perle, interview.

43. Bundy, *Tangled Web*, 544.

[Handwritten notes:]

definetly had personality @ play: anti-totalitarian, cold warrior, crusader for human rights + is narrow view of SU

bigger though is he knew the rules + procedures of congress

the arms control committe {
- there for so long
- chaired influential committees
- could gain bipartisan support
- often a needed vote for legislation
- had ear of president + advisor (personally)
- mentored future president advisors

also not against Nixon or Kissinger personally just what stood for which counter his beliefs + possibly hurt his voters money

5

Zbigniew Brzezinski and Afghanistan

Patrick Vaughan

$\mathscr{T}$he first week of January 1980, National Security Adviser Zbigniew Brzezinski arrived at his office to prepare his morning briefing for President Jimmy Carter. As he did each day, Brzezinski had arrived at 6:45 A.M. and studied the overnight intelligence reports. At 8:15, Brzezinski walked into the Oval Office to brief Carter on what had transpired in the past twelve hours. The meetings were usually formal and businesslike—with a minimum of external conversation. Yet this meeting was different. Carter seemed frustrated and began to ruminate in grave tones about the broader ramifications of the U.S.–Soviet relationship.

As Carter and Brzezinski talked that morning, Soviet combat divisions continued to roll southward into neighboring Afghanistan. The Soviet move was an impressive display of raw military power. On Christmas morning, waves of Soviet transport planes had airlifted combat troops to Kabul airport. Mechanized divisions then moved south across the rugged 1,200-mile Soviet–Afghan border. A few days later, pro-Soviet President Hafizullah Amin was assassinated by Soviet special forces and replaced by a more reliable leadership in Kabul.

Afghanistan had traditionally served as a neutral buffer state between India and the Soviet Union. But a communist coup in April 1978 had triggered a mass revolt among Afghanistan's traditional Islamic population. For more than a year, the Afghan mujahideen had been sustaining a "holy war" against the pro-Soviet governments in Kabul. The Soviet Union now feared that the contagion of a fundamentalist revival might foment separatist impulses within the Soviet Union's already sizable Muslim population.

Brzezinski had not been shocked by the Soviet move into Afghanistan. He had spent his entire life studying the Soviet Union as both an academic and a policy maker and had spent the previous year warning Carter about the likelihood of a full-scale Soviet invasion. Brzezinski told Carter that the Soviet invasion of Afghanistan had dramatically altered the geopolitical balance in what he had begun to term "the arc of crisis." Brzezinski noted that a Soviet-dominated Afghanistan might allow Moscow to gain control of the Middle East simply by implementing a gradual process of Finlandization. This meant that the mere physical presence of the Soviet military—combined with constant threat of political subversion—could frighten key Middle East states into a more compliant relationship with the Soviet Union.

But Brzezinski also warned of more dire scenarios. He understood that the Soviet Union—for all its boasts about overtaking the West—had entered a period of prolonged economic stagnation. Yet it had perhaps the most formidable military force in the world—and was now within 300 miles of the Arabian Sea. This was the lifeline for oil shipments moving out from Saudi Arabia, Iran, and the Persian Gulf. The Western economies would not last long without this supply of oil.

Pakistan, a largely Islamic nation sharing a long border with Afghanistan, was also now in direct range of a potential Soviet advance. Brzezinski noted that the Russians, since the days of the czars, had eyed Afghanistan as a potential path toward the warm-water ports on the Indian Ocean. The Soviet Union was now in position to drive south through the Pakistani province of Baluchistan and reach the gulf regions. He noted that Baluchi tribesmen dispersed throughout Pakistan, Iran, and Afghanistan had long wanted a state of their own. A Soviet advance could be easily justified as a "war of liberation" for an independent Baluchistan. Access to these southern naval bases would then permit the Soviet Union to control the tanker lanes for Middle East oil supplies. Iran, then engaged in its own Islamic revolution, was also exposed to a potential Soviet invasion from the north.

Yet Brzezinski also had reason for optimism. The Soviet Union, he believed, may have fallen into a dangerous trap. At first glance, the battle seemed like a mismatch. The Soviet military entered Afghanistan with five modern motorized divisions—deployed against Islamic guerillas dressed in turbans and sandals. Soviet helicopter gunships hunted the rebels in brutal search-and-destroy tactics. Yet a month after the invasion, Brzezinski's intelligence reports confirmed that the Afghan resistance was proving surprisingly resilient.

The Soviet forces were having difficulties fighting in Afghanistan's mountainous terrain where hundreds of mujahideen units were engaged in small-scale hit-and-run operations. Some Soviet helicopters were even destroyed from Afghan guns firing *down* on them from the mountains. But the Afghan resistance was proving unique in another way. Weeks into the fighting, one observer articulated the dilemma the Soviet Union now faced in Afghanistan. "In the jihad—the holy war—that they are waging, life is of little importance. If they die in battle, then it is an honor; if they live, they keep on fighting."[1]

Brzezinski thought the Afghan rebellion might now be in position to give the Soviet Union its own "Vietnam." But it could do so only if it received external support. The day after the Soviet invasion, Brzezinski dispatched a cautious memo to President Carter. "We should not be too sanguine about Afghanistan becoming a Soviet Vietnam," Brzezinski warned. "The guerrillas are badly organized and poorly led. They have no sanctuary, no organized army, and no central government—all of which North Vietnam had. They have limited foreign support, in contrast to the enormous amount of arms that flowed to the Vietnamese from both the Soviet Union and China. The Soviets are likely to act decisively, unlike the U.S. which pursued in Vietnam a policy of 'inoculating' the enemy."[2]

There were certainly risks involved with supporting such a movement. These were not ordinary soldiers who would return home after the war. They were fighting for something larger than American interests. Yet Brzezinski also believed Muslim outrage against the Soviet Union—coupled with sustained U.S. efforts to achieve a Middle East settlement—would be in America's long-term interest. Brzezinski also believed that funding the Afghan mujahideen would advance the ambitious goal that he had fostered for the previous three decades—the dismantling of the Soviet Union. Whether this was true would in later years become the subject of intense debate.

In the first week of February 1980, a helicopter carrying Zbigniew Brzezinski touched down in a muddy refugee camp tucked along the Pakistan–Afghanistan border. It was now five weeks after the initial Soviet invasion. Some 350,000 Afghan refugees had already fled Soviet forces across the border for sanctuary in Pakistan. The camp was cold and dismal. The refugees were restless and angry. Brzezinski listened as they told stories about Red Army forces attacking their mullahs and Soviet helicopter gunships decimating their mosques and villages. "We don't want wheat or tents," one told Brzezinski. "We want arms and ammunition to fight with. We have fled from terror and cruelty perpetrated by the Communists. We don't want food and rations but arms and ammunition."[3]

Brzezinski had little doubt about the motivation of the soldiers in front of him. He listened to stories that day that reminded him of stories he had heard about the Soviets from Poles in World War II, Hungarians in 1956, and Czechoslovaks in 1968. He now used an interpreter to tell the Afghans standing in front of him just what he thought. "That land over there is yours," Brzezinski declared, pointing his finger across the border to Afghanistan.

"And you will go back one day because your cause is right and God is on your side. You should know that the whole world is outraged. Not only the world of Islam but the world of Christianity is outraged."[4]

Brzezinski's trip to Pakistan proved a symbolic turning point in the Cold War. Toward the end of the visit, a reporter asked Brzezinski if the United States was now willing to supply arms to the Afghan resistance. Brzezinski, though not committing formally, indicated where he stood on the issue. But the real question, in Brzezinski's mind, had been formulated early in his life. "Will the Pakistanis act like Poles or Czechs?" he asked a reporter. He explained that in World War II, the Poles fought an underground resistance against both the Soviet Union and the Nazis. The Czechs—betrayed by the West at the Munich Conference—had largely capitulated. "It's a fact that people who are determined to fight for their own freedom end up winning the respect and sympathy and something more than that from the rest of the world," Brzezinski concluded. "That's a historical fact, not a statement of policy."[5]

Zbigniew Brzezinski had been thinking about the Soviet Union for most of his adult life. Before he entered the Carter administration, he was among America's preeminent specialists on the Soviet Union. This profession was only slightly less contentious than the disputes that had divided the Carter administration. Western academics had long engaged in bitter debates about one of the grander questions of the twentieth century: What was the "true" meaning of Lenin's "Great October Revolution"? One school, generally sympathetic to the noble ideals of social justice and a "worker revolution," believed that something had gone "wrong" with Lenin's original vision—and might one day be corrected.

Brzezinski belonged firmly to another school. His academic work was rooted in his view that nothing had ever gone "wrong" with Lenin's vision. The entire Soviet venture was simply "wrong" from the outset. Brzezinski saw Lenin's revolution as a conspiratorial coup d'état carried out by a ruthless Bolshevik Party. It was thus not a part of the "ineluctable forces of history" as claimed by Soviet dogma. It was a murderous one-party dictatorship whose system of institutionalized terror had introduced the foundations of the modern "totalitarian" state.

Brzezinski argued that Lenin's original brand of "socialism" had far more in common with the pathologies of Nazi Germany and fascist Italy. These basic characteristics marked a "straight line" from Lenin's revolution through the staid and bureaucratic gerontocracy that had unleashed the Soviet invasion of Afghanistan in December 1979.

Zbigniew Brzezinski was born in Warsaw, Poland, a decade after the October Revolution. The year was 1928. This was the year Joseph Stalin had brutally consolidated his power in Moscow—and a year before the crash of the U.S. stock market spiraled the West into a decade of economic depression. Many Western intellectuals were thus optimistic about Stalin's "experiment." They pointed to the full employment, smoke-belching factories, and heroic state workers—as a sign of the "New Civilization" that would soon level the vast inequities of modern industrial capitalism.

George Bernard Shaw visited the Soviet Union in the summer of 1931 and returned convinced that Soviet Russia was the wave of the future. "We had better follow Russia's example as soon as possible," Shaw said. "On the whole, I should advise a young man to go to Russia and settle there."[6] Sidney and Beatrice Webb, the founders of the London School of Economics, rationalized Stalin's liquidation of some 1 million kulaks with the aside that "the Soviet government could hardly have enacted otherwise."[7]

Zbigniew Brzezinski received his education from another source. His father, Tadeusz Brzezinski, had fought in the Polish-Soviet War of 1920 when Polish forces repelled Lenin's attempt to use Poland as a "red bridge" to export the Bolshevik revolution to the West. Some Poles attributed this "Miracle on the Vistula" to divine intervention. It was the only defeat in the history of the Red Army. Tadeusz Brzezinski was among many Poles who believed it had saved not only Poland but also all of "Western civilization." Poles were thus often surprised when people in the West had not heard of it.

In 1936, Tadeusz Brzezinski, now a Polish diplomat, was posted to the Soviet Ukraine. At the time, millions of ordinary peasants and workers were being summarily executed as "enemies of the people." The young Zbigniew Brzezinski believed he had a better understanding of the Soviet Union than the editorial pages of *The Nation* or *The New Republic*. "My father told me stories," Brzezinski recalled. "About the mass disappearances, people he would deal with, about how he would have some elite in the Ukraine to dinner, and he would learn within weeks that they had been arrested and then shot. There is no doubt that this had an enormous impression on me at a very young age."[8]

In 1938, Tadeusz Brzezinski was assigned to a more tranquil posting in Montreal. The ten-year-old Zbigniew Brzezinski spent his first year in Canada bothering his father about when the family might return to Poland for the holidays. On August 23, 1939, came the stunning announcement that Hitler and Stalin had agreed to a "nonaggression" pact. In the early morning of September 1, 1939, sixty German divisions of the blitzkrieg broke through the Polish borders and raced toward Warsaw. World War II had begun.

At 3:00 A.M., Tadeusz Brzezinski received a phone call at his home from the Polish consulate general in New York. The young Zbigniew Brzezinski woke up and pondered what was happening. He felt a curious sense of euphoria. He had always been impressed watching the Polish army march through the streets of Warsaw. He also knew the French and the British had formally guaranteed Poland's security against Nazi aggression. A week after the Nazi incursion, he and his siblings were confident the Nazi advance would be resisted. But it soon became clear that the French and the British were prepared to do little beyond voice their support for the Poles. Poland now faced the Nazi blitzkrieg on its own.

On September 17, Stalin, completing his secret arrangement with Hitler, sent six Soviet armies into Poland from the east. An estimated 1.5 million Poles were quickly deported to the Soviet Union. Half that number died en route—or later from starvation or forced labor in Stalin's gulags. By late autumn, cameras caught Soviet and Nazi armies mingling together in the Polish forests—together with Gestapo and the NKVD officials. "One swift blow to Poland," boasted Soviet foreign minister Molotov, "first by the Germans and then by the Red Army, and nothing was left of this ugly bastard of the Versailles Treaty."⁹

Zbigniew Brzezinski followed World War II as a youth growing up in Canada. He began learning Russian using a copy of Pushkin's *The Captain's Daughter*. He had been a member of the Polish Boy Scouts and had a vicarious experience when many Polish children went into the Polish underground guerilla resistance. He also kept a diary composed almost entirely of a chronology of the war.

The war took a dramatic turn in the summer of 1941—when Hitler betrayed his erstwhile Soviet ally and drove the Nazi blitzkrieg toward Moscow. In December 1941, Japanese forces bombed Pearl Harbor. The United States and Great Britain—two Western democracies—were now locked in a curious alliance with Stalin and the Soviet Union.

In later years, Zbigniew Brzezinski would credit the genius of Franklin Roosevelt's New Deal for allowing America to adjust to the industrial age. Yet the young Brzezinski believed Roosevelt was exceedingly naive in his negotiations with Stalin. The Americans, noted one historian, were ill prepared to respond to Stalin's ruthless brand of realpolitik. Instead, the Americans displayed an "infectious, childlike desire to see the Alliance as one great happy family."

"They wanted a moral crusade, the victory of Good over Evil. It was they who introduced the dominant mood, in which the Soviet dictator became 'Uncle Joe,' in which, in discussing the Soviet Union, one talked only of the Red Army's heroism, in which 'the Russians' could be seen as 'freedom-loving democrats,' and in which events before 1941 were not mentioned. Indeed, since the Americans had played no part in the first stage of the war, they were genuinely uninterested in events prior to their involvement. Nothing could have suited Stalin better."¹⁰

Perhaps nothing symbolized this more clearly than the discovery of the mass grave of Polish reserve soldiers in the spring of 1943. On March 5, 1940, Lavrenti Beria, the head of the NKVD, submitted a memo to Stalin about the fate of the 20,000 captured Polish officers. Stalin ordered all to be shot as "committed enemies of the Soviet Union." NKVD death squads then began a mass execution of 21,587 Polish army reservists. The details of the operation were revealed only after documents surfaced in the early 1990s.

The Polish officers were forced to their knees near the edge of the mass graves. They were gagged and bound before being shot in the back of the head at close range. One journalist, after seeing the documents, described the details uncovered. "Many younger men resisted and were stabbed with bayonets, often several times. The NKVD reserved a macabre death for those most difficult to subdue. Their mouths were stuffed with sawdust and gagged; their overcoats were then yanked above their heads and fastened with choke knots about the neck. Their hands were lashed tightly behind the back and pulled sharply toward the shoulder blades. Finally, a cord connected their raised hands to the choke knot around the neck. If these victims continued to struggle, they strangled themselves to death."[11]

The Brzezinski family, like many Poles, had been curious about the whereabouts of the "missing" Polish officers. On April 13, 1943, Berlin Radio announced the gruesome discovery of some 4,000 Polish corpses in a mass grave near Smolensk. A young Zbigniew Brzezinski was sitting at home in Montreal when he first heard the news. "Precisely because I knew of the Soviets from my father," recalled Brzezinski, "there was not the slightest doubt in my mind that the Soviets did it, although the Nazis were quite capable of doing it, and did many things rather similar. But in that particular case, I had no doubt, whatsoever, that that the Soviets did it."[12]

The Polish government in London asked the International Red Cross to open a formal inquiry into the matter. Stalin, charging that the Poles were spreading "Nazi propaganda," severed diplomatic relations with the Polish government. Roosevelt and Churchill were reluctant to implicate their ally in such a gruesome crime. Roosevelt seemed not to want to believe it. The "graves question," he fumed, "wasn't worth such a fuss." "Wow," Roosevelt was heard to say, "what fools [the London Poles] are! I've no patience with them." Roosevelt later cabled Stalin offering that he "fully understood" his problem with the Poles.[13]

The Brzezinski family in Montreal was beginning to fear that Poland was being sacrificed in a spheres of influence deal with Stalin. At Yalta, Roosevelt and Churchill accepted Stalin's vague promises to hold "free and unfettered" elections in Poland at some point in the future. Zbigniew Brzezinski believed Yalta was only the most visible incident where the Americans grossly misread the Soviet mind-set. Brzezinski later noted that Roosevelt's attempts at personal charm with Stalin had not "ingratiated" him to the Soviet leader. They had, suggested Brzezinski, merely earned Stalin's "quiet contempt."

Brzezinski argued it would have been far better for the West to negotiate from a position of strength—which the Soviets tended to display a measure of respect. "We do not know whether the Soviets would have yielded," Brzezinski wrote years later. "But we do know that they were not tested. The West showed neither foresight nor courage, and this is why Yalta is not only a symbol of subsequent division of Europe but a major historical blot on the record of Anglo-American leadership."[14]

The Brzezinski family was not returning to Poland. In the fall of 1945, Brzezinski enrolled at Montreal's McGill University. Now a young man, his academic views toward the Soviet Union began to take form. In 1950, Brzezinski submitted an M.A. thesis titled "Russo-Soviet Nationalism." He argued that the Soviet Union was not the monolith pink mass displayed on schoolroom maps after the war. It was better understood as a fragile multinational empire—a vast expanse of conquered nationalities brutally centralized under a centuries-long process of "Russification."

In 1950, Zbigniew Brzezinski entered Harvard University, where his academic work continued to challenge the idea of a "monolithic" communist world. But he also sought to implement his academic work into formal American policy. Brzezinski's research convinced him that the Soviet Union's "Achilles' heel" was rooted in its multinational character. "Once I grasped that in my M.A. thesis at McGill," Brzezinski recalled, "I began to formulate a strategy to expose the weaknesses of the Soviet system. This strategy would move to detach the countries of the Soviet bloc from the Soviet Union—and after detaching them—accomplish the dismantling of the Soviet Union itself."[15]

In the summer of 1953, a twenty-five-year-old Zbigniew Brzezinski dropped by Radio Free Europe headquarters in Munich. It was there that he first met Jan Nowak-Jezioranski, the head of the Polish desk of RFE. Nowak-Jezioranski was astonished by Brzezinski's encyclopedic knowledge of the Polish wartime underground and his dedication to the radio services. He was stunned. "For God's sake, you are so very young!" Nowak-Jezioranski told the Harvard student. "How can you explain your dedication to this instrument?!" Nowak-Jezioranski later found his answer. "His father later told me that since he was a child, his son was determined to play a personal role in liberating Poland from the Soviet Union."[16]

In November 1956, the Soviet Union sent tanks into Budapest to crush a rebellion in its Soviet satellite. Brzezinski argued that Eisenhower's silence had signaled to the Soviet Union that a military response would meet no opposition from the West. Given the overt American passivity and "advance declarations of non-interference," Brzezinski concluded, "The Soviets would have been foolish not to intervene."[17]

In the early 1960s, Brzezinski wrote speeches for the Kennedy administration advocating a strategy of "peaceful engagement" toward Eastern Europe—as a means to gradually wean the region out of the Soviet Empire. In early 1960, Harvard University Press released Brzezinski's *Soviet Bloc: Unity and Conflict*. Brzezinski noted that Stalin's monolithic "bloc" had been transformed into a more loosely configured group of states with their own visions of "national communism." China's highly militant challenge to the Soviet Union, argued Brzezinski, was likely to further the disunity in the communist world.[18]

Roman Szporluk, a leading authority on Ukraine, recalled the novelty of Brzezinski's ideas at the time. "Brzezinski was one of the only people at that time," said Szporluk, "who understood that the existence of nationalism in Eastern Europe tended to stimulate the nationalist sentiments within the USSR. He grasped onto the idea very early that national communism in countries like Romania and Poland—would inevitably spread to stimulate national consciousness in the Ukraine, Latvia and Estonia—and on to the other Soviet republics."[19]

Brzezinski began to articulate his view that the Soviet Union had entered a prolonged era of economic stagnation and was likely to collapse along nationalist lines. Brzezinski noted that most of the true innovators in the Soviet Union had likely perished in Stalin's purges. Over time, this had created a case of "reverse natural selection" whereby only the most colorless apparatchiks were able to rise through the power ranks. The result, Brzezinski noted, did not bode well for the Soviet future.

By the mid-1960s, Brzezinski's writing began to emphasize the importance of technology in the postindustrial "technotronic world." He noted that the Soviet Union was not keeping up with the dramatic socioeconomic changes brought about by the age of the computer. This was especially true after 1964, when Nikita Khrushchev was deposed in an interparty coup d'état. Brzezinski immediately dismissed the incoming Brezhnev leadership as a "generation of clerks" whose bureaucratic nature might very well expedite the collapse of the Soviet Union.

At the same time, Brzezinski believed that too many Western scholars were overlooking the festering nationalities seeking greater independence from Moscow. "This omission," wrote Brzezinski in 1968, "is indicative of the inclination of many Western scholars of Soviet affairs to minimize what I fear may be potentially a very explosive issue in the Soviet polity. We still live in an age of nationalism, and my own highly generalized feeling is that it is going to be exceedingly difficult for the Soviet Union to avoid having some of its many nationalities go through a phase of assertive nationalism. History teaches us, be it in Algeria or in Indonesia or in Africa that these demands grow rather than decline. If they are not met or are suppressed, it is likely that the demands will become sharper and more self-assertive. If they are satisfied, they will grow with the eating."[20]

On Sunday, August 20, 1968, Brzezinski was working at his home in New Jersey when he heard on the radio that Soviet tanks had invaded Czechoslovakia to crush Alexander Dubcek's attempt to build "socialism with a human face. " Brzezinski's first response was that he had witnessed the death knell for the Soviet Union. Brzezinski, as he had with the case of Hungary in 1956, also believed Washington's conspicuous silence before the invasion had given the Soviet Union an implicit signal that "détente" with the United States could withstand a Soviet military invasion. Brzezinski's analysis appeared a few days later on the front page of the *Washington Post*:

> The present Soviet leadership is acting more like a fascist than a Communist government. It is to be remembered that fascism was a radical, socialist, nationalist, and imperialistic movement. The invasion of Czechoslovakia will hasten the process not only of disintegration of international communism but in all probability also of the internal decay of the Soviet political system. Without a doubt, the more enlightened segments of Soviet society are as outraged and disgusted as the rest of the world. Before long, the contagion of freedom which is temporarily being snuffed out in Prague will spread to Kiev and Moscow.[21]

A few months later, Richard Nixon defeated Hubert Humphrey in one of the closest presidential elections in American history. Nixon surprised many by naming Henry Kissinger, Brzezinski's old Harvard rival, as his national security adviser. Nixon and Kissinger came into office with a dramatic new approach toward dealing with the Soviet Union. Kissinger was a proponent of "realism." This historically European worldview favored unsentimental "balance of power" over moral crusades. Under Nixon and Kissinger, the Soviet Union would no longer be treated as an ideological rival but as a traditional "great power" with its own legitimate interests to protect.

In the ensuing eight years, Kissinger began a new relationship with the Soviet Union—often orchestrated privately through secret back channels—with the end goal of capping the rapidly escalating nuclear arms race and achieving some sort of geopolitical stability.

The era of "détente" was at its zenith in May 1972 when Nixon and Kissinger arrived in Moscow for a dramatic summit meeting. Nixon and Leonid Brezhnev engaged amiably over vodka and caviar in the glittering surroundings of St. George's Hall in the Great Kremlin Palace. The highlight of the eight-day summit was the signing of the first Strategic Arms Limitation Treaty (SALT I). This pledged each superpower to set limits on the arms race. The new spirit of superpower cordiality seemed to have put an end to the Cold War. Nixon returned home hailing the summit as a key step toward a "generation of peace."

Brzezinski countered that Nixon and Kissinger were dramatically overestimating the virtues of détente—especially the claim that it had introduced a "generation of peace." Brzezinski cautioned there was a dangerous new element of self-confidence emanating from Moscow—not unlike the concept of "manifest destiny" that justified American westward expansion in the nineteenth century. The Soviet Union now saw itself as an ascendant power with an international mission. The American paralysis over Vietnam would likely embolden these views. Brzezinski warned that in the ensuing years, Moscow was quite likely to test America's global resolve.

Brzezinski's alternative foreign policy vision took form in 1973. That year, Brzezinski and David Rockefeller cofounded the Trilateral Commission—a group designed to promote closer "trilateral" ties between North America, Japan, and Western Europe. Brzezinski believed that America's future lay not with a condominium arrangement with the "historically irrelevant" regime in Moscow. A better solution would be to strengthen relations with the world's industrial democracies that were more capable of cooperating to solve the global problems likely to emerge as America moved toward the twenty-first century. Brzezinski favored a more "reciprocal" détente where credits and technology would be linked to Soviet restraint around the world and its willingness to loosen its grip on Eastern Europe.[22]

In July 1973, Brzezinski took a leave from his post at Columbia University to oversee the selection of the Trilateral Commission's first 200 members. His most significant selection turned out to be a rather obscure one-term governor from Georgia. "We wanted a forward-looking Democratic governor who would be congenial to the trilateral perspective," Brzezinski recalled. One of Brzezinski's colleagues mentioned that Jimmy Carter, the current governor of Georgia, had been courageous on civil rights and had shown interest in developing trade relations between Georgia and the Common Market and Japan. "Well, he's obviously our man," replied Brzezinski.[23]

There were few commentators who took Governor Jimmy Carter seriously when he announced his intention to run for the White House in December 1974. The stories that did cover the event noted that a one-term governor from the South had virtually no chance in winning the nomination. *Newsweek* ran a small feature titled "Jimmy Who?"[24] Brzezinski was one of the few in the so-called Washington establishment who did take notice.

In May 1975, the Trilateral Commission held its annual conference in Kyoto, Japan. Brzezinski had been dismayed by the dovish turn of the Democratic Party in 1972. He was critical of both parties for refusing to initiate a comprehensive settlement in the Middle East. After the 1973 Yom Kippur War, Brzezinski believed there was a very narrow window within which to reach a settlement before the tensions spun out of control. At Kyoto, Carter's speech called for a "comprehensive" Middle East peace plan to settle the tensions between Israel and the Palestinians. "It's nice," Brzezinski observed from the rostrum, "to see a Democratic candidate for President who has guts."[25]

Following the Kyoto conference, Brzezinski sent Carter a $20 check and began to submit strategic memos on a more formal basis. By late 1975, Brzezinski emerged as Carter's primary foreign policy adviser. "Brzezinski was the first guy in the Community to pay attention to Carter, to take him seriously," noted one Washington insider. "He spent time with Carter, talked to him, sent him books and articles, educated him."[26]

About the same time, the détente orchestrated by Nixon and Kissinger had come under increasing criticism. In November 1975, the Soviet-backed regime came to power in Angola—supported by Soviet arms and a massive airlift of some 12,000 Cuban combat troops. The boldness of the Soviet move seemed to shock the new Ford administration. Ronald Reagan, now actively challenging Ford for the Republican nomination, was the symbol of the suddenly revived anti-détente wing of the Republican Party. "It's time to straighten up and eyeball it with Russia, and the time to start is in Angola."[27]

Brzezinski, now advising Carter's presidential campaign, took a more cautious tone. Brzezinski believed that the best path toward weakening the Soviet Union was engagement combined with a firm response to Soviet moves around the globe. Brzezinski saw the Soviet move into Angola as confirmation that the Soviets were using détente as a cover to expand their interests throughout the globe. "The sweeping generalizations made by the Administration, about a 'generation of peace' were wrong and misleading," noted Brzezinski. "Détente is going to be a mixed relationship with elements of both conflict and cooperation."[28]

By March 1976, Jimmy Carter had used a string of stunning primary victories to emerge as the unlikely front-runner for the Democratic nomination. Brzezinski believed that Carter had to diffuse the idea that he was a neophyte in foreign policy. The best way to do that was to attack the Kissinger "legend" with a frontal attack. Brzezinski penned Carter's first major foreign policy speech to be delivered at the Chicago Council on Foreign Relations. Carter charged that the United States was simply "giving up too much and asking for too little" in dealing with the Soviet Union. "For too long," Carter noted in a clear jab at Kissinger, "our policy has been maneuver and manipulation, which may have worked in 1815 or even 1945, but has a much less significant role in today's world, where there are increasing mutual interests of all nations, such as protecting natural resources and stopping pollution and international terrorism."[29]

Brzezinski also believed that Kissinger's version of détente had neglected the increasingly visible dissident movements in the Soviet Union and Eastern Europe. This was amplified with the signing of the Helsinki Accords in the summer of 1975. Throughout the previous year, American conservatives had denounced the Helsinki Final Act as a Yalta-like sellout toward Eastern Europe. Indeed, on August 1, 1976, the Soviet leadership commemorated the first anniversary of the Helsinki Final Act as a resounding triumph.[30]

Brzezinski began to advise Carter to change the focus of Helsinki. He should move away from the view that the Final Act had accepted the postwar frontiers—and thus Soviet control over Eastern Europe—and begin to emphasize the still little known "Basket Three" aspects of the Helsinki Accords that committed all signatories to respect "civil, economic, social, cultural, and other rights and freedoms."

"This gave us a real opportunity to press them at the point of greater vulnerability to them," Brzezinski recalled. "And at the same time to do it in a manner which at the same time didn't make us look as if we were just some sort of crude anti-communists interested in inflaming or re-flaming the Cold War. Carter seemed to be killing the Soviets with kindness. Because he was talking about engagement, human rights, disarmament. But the Soviets knew what he was talking about it. Or at least they knew what I was *thinking* about."[31]

Carter's emphasis on the Helsinki Final Act had an additional benefit. Midway through the second presidential debate, President Ford volunteered one of the more infamous gaffes in debate history. Ford, in defending his signature on the Helsinki Final Act, offered the stunning claim that there was "no Soviet domination over Eastern Europe." Carter, bolstered by Ford's blunder, was able to hold on to win one of the closest presidential elections in history.

In the ensuing weeks, Carter foreshadowed the fissions that would emerge in his foreign policy team over the next four years. As secretary of state, Carter selected Cyrus Vance, a highly respected diplomat and lawyer who had served with distinction in the Kennedy and Johnson administrations. A few weeks later, Carter stood in a muddy press field in Plains, Georgia, to introduce Brzezinski as his new national security adviser. Thus were born the disputes that would divide the Carter foreign policy for the next four years.

Vance was a patient and skilled negotiator who made it clear that his main goal as secretary of state was to reach an agreement on the stalled SALT II negotiations. Vance ruled out any form of "linkage" that had been invoked by Nixon and Kissinger. Each subject, said Vance, "should be discussed on its own footing." Vance was especially wary of the precedent set by Kissinger, who used his proximity to Richard Nixon to steamroll the more amiable secretary of state, William Rogers.

Brzezinski, in turn, was determined from the outset to implement a more "reciprocal" form of détente. Few observers at the time knew what he had in mind. Brzezinski's version of "détente," he would admit in later years, was designed not only to contain the Soviet Union but also to engineer its demise. This involved an increased effort to promote human rights, support dissidents, and stir up the nationalities—and contest the Soviet Union militarily around the world. Robert Gates, then working under Brzezinski in the Carter national security team, noted the dramatic break with the Nixon–Kissinger approach. "Beginning early in the administration, and going beyond the human rights campaign, Brzezinski initiated, and Carter approved, an unprecedented White House effort to attack the internal legitimacy of the Soviet government."[32]

Adam Michnik, at the time an intellectual force behind Poland's nascent opposition movement that would soon grow into the Solidarity movement, recalled the impact of Carter's human rights policy. "Kissinger had a vision like Metternich—'we divide the world into spheres of influence and we talk with governments.' But Brzezinski and Carter came to office and said, 'There were not only governments but civil societies, who very often think different than the government, but they are gagged.' And Brzezinski understood what hardly anybody could understand at that time in America—that an ideological confrontation with the Soviet bloc had to be undertaken—and the American slogan in this confrontation should be human rights."[33]

Brzezinski was also intensely interested in exploiting the Soviet nationality problem—what he had referred to in his M.A. thesis as the Soviet Union's "Achilles' heel." The Carter administration unveiled a minorities program aimed at infiltrating written materials into the various Soviet republics, primarily Ukraine. Brzezinski also initiated a covert program targeting Soviet Muslims and Ukrainians as well as efforts at supporting human rights activists. Brzezinski placed Paul Henze, a former colleague who worked at Radio Free Europe, in charge of seeking a more engaged policy toward the Soviet nationalities. "Brzezinski took me aside right away," recalled Henze. "He simply said 'I want you to see what you can do to really get some attention to non-Russian nationalities in the Soviet Union. They're important, and they're going to be more important, and we need to have ourselves equipped to do something about them.'"[34,35]

Such policies were taking place largely under the radar of the public. In was not until early 1978 that Brzezinski and Vance emerged in a public debate over how best to engage the Soviet Union. In late 1977, the Soviet Union began to intervene more assertively in a border dispute between Somalia and Ethiopia. In November 1977, Soviet military transport flights began to airlift of Cuban forces into Ethiopia. Brzezinski saw this as far more than supporting one side in an African civil war—he saw it as a continuation of the Soviet Union's challenge to America and its strategic partners in the region.

Brzezinski now linked the Horn of Africa to the broader concerns in what he termed the "arc of crisis" throughout the Middle East. Ethiopia was located on one of the key choke points of the Middle East, bordering on the Red Sea and the Gulf of Aden across from Saudi Arabia. Brzezinski argued that Iran, Egypt, Saudi Arabia, Sudan, Kenya, and North Yemen all felt threatened by the scale and boldness of the Soviet move. Brzezinski argued that the United States might deploy an aircraft carrier to the region as a tangible sign of American concern. Vance argued the SALT treaty was of vital importance and that a "regional" issue could not get in the way of the broader U.S.–Soviet détente. Andrew Young, U.S. ambassador to the United Nations, publicly rebuked Brzezinski, noting that "the Ogaden is really nothing more than a thousand miles of sand."[36] President Carter, taking Vance's view, rejected Brzezinski's proposals.

By March 1978, the Soviets had airlifted some 10,000 Cuban troops into Ethiopia. Brzezinski's military adviser Colonel William Odom recalls the tension that had emerged between Vance and Brzezinski at the time. "Brzezinski was asking some key questions. What is the long-term significance of letting the Soviets get away with moving two Cuban divisions in there? What is the significance of making no linkage to arms control? Can we really do this? Do we understand what we're going to get into if we allow this? Are we not blessing assertiveness from the Russians in these other areas? But Vance and his adviser Marshall Shulman were always there to insist that it was a local issue—and we shouldn't be alarmed."[37]

Brzezinski responded by taking an increasingly visible profile in the administration. In May 1978, Brzezinski embarked on a high-profile trip to the People's Republic of China. He had mounted an assiduous campaign with Carter to make the trip. In the end, Carter acceded but over the vocal objections of Vance, who was attempting to negotiate the SALT treaty at the time. Vance had traveled to China the previous year and was careful to emphasize that the United States had no agenda to use one communist power against the other.

Brzezinski had a very different view. Brzezinski now saw the development of closer relations with China as a way to challenge the Soviet Union. His trip had an overt agenda to bring the United States and China in into a closer relationship to combat "Soviet hegemony." "Neither of us dispatches international marauders to advance big-power ambitions in Africa," Brzezinski told his Chinese hosts. "Neither of us seeks to enforce the political obedience of our neighbors through military force." At one point, Brzezinski toured the Great Wall and quipped that the last one to the top had to "fight the Soviets in Ethiopia." China's new leadership appeared to have taken a pragmatic turn. A group of Chinese sailors asked Brzezinski to stand with them for a photo. "Do you know you are posing with an imperialist?" asked Brzezinski. Not so, said the sailors, using a colloquial reference to the Soviet Union. "We are having a photograph taken with the polar-bear tamer."[38]

Vance was said to have visibly grimaced when he heard about Brzezinski's flippant and overtly anti-Soviet jibes in China. But the policy tilt toward China had gone Brzezinski's way. On December 15, 1978, President Carter issued a dramatic announcement that the United States and China would establish formal diplomatic ties.

Brzezinski's trip to China overlapped with a burgeoning political crisis in the Middle East. Iran had been a pillar of American security interests in the region since a coup backed by the Central Intelligence Agency (CIA) had brought Shah Mohammed Riza Pahlevi to power in 1953. This relationship became even stronger during the Nixon–Kissinger years—and Carter appeared anxious to continue the relationship. Yet by the late 1970s, the shah was being challenged by a rising tide of Islamic fundamentalism. By 1978, Ayatollah Rubollah Khomeini—a fiery Islamic spiritual leader who had spent the previous fourteen years in exile—began to gather popular support within Iran.

Brzezinski favored a full backing of the shah, even if it entailed an American-backed military coup. He dismissed the State Department's more hopeful conclusions that Khomeini might emerge as a "Ghandi like figure" to preside over a moderate coalition government. On January 15, 1979, the ailing shah—besieged by street mobs and unsure of the true level of American backing—fled Iran. Two weeks later, Khomeini returned to Tehran in triumph. On November 4, 1979, Iranian militants loyal to Khomeini stormed the American embassy in Tehran and took sixty-six Americans hostage. The nightly displays of the captives on American television had spawned a rash of critical commentaries postulating that America was no longer respected in the world. Republican Ronald Reagan announced his candidacy for the White House days after the hostages had been seized in Tehran.

Brzezinski was dismayed by the strategic loss of Iran in an increasingly turbulent region. He nevertheless advised President Carter to refrain from a blanket confrontation with all of "Islam." Much of the resentment in the Islamic world, Brzezinski noted, was based on the widespread belief that the United States was the colonial successor to Britain and France in the Middle East. To amplify these suspicions with a rhetorical attack on all of "Islam," Brzezinski cautioned, was to invite a dangerous self-fulfilling prophecy.

Brzezinski understood that America was not the only superpower troubled by the rise of Islamic fundamentalism. The Muslim territories on the Soviet Union's southern frontier suffered greatly under Bolshevik rule. Lenin's Bolshevik regime had razed mosques, broke up feudal estates, and sought to crush all resistance among local tribesmen. Soviet forces frequently executed the mullahs, banned the Holy Koran, and the hajj. This created a sustained rebellion in the 1920s involving Uzbek, Kazakh, Krygyz, Turkmen, and Tajik *basmachi* (bandits). Yet by the late 1970s, Moscow saw this issue being revived along its southern border with Afghanistan.

In the early years of the Cold War, Afghanistan was generally regarded as a buffer between the Soviet Union and America's strategic interests in Iran and Pakistan. By the late 1960s, the Soviets had taken more active measures—training and equipping its armed forces—in an effort to draw Afghanistan closer into its own version of a collective security system for Asia. This relationship took a turn in July 1973 when a group of army officers staged a coup in Afghanistan. Mohammed Daoud Khan's new government banned the Communist Party and soon began to lean toward a more neutral role for Afghanistan. Daoud's efforts to steer Afghanistan more toward the West became a vital concern for the Soviet leadership. By the time Carter took office in early 1977, Moscow feared that Afghanistan was about to follow the path of Egypt in breaking free of its client status to move closer toward America's strategic interests in the region.

On April 27, 1978, the Afghan Communist Party launched a bloody coup d'état that brought the Communist Party to power. The sixty-eight-year-old Daoud, many members of his family, and ranking officials were slain by the rebels. The new ruling group represented a break from the elite group of the Mohammadzai clan that had ruled the country since the nineteenth century. The new government, headed by Nur Mohammed Taraki, was a faction of the Communist Party that had emerged in the 1960s. Some thought the Soviets had viewed United States as simply too weak to do much about it. "The simple truth," quipped one French intelligence officer, "is that the Soviets are able to get away with practically anything these days."[39]

The Soviet-backed government attempted to bring secularizing reforms to Afghanistan. Some of these—like land reform and introducing literacy classes for women—were designed to bring Afghanistan into the modern age. Yet the draconian measures in which they were enforced resulted in fierce resistance from the country's largely Islamic population. The Soviet-style "cult of personality" that accompanied Nur Mohammed Taraki's ascension to power did not help matters. "Taraki is getting more praise than the Prophet Mohammed these days," said one observer. "And that's very dangerous for a politician."[40]

The Afghan government met the Islamic resistance with brutal countermeasures. Some 27,000 political prisoners were executed at the Pul-I-Charki prison outside Kabul. The level of brutality alarmed even the Soviet leadership. Taraki told his Soviet sponsors that he was only following the Soviet example. "Lenin taught us to be merciless towards the enemies of the revolution," Taraki confided to a KGB official, "and millions of people had to be eliminated in order to secure the victory of the October Revolution."[41]

In March 1979, Islamic resistance responded with a grisly attack on dozens of Soviet advisers as well as their wives and children in the western city of Herat. The mutilated Russian corpses were impaled on spikes and displayed in the city streets. Soviet-trained Afghan bomber pilots then responded with a relentless wave of revenge attacks that took the lives of some 20,000 Afghan citizens. The events in Herat seemed only to harden the Soviet resolve to establish control over the Afghan countryside. "Under no circumstances can we lose Afghanistan," KGB chief Yuri Andropov informed the Soviet Politburo.[42]

In Washington, Brzezinski began to contemplate taking a greater role in aiding the Afghan resistance. On March 30, 1979, David Aaron, Brzezinski's deputy national security adviser, chaired a meeting to discuss the idea of providing covert assistance to the Afghan resistance. Aaron's group discussed the fundamental issue. "Is there interest in maintaining and assisting the insurgency, or is the risk that we will provoke the Soviets too great?"[43]

On July 3, 1979, President Carter signed a presidential finding authorizing the CIA to funnel "nonlethal" covert support to the Afghan insurgents. No weapons were to be supplied, but the CIA was authorized to spend some $500,000 on propaganda and psychological operations, provide medical supplies and radio equipment, and supply funds to the Afghan rebels; CIA officers from the Near East Division soon began to import medical equipment and radios to the Pakistan intelligence service—where they were distributed across the border to the Afghan guerillas.

Brzezinski also believed it important to inform the Soviets of American concern for their creeping intervention. Brzezinski believed that the U.S. silence before the Soviet invasions of Hungary and Czechoslovakia had provided an implied green light to invade. In August 1979, Brzezinski gave a speech warning the Soviet Union against deepening its involvement in Afghanistan. He took note of the "prudent" American restraint during the crisis in Iran. "We expect others," Brzezinski noted, "similarly to abstain from intervention and from efforts to impose alien doctrines on deeply religious and nationally conscious peoples." The next day, the speech appeared on the front page of the *New York Times* under the headline "U.S. Is Indirectly Pressing Russians to Halt Afghanistan Intervention."[44]

In September 1979, Brzezinski sent Carter a personal five-page essay titled "Acquiescence vs. Assertiveness," noting Moscow had traditionally been more cautious when confronted with the latter. (Anatoly Dobrynin, the longtime Soviet ambassador in Washington, later conceded that the "relatively weak Western reaction" to the invasion of Czechoslovakia played a significant role in Moscow's later decision to invade Afghanistan.[45])

The crisis deepened in September 1979 when Taraki was killed in a murky power struggle within the Afghan leadership. His successor, Hafizullah Amin, pursued even more aggressive policies against the mujahideen. Yet the Soviet leadership had come to view Amin with suspicion. At the same time, the KGB believed that the United States was seeking to replace its loss in Iran with a new strategic relationship with Afghanistan. There were rumors that Amin was a CIA plant, willing to make a deal with the West or perhaps follow the Egyptian precedent or even establish an anti-Soviet alliance with Pakistan or China.

In early December 1979, the Soviet Union had made its fateful decision. The Politburo met on the evening of December 12, 1979—the same day that NATO had announced it would introduce cruise and Pershing missiles into Western Europe. Brezhnev was now an aging and ailing leader. He entered the room drunk and visibly irritated at the events transpiring on the Soviet southern frontier. After hearing the news from Afghanistan, the Soviet leader banged his fist on the table and shouted insults at the Afghan leadership before leaving the room. The Politburo had now committed itself to launch a full-scale invasion.

On December 22, 1979, Brzezinski received a phone call from deputy CIA director Bobby Inman warning that a Soviet invasion of Afghanistan was likely within seventy-two hours. On December 25, waves of Soviet transport planes began landing at the Kabul airport discharging some 5,000 combat troops along with their artillery and armored vehicles. On December 27, KGB paramilitaries, dressed as Afghan soldiers, hunted down and assassinated President Hafizullah Amin. The Afghan government was then handed to the more reliable Babrak Karmal, who had been held under Soviet protection before the coup.

The Cold War had taken a dramatic turn. Brzezinski now sought every opportunity to make the Soviet Union pay a price for the transgression. Brzezinski knew that Carter was disappointed that his original foreign policy ideals had not materialized. Yet he also believed that the administration was partly at fault. Brzezinski told Carter that the men in the Kremlin had come to view the Carter administration's version of "détente" as a sign of weakness. Brzezinski advised Carter that he must take the hard line of Harry Truman before he could return to the more idealistic visions of Woodrow Wilson.

On December 26, 1979, Brzezinski sent a memo to Carter titled "Reflections on Soviet Intervention in Afghanistan." "It is essential that Afghanistan's resistance continues," he wrote. "This means more money as well as arms shipments to the rebels, and some technical advice. . . . We should concert with Islamic countries both in a propaganda campaign and in a covert action campaign to help the rebels." Brzezinski continued. "Our ultimate goal is the withdrawal of Soviet troops from Afghanistan. . . . Even if this is not attainable," Brzezinski noted, "we should make Soviet involvement as costly as possible."[46]

A key question centered on whether the United States—short of nuclear war—had the military strength to curb further Soviet incursions into the Persian Gulf. Brzezinski had taken the lead in drafting President Carter's State of the Union Address. On January 23, 1980, Carter gave a speech deliberately echoing the tone of substance of Harry Truman's initial call for containment of the Soviet Union in Europe. "Any attempt by any outside force to gain control of the Persian Gulf region," Carter announced, "will be regarded as an assault on the vital interests of the United States of America and such an assault will be repelled by any means necessary, including military force."

But Carter's problem was indeed more delicate than Truman's. The United States was now relying on the good faith of Islamic nations engulfed in a rising tide of fundamentalism. Brzezinski thought that the risk could be managed. In January 1980, a summit of thirty-five Islamic countries convened in Islamabad. They released a unanimous condemnation of the Soviet intervention of Afghanistan and demanded "immediate, unconditional and total withdrawal of Soviet troops." But there were also obvious risks for the United States becoming too involved in what many were now referring to as an Islamic jihad. One member of the Islamic conference voiced his anger at the Soviet invasion with an ominous caveat. "The message to the West is clear," said one Pakistani academic. "Islamic anti-Sovietism springs from Islamic interests, and not from pro-Westernism."[47]

Pakistan was now was the only buffer state between the Soviets and the Indian subcontinent. Yet some analysts in the region questioned the wisdom of courting General Zia. He was known in diplomatic circles as being "devious." In November 1979, many in the American diplomatic corps claimed that he had deliberately failed to halt Islamic militants from burning the U.S. embassy in Islamabad. Zia was also a problem in the realm of public relations. Carter received a great deal of publicity by requesting $400 million from Congress to provide economic and military aid for Pakistan. Zia publicly embarrassed Carter by dismissing the offer as "peanuts."

Carter sent Brzezinski to Pakistan as a way to assure Zia of the seriousness of the American commitment. On arrival, Brzezinski handed Zia a personal letter from President Carter, pledging firm American support against further Soviet encroachments. Brzezinski then made headlines in the American newspapers while toting an AK-47 while touring the Afghan border with Pakistani military advisers. Brzezinski was probing his hosts on the situation. "Have the Soviets come up to the border?" "No," his military escort replied. "As far as we can tell they have come no further than Jalalabad." "Can you hold them here?" asked Brzezinski, standing near the border with Afghanistan. "Not really," said the general. "We'd try to slow them down, down there," the general said while pointing to the terrain below the Khyber Pass.[48]

Thus began the secret conduit that supplied the Afghan resistance for the rest of the 1980s. By the spring of 1980, the Afghan mujahideen was proving surprisingly effective in neutralizing the raw military power of the Soviet Union. The Afghan army was plagued by mass desertions to the resistance. And, like the failed U.S. military strategy in Vietnam, the Soviet military abandoned any attempt to win "hearts and minds" by unleashing devastating search-and-destroy helicopter missions.

A week before the 1980 election, the Soviet leadership hosted Afghanistan's President Barrack Karma. "The revolutionary process in Afghanistan," Leonid Brezhnev assured his Afghan client, "was irreversible."[49] That very same week, Brzezinski sent a memo to the CIA urging a more sustained effort to arm the Afghan insurgents.[50]

In November 1980, Ronald Reagan defeated Jimmy Carter in an electoral landslide. Reagan's campaign was based largely on the charge that Carter had been "soft" on the Soviet Union. Brzezinski, citing the rise of Solidarity in Poland and the Soviet quagmire in Afghanistan, thought this was grossly overstated. But perceptions mattered more than the reality.

Brzezinski warned of the dangers as the bitter Afghan war stretched further into the decade. On Brezhnev's death in 1982, Brzezinski proposed that a genuinely "neutral" Afghanistan might be ensured by the presence of "Islamic peacekeeping forces" from various countries. Brzezinski elevated these concerns as Mikhail Gorbachev assumed power in the mid-1980s.

"To achieve the external neutralization of Afghanistan," Brzezinski warned in 1985, "the United States must be ready to participate—with the

Soviet Union, China, Pakistan, Iran and possibly India—in a five- or six-power guarantee of the genuine neutrality of Afghanistan." This, Brzezinski noted, might also assure the Soviet Union that their departure would not prompt "immediate massacres of the pro-Soviet minority in Afghanistan."[51]

By the late 1980s, the war in Afghanistan had taken on a more radical character. In 1986, the CIA agreed to a long-standing Pakistani request to recruit radical Muslims from around the world to come to Pakistan and fight alongside the Afghan mujahideen. Saudi Arabia, in particular, saw this as an opportunity to export its extreme form of Wahhabism and to divert the energies of its more militant domestic critics.

Although the Arabs in Afghanistan were widely viewed as a distraction by their Afghan military commanders, they could raise vast amounts of cash to fund the resistance. Among the more prominent of these Arab fund-raisers was Osama bin Laden, the pious scion of a Saudi construction magnate.

By the time Ronald Reagan left office, Brzezinski's longtime predictions about the eventual collapse of the Soviet Union appeared to be coming to fruition. "It is not an exaggeration," Brzezinski predicted in early 1988, "to affirm that there are five countries now in Eastern Europe all of which are ripe for revolutionary explosion. Nor is it an exaggeration to say that this could happen in more than one simultaneously."[52] He also agreed with those who saw this revolutionary turmoil in Eastern Europe as an indirect result of the Soviet defeat in Afghanistan.

On February 15, 1989, the new George H. W. Bush administration watched triumphantly as the last Soviet soldiers filed across the bridge linking the last Afghan town with the Soviet Union.

"From the overall strategic point of view," said one U.S. official at the time, "driving the Soviets out is a tremendous success, and we deserve a lot of credit for the rebels winning this victory. It's not the United States' fault if the Mujahedeen have some rough periods sorting out their internal affairs. It's not necessarily a failure of American foreign policy."[53] Disturbed by the implications of such statements, he noted that Afghanistan had been utterly devastated by the Soviet invasion. Some 20 percent of the Afghan population had fled to refugee camps in Pakistan and Iran where many had become politically radicalized.

As the Soviet Empire began to crumble, Strobe Talbott conducted an interview with Brzezinski titled "Vindication of a Hardliner." Brzezinski may have indeed felt "vindicated" regarding his long-held views toward the Soviet Union. But he also stressed the dangers of the increasingly inflamed political situation in the region he once termed the "arc of crisis."

"Now is the time to ask ourselves," he cautioned, "creatively and historically, how do we respond to the apparent collapse of the Soviet Union? We can either deliberately shape a new world or simply let the old disintegrate—with some of the wreckage possibly even endangering us."[54]

NOTES

1. "Afghan Report: A War Russians Can't Win," *U.S. News and World Report*, March 3, 1980.

2. Steve Coll, *Ghost Wars: The Secret History of the CIA, Afghanistan, and Bin Laden, from the Soviet Invasion to September 10, 2001* (New York: Penguin Books, 2004), 52.

3. "Brzezinski at the Pass: Bonhomie, Bullets," *New York Times*, February 4, 1980.

4. "Brzezinski at the Pass."

5. "Brzezinski at the Pass."

6. "Shaw Urges World to Imitate Soviet," *New York Times*, August 31, 1931.

7. See Robert Conquest, "Academe and the Soviet Myth," *The National Interest*, no. 31 (spring 1993): 92.

8. Zbigniew Brzezinski interview with author, June 28, 2001.

9. Lynn Olson and Stanley Cloud, *For Your Freedom and Ours: The Kościuszko Squadron; Forgotten Heroes of World War II* (London: Arrow Books, 2003), 72.

10. Norman Davies, *Rising '44, "The Battle for Warsaw"* (London: Pan Books, 2003), 41.

11. "Death in the Forest," *New York Times*, September 1, 1991.

12. Zbigniew Brzezinski, interview with author, June 28, 2001.

13. Olson and Cloud, *For Your Freedom and Ours*, 270.

14. Zbigniew Brzezinski, "The Future of Yalta," *Foreign Affairs* 63, no. 2 (winter 1984–1985): 279.

15. Zbigniew Brzezinski, interview with author, June 28, 2001.

16. Jan Nowak-Jezioranski, interview with author, September 4, 2003.

17. Zbigniew Brzezinski, "U.S. Foreign Policy in East Central Europe—A Study in Contradiction," *Journal of International Affairs* 11, no. 1 (1957): 70.

18. Zbigniew Brzezinski, *Soviet Bloc: Unity and Conflict* (Cambridge, Mass.: Harvard University Press, 1960).

19. Roman Szporluk, telephone interview with author, January 27, 2005.

20. Zbigniew Brzezinski, "Reflections on the Soviet System," *Problems of Communism* 17 (May–June 1968): 47.

21. Zbigniew Brzezinski, "Invasion Revives a Stalin Credo," *Washington Post*, August 25, 1968.

22. Zbigniew Brzezinski, "The International and the Planetary," *Encounter*, 39, no. 2 (August 1972): 49–55.

23. Brzezinski, *Power and Principle: Memoirs of the National Security Adviser 1977–1981* (New York: Farrar, Straus and Giroux, 1983), 5.

24. "Jimmy Who?," *Newsweek*, December 23, 1974, 24.

25. Brzezinski, *Power and Principle*, 6.

26. Leslie Gelb, "The Secretary of State Sweepstakes," *New York Times Magazine*, May 23, 1976.

27. "Angola: Détente Under Fire," *Newsweek*, January 19, 1976, 21.

28. "Angola," 24.

29. Christopher Lydon, "Carter, Outlining Foreign Policy Views, Urges Wider Discussion," *New York Times*, March 16, 1976.

30. "A Year after Helsinki: Despite Moscow's Promises, No Greater Freedom for East Europe," *U.S. News and World Report*, August 9, 1976.

31. Zbigniew Brzezinski, interview with author, March 29, 2000.

32. Robert Gates, *From the Shadows: The Ultimate Insider's Story of Five Presidents and How They Won the Cold War* (New York: Simon & Schuster, 1996), 90–91.

33. Adam Michnik, interview with author, March 30, 2001.

34. Paul Henze, interview with author, June 7, 2000.

35. Paul Henze, interview with author, June 7, 2000.

36. "Andrew Young on Africa: Still the Voice of Dissent," *U.S. News and World Report*, June 12, 1978.

37. Zbigniew Brzezinski, interview with author, September 23, 2004.

38. "Making Friends in Peking," *Time*, June 5, 1978, 19.

39. "After Kabul's Coup," *Newsweek*, May 15, 1978, 39.

40. Robin Knight, "Afghanistan's Shaky Venture into Marxism," *U.S. News and World Report*, December 11, 1978.

41. Coll, *Ghost Wars*, 41.

42. Coll, *Ghost Wars*, 40.

43. Coll, *Ghost Wars*, 44–45.

44. Hedrick Smith, "U.S. Is Indirectly Pressing Russians to Halt Afghanistan Intervention," *New York Times*, August 3, 1979.

45. Anatoly Dobrynin, *In Confidence: Moscow's Ambassador to America's Six Cold War Presidents* (New York: Times Books, 1995), 184.

46. Coll, *Ghost Wars*, 52.

47. "Selling the Doctrine," *Newsweek*, February 11, 1980, 42.

48. "Brzezinski at the Pass."

49. "Afghanistan: Moscow's Friend in Need," *Newsweek*, October 27, 1980, 73.

50. Robert Gates, *From the Shadows: The Ultimate Insider's Story of Five Presidents and How They Won the Cold War* (New York: Simon & Schuster, 1996), 149.

51. Zbigniew Brzezinski, "Linking Two Crisis," *New York Times*, October 6, 1985.

52. Timothy Garton Ash, "The Empire in Decay," *New York Review of Books*, September 29, 1988, 54.

53. Elaine Sciolino, "On the Brink: What Was Lost in Afghanistan," *New York Times*, February 5, 1989.

54. Strobe Talbott and Robert T. Zintl, "Vindication of a Hard-Liner," *Time*, December 18, 1989, 13.

· 6 ·

The Wave Maker:
Bill Casey in the Reagan Years

John Prados

In an administration dominated by underlings, a series of policy entrepreneurs following their own agendas, William J. Casey stood out. Action oriented, a lawyer but willing to skirt rules, a longtime political operative, it would seem as if Bill Casey had a finger in almost every pie. Of course, Casey is best known for his role in the affair that reached the edge of a constitutional crisis, Iran-Contra, but in truth he cut a much deeper and wider swath and had done so for many years. As far back as the 1960 presidential campaign of Richard M. Nixon against John F. Kennedy, remembers William Safire, "I would write some gut-kicking ad and trust to Casey to set up the committee to sign it."[1] At the time, Casey had merely been law partner to the man who chaired the Republican National Committee. By the 1980s, the New York lawyer was doing the gut kicking himself.

Casey stood among that crowd of Americans fiercely determined to rise above their roots, in his case Elmhurst, Queens, an outer borough of New York, where his dad worked for the city department responsible for street cleaning and his mother was a former retail salesgirl. Both the parents were Democrats, indeed William Joseph Casey Sr. was an activist in the party's machinery, which led him to a pension fund management job when Bill Jr. was still a boy. The young Casey went to Catholic school until the final year of his secondary education, then studied with the Jesuits at Fordham University and, after a brief attempt at social work, went on to St. John's Law School. Notorious for his mumbling at meetings during his government years, this trait of Casey's was already evident in secondary school and on the Fordham debate team. He married his college sweetheart, Sophia Kurz. In a letter to her, he once wrote that he preferred "unlimited space, unlimited freedom, and unlimited possibilities, all perfection and no imperfections or obstacles."[2]

Casey would succeed in casting off the limits but never attain the other element of his equation.

Casey made his crucial alliance early, at twenty-seven years old in 1938, when he met Leo Cherne. The latter had created a business publishing venture with an associate, eventually known as the Research Institute of America (RIA), and hired Casey to write material on law and ethics. Casey also formed a law partnership on the side and, souring on Franklin Roosevelt's New Deal, became involved in Republican politics beginning with the 1940 campaign. Remaining with RIA and as an economic consultant after Pearl Harbor, at midwar he decided to join the service and was commissioned a lieutenant (junior grade) in the navy.

One of Casey's former law partners had gone to work for the Wall Street firm Donovan, Leisure, Newton, and Lombard, and William J. ("Wild Bill") Donovan of that firm now headed the U.S. wartime intelligence unit Office of Strategic Services (OSS). Lieutenant Casey used that connection to escape an assignment to naval procurement, joining the OSS in September 1943. Casey would later tell his biographer that one of Donovan's sayings had impressed him, "The perfect is the enemy of the good."[3] It would be during his OSS period that Bill Casey abandoned the desire for perfection he had previously expressed. Donovan took a liking to Casey and soon sent him to London under David K. E. Bruce, where Casey became an important staff aide. Later Bruce went to the Continent to establish an OSS element in Paris. Casey moved back and forth from the end of 1944, when Donovan made him intelligence collection chief for Europe with the mission of penetrating Nazi Germany. According to OSS official figures, which were, however, based on Casey's own report, 60 percent of the 102 missions mounted had been successful. This is difficult to judge since by this point in World War II, Hitler's Germany was already collapsing. Bill Casey expected reassignment to Kunming, China, to work on Pacific intelligence, but the war ended several weeks before his expected departure date.

Casey returned to the Cherne business, RIA, intent on amassing a fortune. In 1948 he enlisted as associate general counsel in the Economic Cooperation Administration, the entity then being established to administer the Marshall Plan, but he saw little opportunity for advancement and resigned after about six months, returning again to RIA. In the summer of 1950, Casey left to create a competitor, the Institute for Business Planning (IBP). At IBP, Casey wrote or packaged a series of books interpreting business law for laymen that made him a millionaire. He made even more from his law practice, which he re-created, and from assorted venture capital investments.

Leo Cherne is reported to have been stunned at the betrayal, considering Casey "a ruthless and not terribly sensitive former friend,"[4] but it would not in fact end their relationship. Both were active in the privately funded International Rescue Committee (IRC), an organization that helped refugees.[5] The somewhat shadowy IRC was at least a fellow traveler of the Central Intelligence Agency (CIA)[6] and may have had agency connections in the form of money and help and may have furnished cover for intelligence officers, though this has not been authoritatively established. Organizations with which it worked closely, including the National Committee for a Free Europe, *were* CIA proprietaries, and in the 1950s the IRC sponsored formation of the German entity Fighting Group Against Inhumanity, which is widely believed to have been a CIA covert action project.[7] In any case, Leo Cherne would be IRC's long-service chair, and from 1966 to 1970, Casey was its executive committee chairman as well as president for more than a year afterward. It was in that capacity that he visited Vietnam at the height of the American war and Czechoslovakia around the time of the Soviet intervention against the "Prague Spring." Casey would also become a prime mover in the formation of conservative pressure groups like the American Friends for Russian Freedom, the Citizens' Committee for Peace and Security, and the similarly inclined think tank National Strategy and Information Center (NSIC). Political scientist Frank Barnett, whom Casey had personally recruited for the Russian freedom group, became one of the chief NSIC analysts. This group produced a stream of reports extolling the Soviet threat—in the Indian Ocean, to the Middle East, on nuclear weapons, and so on. Casey was a major contributor to the groups' funding. He was able to use donations to the advocacy groups to offset taxes on his earnings from his law practice, his major company, and the Institute of Business Planning; successful stock purchases; and venture capital endeavors in computers, media, and elsewhere.

As noted, Casey participated in Richard Nixon's 1960 presidential campaign and supported Nixon again for the nomination in 1964 when Barry Goldwater became the candidate. He ran for Congress himself in 1966 but lost. In the Nixon campaign of 1968, Casey was a major campaign contributor and also headed a team that produced an instant book publicizing the candidate's positions on a variety of issues. Casey had involved himself in OSS veterans groups but played no identifiable role in the push spearheaded by General Donovan, Allen Dulles, and others to create a peacetime unit, the one that became the CIA. In angling for a job appointment from Nixon, however, Casey suddenly put himself into agency shoes, suggesting that he could function as an armed service secretary, assistant secretary of state, or as the CIA director, a position then held by Richard Helms. The Nixon transition group offered Casey a subordinate job at the Internal Revenue Service that he rejected, then the second top slot at the CIA. The New York potentate had no desire to work for Helms, someone who had been under him in the OSS. Casey's administration position did not materialize until 1971 when Nixon appointed him chairman of the Securities Exchange Commission (SEC). The lawyer left the International Rescue Committee for that job.

Appointment to the SEC required U.S. Senate confirmation. In preparing himself for confirmation hearings, Casey found that his work on certain advertising campaigns for companies he owned posed potential hazards for his testimony. He contrived to sell the companies off, including one run by his younger brother, prior to going before the Senate. This action evidences the wheeler-dealer approach typical of the man. At the hearings, Casey did have trouble because of some of his companies' activities that had brushed up against SEC regulations. In office there would be a controversy over Casey's actions in handling the international fraud and embezzlement case against financier Robert Vesco, who eventually became a fugitive from justice.

Meanwhile, the Nixon administration had faced a tough political battle very early on when it attempted to secure congressional approval for the Safeguard Anti-Ballistic Missile (ABM) system, another area where Bill Casey involved himself. The citizens' committee that Casey created actually had the purpose of lobbying for ABM. His reward for that was an appointment to the General Advisory Committee to the Arms Control and Disarmament Agency. Needless to say, the new member had little use for arms control, and his job amounted more to bird-dogging agency negotiators to make sure they did not give away the store in talks with the Soviets. Casey finally got a chance to actually work in a national security position in 1973 when he served for a year as undersecretary of state for economic affairs, but he left to become president of the Import-Export Bank. He also sat as a member of the Murphy Commission, a presidential commission headed by former Ambassador Robert D. Murphy that conducted a broad review of U.S. national security mechanisms and policy for the Ford administration.

Meanwhile, Nixon had selected Leo Cherne as chairman of the President's Foreign Intelligence Advisory Board (PFIAB), the civilian committee that functioned as the White House's intelligence oversight mechanism. An opening on PFIAB materialized after Nixon left office. In early 1976, Cherne recommended to President Gerald Ford that he bring Bill Casey onto the board. Ford agreed, and Casey arrived at PFIAB with a special watching brief on economic intelligence. Casey was among those board members who approved the "experiment" in intelligence analysis called the Team B report, which amounted to a skewering of the official estimates by a group of hand-picked conservative experts.[8] Within months of James Earl Carter replacing Ford as president and largely because of the embarrassment of the Team B experiment, Carter abolished the PFIAB, ejecting Casey from this monitoring seat over the intelligence world. As a private board, PFIAB had typically met for a couple of days at a time every two months. These dozen days over a year of service were the full extent of William J. Casey's spy experience between leaving the OSS in 1945 and coming to the head of the CIA—and the entire U.S. intelligence community—in 1981.

The essential Bill Casey was smart, perhaps brilliant, opinionated, gruff but inarticulate, secretive and purposeful, ruthless and willing to skirt the norms, and an original Cold Warrior. These traits were on display during the Carter era, from 1977 to 1981, particularly during the last two years, when Casey labored mightily to return a Republican to the White House. First came the sequel to the Team B affair, and then, in the high campaign season, would be Casey's full tilt move to back Republican candidate Ronald Reagan.

In the first of these episodes, those former members of Team B who remained outside of government, concerned that their critique was being buried, contrived to spark a public debate. They placed articles in the media, did interviews, and, when this did not result in enough traction, recruited a galaxy of well-known political and business figures to join something they called the Committee on the Present Danger, a revival of a public interest group that had formed in the days of NSC-68. Paul Nitze or Richard Pipes are usually the persons named in discussions of the Committee on the Present Danger, but William J. Casey became a prominent member of its board, willing to encourage the involvement of Frank Barnett of the National Strategy Information Center, who now became a founding member of the group.[9]

Many of the criticisms popularized by the Committee on the Present Danger involved arcana of nuclear weapons and are not necessary to this discussion, but all their points went to one central argument—that the Soviet Union had sought strategic superiority and was decisively ahead of the United States on nuclear arms. In particular, Casey's gladiators thundered, the Russians had deployed so many nuclear-tipped missiles that were so accurate that U.S. land-based missile forces were vulnerable to a nuclear first strike in consequence of which the Soviets could fight and win a nuclear war.[10] Thus, a "window of vulnerability" existed that critics blamed on the Carter administration; it needed redress—and only a Republican president could adequately do this in their view. The "window of vulnerability" gained great currency in the 1980 presidential campaign, and the issue worked very much like the "missile gap" argument had during the Kennedy–Nixon election in 1960.

For the 1980 campaign, Bill Casey went far beyond his previous efforts on behalf of Republicans. He supported Ronald Reagan, becoming one of the candidate's "kitchen cabinet" of advisers, and performed a review of the Reagan organization. Then he was asked to lead the Reagan campaign staff. Casey agreed. From early 1980, he worked full time on the election. Casey streamlined the operation, cutting away loose people, focusing those who remained, and getting Reagan past the primaries with a commanding lead over his competitor, George Herbert Walker Bush. In the lead primary, that in New Hampshire, the state campaign chief especially impressed Casey. That man was Max Hugel, like Casey himself an entrepreneur and venture capitalist. Casey hired Hugel to replicate on a national level the techniques he had used in New Hampshire. He and Hugel shared an apartment during their time at Reagan's California headquarters. Months before the Republican convention, all Reagan's opponents had dropped out of the race. His nomination was assured. Reagan took on George H. W. Bush as vice-presidential candidate on the Republican ticket.

A highlight of the election campaign would be the televised debates between candidates that had become standard fare in American politics. Casey hired James A. Baker III to supervise the work of preparing Reagan for the debates. Republican congressman David Stockman played the role of opponent Jimmy Carter in debate rehearsals held by the Reagan camp. Stockman revealed later that he had had access to Carter's actual briefing book for the debate on national security. This story inevitably led to controversy. Once it came under investigation, Baker recalled receiving the debate materials directly from Bill Casey. Casey denied it. Reagan White House aides—by then Ronald Reagan had won the presidency—established that there had been not one but at least five documents purloined from the Carter campaign and that someone had fed Casey's campaign organization with inside information on Carter's schedule as well. Inquiries by the Federal Bureau of Investigation and Congress eventually looked into the allegations. They could not determine the exact truth but did find links between the Casey staff and a political consultant as well as a National Security Council (NSC) official, both of whom had access to the material.[11]

Another major campaign scandal from 1980 concerned American hostages in Iran who had been held captive since Iranian militants took over the U.S. embassy in Tehran the previous year. The Carter administration had mounted an abortive rescue mission to free the hostages and was now negotiating to secure their release. The liberation of the hostages prior to the election would have been a key political event favoring Carter. Allegations of an "October Surprise" effort by Casey and Reagan campaign officials in an effort to dissuade the Iranians from taking any action before the election were made and became the subject of several inquiries. Casey is supposed to have traveled to Madrid and Paris to meet Iranians in the course of this activity. Again the actual truth was never established. At a minimum it is clear that Casey's staff did create an extensive political intelligence network to watch for Carter administration actions in this regard. Gary Sick, the NSC staff director for

Iranian affairs, looked into these reports and concluded that an "October Surprise" did occur. A congressional report found that "the evidence supports the conclusion that William Casey, while director of the Reagan campaign, was intensely involved in the hostage crisis and likely was dealing with [Iranian intermediary] Cyrus Hashemi, either directly or indirectly."[12]

In an odd piece of history, the American hostages were released on the day Ronald Reagan was inaugurated as president. Whether this event resulted from the success of Carter administration negotiations or reflected some private deal with the Reagan people remains unknown. In the meantime, the transition to Reagan's presidency offered William Casey a new opportunity. He wanted to be secretary of state. Reagan instead offered him the post of director of central intelligence (DCI), directing both the CIA and the larger U.S. intelligence community. To ensure his ability to make policy, not merely provide intelligence, Casey sought and obtained the president's assurances that he would have a full voice in administration deliberations, and Casey was given cabinet rank, an elevation of the status of the DCI. In turn, Casey told President Reagan that, while he might speak to policy, he would provide the intelligence straight: "I wouldn't bend it to fit the policy. But I expect to be part of the foreign policy team."[13]

Two last points are in order before the discussions moves to Casey's CIA years. First, the presidential transition teams reflected William J. Casey's influence even before he secured the DCI job. The leader of the Pentagon team, William R. Van Cleave, had been a member of Team B and an executive committee member of the Committee on the Present Danger (in fact, thirty-three of the committee's members, including Casey himself, would get jobs in the Reagan administration). The intelligence transition team was under John Bross, Casey's direct subordinate at the OSS in 1945, postwar friend, and a career CIA officer who came back from retirement to serve Casey again. Although other professionals were involved, the exercise was dominated by firebrand conservatives to whom Team B's views were gospel. The team approached the CIA with an eye to a purge that Bross rejected and was even too much for Casey, who shelved a great number of its recommendations, which included firing hundreds of its officers, the entire top echelon, including everyone involved in the Soviet estimates.

Finally, in securing Senate confirmation for his appointment as DCI, William J. Casey again encountered trouble on Capitol Hill. He received initial approval, but very soon afterward a New York court ruled that Casey had engaged in misleading stock offerings in the 1960s. A Senate intelligence committee inquiry began, then it came out that Casey's disclosure forms had been, to put it charitably, incomplete, failing to list more than half his accounts, including the governments of Indonesia and South Korea, the City of

New York, and many more. He had also failed to list certain assets and liabilities or to register as an agent of a foreign government as required by U.S. law. The New Yorker intended to continue managing his own stock portfolio, though Casey owned stock in a number of companies that did business with the CIA. These irregularities raised eyebrows. The committee initially cleared Casey, after which more charges arose. Committee chairman (later vice chairman, then again chairman) Senator Barry Goldwater went to bat for Casey, and toward the end of 1981 he would be found "not unfit" to serve as DCI.[14] This early brush with congressional overseers would become characteristic of Casey's tenure at the CIA.

William J. Casey came to CIA headquarters at Langley, Virginia, swathed in the glories of the Good War and the old OSS. Outside the agency this romantic coloration served Casey's purposes. Inside, CIA officers were discomfited by the excesses of the Reagan transition and feared for their jobs—even harder-line Kremlin watchers like analyst Robert Gates.[15] Director Casey provided some reassurance, but he also took actions that seemed to confirm fears. Principal among these was his selection of a complete outsider, the political operative Max Hugel, to head the clandestine service, passing over a widely experienced professional officer. The Hugel appointment crashed and burned within months, victim of allegations of insider stock trading, amid the summertime uproar over Casey's own business dealings. The director turned then to the pros, but in some ways the message got across: CIA employees were on notice both that their boss had been advised to get rid of them and that Casey was not afraid to hire outsiders in their stead. That sense of vulnerability would have much to do with what happened to the Reagan-era CIA.

In the first place, unlike previous CIA directors, William J. Casey worked hard to stake out a policy position, a public one. No DCI had ever done this before. In dozens of speeches and interviews, Casey commented on everything from military power to the Middle East to immigration, all from the perspective that the Soviet Union was on the march and needed to be countered. In May 1981, just four months after reaching Langley, Casey spoke to a business group about Soviet tanks and guns, stockpiled around the Arabian peninsula and "*used*" (his italics) in Chad, Lebanon, El Salvador, and Guatemala, while Russian military strength grew and America's diminished. Casey made claims about Soviet missile forces, subversion, economic, and industrial espionage; about his favorite theaters for covert operations in Nicaragua, Afghanistan, and Angola; about Soviet use of chemical weapons in Laos, Cambodia, and elsewhere; about penetration in the Third World; and much more. Moscow, in Casey's view, controlled worldwide terrorism by financing, arming, and training the terrorists. Casey approvingly cited a book by journalist Claire Sterling that made this claim more extravagantly. Even liberation theology he pictured as an organizing tool for Cuban communism. He spoke of a plethora of threats and, beyond U.S. intelligence, of his view of necessary policy action.[16]

Far from providing President Reagan with objective intelligence reporting, Bill Casey's CIA furnished intelligence to please. But it would not simply be intelligence to support Reagan's policy, the CIA's data would be in support of *Bill Casey's* policy *preferences*. This statement applies to the community's flagship products, the National Intelligence Estimates (NIEs), though Casey lacked the time or energy to interfere with more routine products. With the President's Daily Brief (PDB), Casey usually did not see the publication until it had already gone to the White House. Robert M. Gates, whom Casey made his deputy director for intelligence, informed Casey in advance of items that would run only when he knew they were likely to kick up dust among one or another senior administration figure. Even here, though, Casey contrived changes, inducing President Reagan to assent to a wider distribution of the PDBs and to having them presented by CIA briefers rather than left in the office of the national security adviser. Given President Reagan's relative ignorance on key issues that arose on Casey's watch, however, one has to question either the president's attentiveness, Casey's efforts to ensure a pristine PDB flow, or alternatively his purposefulness in advancing certain issues through the PDBs.

Another of Gates's roles was to chair the National Intelligence Council, which drafted the NIEs, however, and here "I was much less in control of my . . . job." Here Gates writes of Casey, "He rode the process hard, pushed his own views, and was often very tough for people to deal with or talk to."[17] In the spring of 1982, the director fired off a note to Gates and his predecessor as council chair, Henry Rowen, demanding that the NIEs be "more aggressive and more timely."[18] Casey also developed the technique of showing papers he questioned to trusted friends, some of them former CIA people or outsiders, and getting comments he could throw back at estimators.[19] He also brought in a complete outsider, Herbert E. Meyer, a magazine editor (*Fortune*), ostensibly for writing style, but in fact the conservative Meyer acted as another filter vetting the drafts. When Director Casey lacked the time or reason for personal involvement, the process worked much as it had under previous DCIs. But when Casey had an ax to grind, the result could be very different.

The director told his senior analysts in December 1983, "Our estimating program has become a powerful tool in forcing the pace in the policy area."[20] The evidence suggests that Casey used the PDBs to keep his agency on the radar screen and the NIEs to lay a basis for his policy predilections. This is very different from what Casey told the public in speech after speech, such as the Commonwealth Club of California, to whom he declared, "We have taken steps to assure standards of integrity and objectivity, relevance and timeliness, accuracy and independence to the national estimate process." Director Casey in fact called that "my highest responsibility."[21] It was. But he did not do as he said.

The Casey method was apparent from the very first estimate of his period, that being on Soviet sponsorship of terrorism. The draft of the National Intelligence Council (NIC), though citing Russian help to terrorists and that of Eastern European satellite countries, fell far short of Claire Sterling's version of Kremlin central control. In fact, the initial draft said, "The Soviets have opposed international terrorist activity in public and in private."[22] Casey rejected the draft, failed to get something more to his liking, then sent it over to the Defense Intelligence Agency (DIA) for an edgier version. A fight ensued between the competing views of the DIA and CIA, making it impossible for Casey to sign off on the Pentagon draft. Casey then ordered the scope of the paper expanded to generic revolutionary violence, where he supposed a stronger case could be made for Russian meddling, and had Ambassador Lincoln Gordon, a distinguished estimator from the agency's past, do a fresh version. The revision concluded, "The Soviets are deeply involved in support of revolutionary violence worldwide."[23]

The Casey method did not always work out, especially early on. An example here would be the Special National Intelligence Estimate (SNIE) that appeared in 1981 on the Soviet project to build a natural gas pipeline to Western Europe. The Reagan people were concerned that the pipeline would weaken European ties to the United States, and they were looking for a lever to stop the project. They had also mounted a massive campaign against Russian acquisition of U.S. technology. Casey opposed the pipeline not only for the European angle but also because with it the Russians would earn cash in hard currencies. An SNIE judgment that the Soviet pipeline would require U.S. technology could be used on Capitol Hill to argue for export controls that might shut down the project. The NIC chairman of the day, Henry Rowen, personally took on managing the estimate. Rowen went to Europe, spoke to local officials, and explored the facts. He came back and told Casey the Russians would build this pipeline no matter what the United States did about it. Casey took the point, and the SNIE went forward with that conclusion.[24]

Another issue was "yellow rain," so called because chemical weapons at issue in allegations of Soviet use of them were said to appear that way as they dispersed over the land. Secretary of State Alexander Haig became the trigger—as he had been in the call for a terrorism NIE—when he claimed that the United States had physical evidence of their use in Laos, Cambodia, and Afghanistan. But laboratory results were inconclusive, and scientific experts who did field studies in Southeast Asia could not confirm the charges. Director Casey ordered up an SNIE that appeared in early 1982 but confined the paper to Afghanistan, where the outsiders had no access. The SNIE concluded the Russians were indeed using the chemical weapons, a violation of Geneva protocols.

In 1982, the CIA did an estimate on the situation in Africa. When that reached him in draft form, it reportedly contained little on the Soviets in Africa, focusing on nationalist movements instead. Casey replaced the manager on the paper and had it rewritten. The new manager had well-known views on Soviet subversion in the Third World, and the estimate he produced, said a source, "reeks of Moscow's footprints in Africa."[25]

Soviet progress on the exotic weaponry for "Star Wars" became a key intelligence question when President Reagan announced his Strategic Defense Initiative (SDI) in March 1983. Suddenly, the treatment of Soviet SDI and ABM systems in the national estimates became darker. Technologies previously projected as coming online only by the 1990s or later were portrayed as possibilities for orbital testing and even deployment within the decade of the 1980s. The NIEs on Soviet strategic forces became gloomier each year of Casey's tenure, and a first NIE specifically devoted to Soviet SDI avoiding making any analysis at all of the huge weight-to-orbit or power generation requirements required for a practical space-based SDI network while repeating the near-term projections for deployment. In addition, the Soviets were reported to be making all this alleged technical progress on the basis of absurd expenditure levels, considerably lower than U.S. spending for an SDI program that yielded no deployable technology.[26]

There were similar problems with the Casey-era NIE depictions of Soviet strategic nuclear forces. The "window of vulnerability" stayed open through the early 1980s as NIC analysts built more alarming claims on the distortions that had been inserted into the estimates in consequence of the Team B exercise. In particular, analysts repeatedly projected that the Soviets would build every weapons system they had in development to the full extent of manufacturing capacity, generating estimates that postulated Soviet strategic nuclear weapons in future years in the tens of thousands, even in the context of arms control negotiations. Douglas MacEachin, who headed the Office of Soviet Analysis through much of this period, concluded that the Soviet economy was incapable of manufacturing all the weapons projected. He ended up trying to insert a dissent into the CIA's *own* NIEs and felt that Director Casey, whose expertise was of course in economics, sympathized with him. But MacEachin ran afoul of a policy that Casey had introduced of not permitting such dissents, and the DCI refused to make an exception.[27] Casey's politicization had become that ingrained.

On Central America, too, the NIEs followed the director's proclivities. A series of briefings to the intelligence oversight committees on Capitol Hill in late 1982 upset legislators so much that the House Permanent Select Committee on Intelligence made an inquiry. Its report found not only that the intelligence had been slanted to back the CIA operations in progress there, that the analytic community was "under pressure to reinforce policy rather than to inform it," but also that Casey had further overstated what the papers themselves said.[28] Gates records, "By the end of 1982, the most fundamental division over Central America within CIA was between the career professionals and Casey."[29] A direct charge of exaggeration was leveled against Casey for testimony he gave the Senate in May 1983. The estimate on the capabilities of the CIA-backed Contra rebels in Nicaragua then in draft was so much different that a month later Director Casey sent it to President Reagan with a cover note that read, "We are losing in Central America."[30] Analysts resorted to laying out the evidence "straight," then giving Casey what he wanted by way of conclusions. In 1985, the NIE "Nicaragua: Prospects for Sandinista Consolidation," after listing a series of obstacles that would prevent the Sandinistas from attaining a Marxist-Leninist state, judged that nothing would prevent them reaching a system that "would retain little more than symbolic remnants of political pluralism."[31]

A 1984 NIE on Mexico is a case that became known at the time. The NIC manager for the estimate, John Horton, a former agency station chief in Mexico City, assigned a Latin America expert to compile the paper. The expert visited the country, incorporated data from casual sources, and decided that Mexico stood at the brink of revolution. He showed the draft to Casey before giving it to Horton, and the DCI liked it. But CIA evidence did not support a judgment of instability in Mexico, and Horton tried to get the offending material out. Casey insisted the estimate should declare there was a one-in-five chance of "a political destabilization of Mexico."[32] Horton talked back. The paper went through nine drafts, one of them by Casey's "editor" Herbert Meyer, plus a critique by a *policy* official, a former Casey associate who had moved on to the NSC staff. It emerged with the alarming prediction intact. A number of intelligence agencies, including military ones, dissented from the assessment. John Horton resigned from the CIA. Casey had an NIE that lent weight to his secret war in Central America.[33]

Finally, it is worth looking at a 1985 SNIE on the Soviets and the entente of Syria, Libya, and Iran. This "entente" was entirely an artifact of the paper, which was itself the product of an outsider, an Israeli, commissioned by the NIC, most likely Vice Chairman Herbert Meyer. By the time CIA professionals had finished with it, the special estimate indicated that while there were examples of bilateral cooperation among these countries, there was little evidence of formal joint operations, especially trilateral ones. A week after the draft arrived in Casey's office, Meyer forwarded it to the intelligence community board of directors (the National Foreign Intelligence Board) with a note indicating that Director Casey had had the Key Judgments of the estimate amended to indicate "pervasive" connections among the radical states, which "shared certain common purposes; . . . were willing to consult regularly and to pursue numerous goals in tandem."[34] The CIA's Directorate of Intelligence was prevented from filing any dissent.

In 1981, some thirty-eight NIEs were written. By the mid-1980s, the U.S. intelligence community was publishing estimates at a rate of fifty or sixty a year, compared to a dozen during the last year of the Carter administration. William J. Casey in several interviews drew attention to the number as an illustration of the usefulness of CIA assessments. But however helpful the NIEs may have been as substantive analyses, they were *more* important to Bill Casey in his quest for a role in U.S. foreign policy. The number of these documents should be seen as corresponding to the depth of Casey's policy involvement.

Bill Casey the policy maker was undoubtedly most comfortable during the early months of the Reagan administration. Later there would be problems, increasing inertia, presidential drift, and a dilution of the Reaganaut core, but at the outset it seemed that the sky was the limit. Reagan had arrived at the White House with a convincing majority and had carried voters on the basis of an assertive program of change. In the national security field, this amounted to challenging the Soviet Union more sharply and building up the U.S. military. Secretary of State Alexander M. Haig, if not a kindred soul, held views similar to Casey's. Secretary of Defense Caspar Weinberger had the same goals and a business background like Casey's. The White House was populated with persons who had worked alongside Casey in the campaign, with Richard V. Allen, who had been foreign policy issues director, Reagan's first national security adviser.

Casey and Haig cooperated on at least four issues. On repositioning the Soviet Union in the public mind as a bitter enemy, Haig's claims on Moscow and terrorism plus Yellow Rain, backed by Casey's NIEs, gained a certain traction. On closing off avenues of technology transfer from the United States and the West to the Russians, Haig and Casey worked in concert. On Russian expansionism in the Third World, Casey was exuberant, if anything going beyond Haig's preference for confining the Soviets within existing spheres of influence. On Cuba, where Casey and Haig agreed that Fidel Castro must be painted with a black hat, Casey worked to support Haig, who effectively scuttled a move toward rapprochement under way in the Carter administration. On technology transfer in particular and on a range of other military issues, Caspar Weinberger's efforts complemented Casey's.

When it comes to policy roles, the CIA's is often seen primarily in terms of its covert operations. Here Casey effectively went beyond many of his colleagues in attempting to roll back the Soviets. On Nicaragua, Secretary Haig traced the root problem to Cuba. He was at least somewhat committed to a diplomatic track with Nicaragua itself when Casey won approval of a covert paramilitary operation that soon required negotiations to be for propaganda purposes and feared them as undercutting the CIA project.[35] In fact, the real diplomacy was to recruit allies to the secret war and bases to conduct it, while Weinberger and the military were recruited to increase coercive pressures on Managua through overt participation in the CIA strategy, conducting highly visible military maneuvers near Nicaragua. In Africa, Casey resurrected the paramilitary project in Angola that had been shut down by Jimmy Carter and kept it running even after the State Department opened complex negotiations with Cuba, Angola, and South Africa to end the civil war there. After a certain point, the CIA and State Department were competitors in Angola, with Casey pandering toward then-racist South Africa.[36] In Afghanistan, Casey continued and escalated the covert operation begun by the Carter administration. Uncertain to a degree about whether the goal ought to be bleeding the Russians or beating them, the Pentagon and Congress eventually pressured Casey into the latter posture.[37] Casey also conducted anti-Soviet covert operations in Mozambique, Cambodia, and Eastern Europe and Russia, where he continued political action efforts started under Carter and reportedly tried a sabotage attempt against the Soviet gas pipeline.[38] In some of this, Casey exhibited his penchant for unilateralism, as when he bypassed the CIA chain of command to directly run an officer assigned to run operations using corporate and private contacts. In fact, CIA's Directorate of Operations finally felt obliged to create a new position of associate deputy director specifically in order to impose some control over Casey's unilateral activities.[39] The array of activities became so broad that some observers were driven to recall Casey's time in the OSS and built an image of him as "a cagey old man with an eye for legal loopholes who is romantically and recklessly bent on reliving his youth."[40]

But Bill Casey's policy role went far beyond covert operations. He was and remained a thorny impediment when it came to arms control—and a supporter of new strategic weapons systems. On the Strategic Defense Initiative (SDI), for instance, Casey threw open his doors to a former Team B and Committee on the Present Danger figure, retired General Daniel O. Graham, who now had a new public advocacy group called Project High Frontier, which plumped for a space-based ABM system. Graham met with Casey to extol his weapons system, making claims about Soviet progress on defense systems. Director Casey not only turned to his own experts, using the Graham claims about the Russians to push their analysis, but also became a voice for ABM research. He encouraged President Reagan on SDI after 1983, and repeatedly intervened with the president when Moscow's negotiators sought limits on SDI. Casey warned Reagan against anything that threatened "his" system.[41]

Another arms control issue during this period was the question of whether the Soviets had violated existing agreements, including the ABM treaty and the Strategic Arms Limitation Treaty (SALT I and II) agreements. Casey pressed CIA analysts for determinations that they had and sent them back their papers when these did not concord with his views. Casey set a benchmark, staking out his position in public speeches. He encouraged a review of Soviet compliance by the General Advisory Committee to the Arms Control and Disarmament Agency, of which he had once been a member. When that review agreed that violations had indeed occurred, Casey supported a Reagan administration decision announcing that it would not feel bound by the SALT agreements, if not the ABM treaty. Reagan decided against moves that actually breached the agreements, but he made the point that the United States could break out of them at any time. This was relevant to SDI, where U.S. research might have (but did not) resulted in deployable technology, and to offensive forces, where the United States was then deploying systems on all three legs of the triad (the Peacekeeper ICBM, the Trident submarine-launched missile, and the B-1 bomber).

Casey warned Reagan against dealing with the Soviet leader Mikhail Gorbachev before the 1985 Geneva Summit, and once it became evident that Reagan, building confidence in Moscow, was ready to seek some nuclear arms limits, the CIA director sided with Joint Chiefs of Staff proposals, which were the most restricted ones. In general Bill Casey's view of arms control was to use it as another device to help disarm the Soviet Union. Robert Gates, the CIA's intelligence chief and Casey's eventual successor, recalls the DCI's approach to arms control matters as "often constructive."[42] This is open to interpretation and may say more about Gates's views on arms control as it does about Bill Casey. In fact, Gates writes elsewhere that Casey and the secretary of state had significant differences on arms control—and it was the State Department that was taking the lead in seeking arms restraints.[43]

Meanwhile, Al Haig became increasingly isolated in the Reagan administration, ironically, as someone too moderate, and by mid-1982 he had no future there. Haig resigned, to be replaced by George P. Shultz. Bill Casey initially thought he could recruit a new ally and plied the secretary with all manner of CIA materials. But Shultz soon viewed Casey—correctly—as in league with Weinberger, who had swiftly become his enemy in the Bush administration. Indeed, at weekly lunches Weinberger and Casey "would grump about Reagan's unwillingness to 'rein in' Shultz."[44] For his part, Shultz notes he saw Casey with increasing unease: "He had very strong policy positions, which were reflected in his intelligence briefings. He claimed he was objective. But his views were so strong and so ideological that they inevitably colored his selection and assessment of materials."[45]

Beginning in 1983, Secretary Shultz fought Casey and Weinberger over working to secure real agreements with Moscow. Casey worked to preserve the hard edge of U.S. suspicions of the Soviets. That fall, after Russian interceptor aircraft shot down the Korean airliner KAL 007, the intensity of U.S. condemnations, combined with certain North Atlantic Treaty Organization (NATO) maneuvers, convinced the Soviets that Washington might actually be pushing for a nuclear war, resulting in a war scare in Moscow. President Reagan began to shift into Shultz's camp a year later, once he realized how close the United States and Soviet Union had come to nuclear war the previous fall,[46] yet there would still be no significant progress for another eighteen months—until the Geneva Summit—despite Reagan's replacing many of the hard-liners in his administration at the start of his second term. This fact suggests the degree of success enjoyed by Casey and his allies until that time.

William J. Casey was himself the author of the policy proposal that led to the most intense political controversy of the administration, the political emasculation of Ronald Reagan and the president's near impeachment. This was the idea of escalating the secret war on Nicaragua by mining that nation's ports. This was an act of war, undeclared, and a violation of statutes that established guidelines for CIA operations in Central America. When the mining was revealed to have been a direct CIA operation in the spring of 1984 and it came out that the agency had been disingenuous in informing Congress of its operations, Capitol Hill zeroed out the budget for the CIA operation and passed explicit restrictions on agency contact with the formerly CIA-backed Contra rebels. Only "humanitarian" funds were to be provided to the Contras. Bill Casey's efforts to circumvent that restriction led to the uproar.

As policy maker and CIA director, Bill Casey had become adept at fashioning situations where President Reagan was asked to approve general, perhaps even generic, instructions that the CIA used to sanction wide-ranging projects. That would become the case with Nicaragua after the mining. Casey expected trouble. In March 1984, before Congress took action, the DCI informed National Security Adviser Robert McFarlane that they needed to explore Contra funding alternatives other than U.S. budgets. McFarlane solicited some money from the government of Saudi Arabia even before President Reagan held a National Security Planning Group meeting to consider the issue on June 25. Bill Casey would continue to control the Nicaragua operation, even after the CIA had been forbidden by law from participating in it. McFarlane assigned one of his staffers, Marine Lieutenant Colonel Oliver L. North, to help Casey. In effect, Casey functioned as both high authority and manager for this activity and North as his main operative.

This is not the place for an extended account of what became an increasingly ramified covert operation and then blossomed into the Iran-Contra affair. But its main outlines show William J. Casey directly conducting policy, with consequences that affected American national security, U.S. foreign policy, and the political viability of the Reagan administration itself.[47] Among the actions that occurred here were that Casey, sometimes with NSC officials, sometimes directly with North, contrived means to direct other U.S. government employees to act in ways benefiting their operation, including both CIA and State Department officers. They solicited money both from foreign governments and from private persons. They recruited individuals who were former military and CIA officers and became known as the "private benefactors" to act in place of CIA personnel in what effectively became two different covert operations. They conducted negotiations with representatives of foreign governments—and got American diplomats to negotiate for them in other instances—including those of Honduras, Costa Rica, El Salvador, Israel, Iran, Portugal, Saudi Arabia, Brunei, Taiwan, South Korea, South Africa, and others. They turned a general presidential concern over American citizens held hostage in Lebanon into a covert operation that sold U.S. weapons to Iran without congressional authorization, using weapons diverted from U.S. and Israeli military stocks. Some U.S. weapons went to Israel, and indeed the Israelis used the transaction to convert a part of their stockpile of an older U.S. missile to the most modern version. Proceeds from the Iranian sales were converted to the use of the Contras and for the profit of the private benefactors, who contracted CIA proprietary airlines to deliver weapons to Iran and move cargoes to Central America. The benefactors also built an infrastructure of bases and aircraft in Central America, the major one at a Salvadoran military facility. And North both solicited offers for weapons to sell from dealers and had the private benefactors organize some arms deals on their own while participating in Contra deliberations on what weapons to purchase. In addition, the private benefactors carried CIA intelligence to the Contras, provided CIA tactical advice to Contras in Costa Rica, and piggybacked some of their military supply activities on humanitarian relief shipments. Between

June 1984 and November 1986, the operation unfolded. That November, the shoot-down over Nicaragua of a plane belonging to the "private bene-factors" and the revelation in a Beirut newspaper of some details on the Mc-Farlane visit to Iran combined to uncover both sides of the operation. The unraveling began with congressional hearings on Nicaragua at which CIA and State Department officials presented false and misleading testimony re-garding their knowledge of events and proceeded through the concoction of a chronology to be given Congress that also contained false information, separate and joint congressional investigations, inquiry by a presidential board, an intensive investigation by an independent prosecutor, and a series of court cases. Some officials and CIA officers were saved from prison or trial only by a pardon from Ronald Reagan's successor.

William J. Casey was not around to witness much of the fallout from his activities. Shortly after presenting testimony at some of the first congressional committee hearings on what became Iran-Contra, Casey suffered a collapse and was rushed to the hospital. He was found to have a brain tumor and in the hospital suffered a further stroke. Casey passed away in May 1987, his legacy a huge scandal for both the CIA and the American government.

Bill Casey at the CIA had been a swashbuckling activist who went far beyond the agency's writ for telling truth to power. His actions were part and parcel of a pattern of privatization of power during the Reagan era in which officials with hard-held beliefs and ready programmatic solutions were able to substitute their agendas for government-wide policy. For Casey, this approach was a natural outgrowth of his business practices. To work among a constel-lation of policy entrepreneurs who cooperated or shifted their alliances to overcome obstacles posed by statutory restrictions, a bureaucracy they viewed as hidebound, or international commitments they saw as inconvenient or counterproductive seemed normal to Casey. Iran-Contra was a consequence of this approach. And Casey supported other Reagan administration policy entrepreneurs in similar excesses on myriad issues of national importance. The net result would be United States policies that were "rational" only at the margins, saved by the unwillingness of allies and adversaries to play along with Reagan brinkmanship and, in some areas, by the president's awakening to the dangers posed by this method. In the 1970s, Americans had worried that the CIA was a "rogue elephant" out to play its own game, and presiden-tial commissions and congressional investigations had ensued. These estab-lished that the agency had in fact operated under tight presidential control, but Congress attempted to strengthen checks and balances by creating a sys-tem of congressional oversight of intelligence. No one had paid much atten-tion to the possibility there might be a rogue CIA director. Bill Casey at the head of the agency showed how easily a strong-willed individual could cir-

cumvent the system. His career is testimony to both the continuing central-
ity of the individual in history and the often-denigrated point that sometimes
bureaucracies are important.

NOTES

1. William Safire, "Casey at the Source," *New York Times*, December 15, 1986,
A23.
2. Joseph Persico, *Casey: From the OSS to the CIA* (New York: Viking, 1990), 30.
3. Persico, *Casey*, 57.
4. Persico, *Casey*, 89.
5. The semiofficial history of the IRC is in Aaron Levenstein, *Escape to Freedom: The
Story of the International Rescue Committee* (Westport, Conn.: Greenwood Press, 1983).
6. When Allen Dulles, then freshly minted CIA director, was asked for an appointment by the IRC's Cherne, he agreed but noted, first, that the IRC was somewhat outside the scope of its proper activities and, second, that he had already been
receiving reports on the IRC *from Bill Casey* and other former OSS personnel. See
Eric T. Chester, *Covert Network: Progressives, the International Rescue Committee, and
the CIA* (Armonk, N.Y.: M. E. Sharpe, 1995), 117.
7. Chester, *Covert Network*, 88–95.
8. See Anne H. Cahn, *Killing Détente: The Right Attacks the CIA* (University Park:
Pennsylvania State University Press, 1988).
9. Committee on the Present Danger, "Common Sense and the Present Danger,"
no date (January 1977). Compare John Prados, *The Soviet Estimate: U.S. Intelligence
and Soviet Strategic Forces* (Princeton, N.J.: Princeton University Press, 1986), 248–57.
For an extended discussion, see Jeffrey Sanders, *Peddlers of Crisis* (Boston: South End
Press, 1983).
10. The Team B analysts had made a series of claims about the accuracy of Russian intercontinental ballistic missiles (ICBMs) that were unfounded. This was crucial in a technical sense because accuracy is far more important than explosive power
(yield) in determining the ability of a nuclear weapon to destroy a hardened target
such as a U.S. ICBM silo. Since there were physical limits on how much a target
could be hardened and at the margin the nth degree of hardening was hugely expensive, U.S. leaders had stopped the ICBM hardening program at a certain point.
However, the Russian ICBMs never demonstrated the degree of accuracy that would
have made silo vulnerability a serious concern, especially in a force posture where the
other "legs" of the U.S. "triad" of forces (sea-launched ballistic missiles and bombers)
were not in danger. The CIA and other U.S. agencies in dealing with the Team B report lent a certain substance to the "window of vulnerability" argument by increasing
their estimate of Russian ICBM accuracy. In the mid-1980s, however, the intelligence estimates took back those assessed increases. The window of vulnerability argument virtually disappeared—studies showed the Soviets theoretically incapable of

executing an attack capable of disarming U.S. ICBMs without exhausting their own force.

In the meantime, in developments never referenced by the popularizers of the Soviet threat, U.S. forces were already at the accuracy levels claimed for the Russians, and the United States was deploying technologies that extended the same degree of accuracy to submarine missile forces (on which the bulk of U.S. warheads resided), plus a further generation of accuracy and nuclear yield improvements on land-based missiles, with the result that *Soviet* ICBM forces were increasingly vulnerable. The truth was that force improvements were making ICBMs vulnerable on both sides of the nuclear balance. There was *no* "window of vulnerability," or at least none that applied only to American forces. And the argument that the Soviets could fight and win a nuclear war required discounting the sea-based and air components of the "triad," which were each more powerful than its land-based leg.

11. The House of Representatives report, as well as William J. Casey's affadavit, are excerpted in the *Washington Post*, May 24, 1984, A16. Compare Walter Shapiro et al., "Case of the Pilfered Papers," *Newsweek*, July 11, 1983, 20–24; Melinda Beck et al., "Reagan: Feeling the Heat," and Tom Morganthau et. al., "The Great Mole Hunt," *Newsweek*, July 18, 1983, 14–21. Some of this reporting relied on details first related by Laurence I. Barrett in his book *Gambling with History: Reagan in the White House* (Garden City, N.Y.: Doubleday, 1983).

12. Gary Sick, *October Surprise: American Hostages in Iran and the Election of Ronald Reagan* (New York: Crown Books, 1992), passim. United States Congress, Senate (102/2), Foreign Relations Committee, *Report of the Special Counsel to Senator Terry Sanford and Senator James F. Jeffords: The "October Surprise" Allegations and the Circumstances Surrounding the Release of the American Hostages Held in Iran* (Washington, D.C.: U.S. Government Printing Office, 1992), 115.

13. Persico, *Casey*, 203.

14. Judith Miller, "Panel Finds Casey Not Unfit for Job," *New York Times*, December 2, 1981, A21. The Justice Department opened a separate investigation of Casey's failure to register as a foreign agent and cleared him in the spring of 1982.

15. Robert M. Gates, *From the Shadows: The Ultimate Insider's Story of Five Presidents and How They Won the Cold War* (New York: Simon & Schuster, 1996), 192.

16. For a collection of Casey's speeches, see Herbert E. Meyer, ed., *Scouting the Future: The Public Speeches of William J. Casey* (Washington, D.C.: Henry Regnery Gateway, 1989). The line on Soviet tanks and artillery is quoted from a May 1981 speech (22). Soviet tanks and artillery were never used in Guatemala or El Salvador, and the only such weapons in Lebanon and Chad were those of the Syrian and Libyan armed forces, not Russian or terrorist groups. The Claire Sterling book is *The Terror Network: The Secret War of International Terrorism* (New York: Holt, Rinehart and Winston, 1981).

17. Gates, *From the Shadows*, 333.

18. Gates, *From the Shadows*, 201.

19. Bob Woodward, *Veil: The Secret Wars of the CIA, 1981–1987* (New York: Pocket Books, 1988), 389.

20. Gates, *From the Shadows*, 286.

21. Casey Speech to the Commonwealth Club of California, May 21, 1982. Herbert Meyer, *Scouting the Future*, 48.

22. United States Congress, Senate (102/1), Select Committee on Intelligence, *Report: Nomination of Robert M. Gates to be Director of Central Intelligence* (hereafter cited as Gates Nomination Report) (Washington, D.C.: U.S. Government Printing Office 1991), 151.

23. Gates Nomination Report, 151.

24. United States Congress, Senate (102/1), Select Committee on Intelligence, *Hearings: Nomination of Robert M. Gates*, vol. 1 (Washington, D.C.: U.S. Government Printing Office, 1991), 718–19.

25. Patrick Tyler and David B. Ottaway, "The CIA in Transition: Casey Strengthens Role under 'Reagan Doctrine,'" *Washington Post*, March 31, 1986, A14.

26. The SDI estimates are examined in depth in John Prados, "The Strategic Defense Initiative: Between Strategy, Diplomacy, and U.S. Intelligence Estimates," in *Back to the Cold War? The Crisis of Détente in Europe 1975–85*, ed. Leopoldo Nuti (London: Routledge, in press).

27. United States Congress, Senate (102/1), Select Committee on Intelligence, *Hearings: Nomination of Robert M. Gates*, vol. 2 (Washington, D.C.: U.S. Government Printing Office, 1991), 273–74.

28. United States Congress, House of Representatives (97/2), Permanent Select Committee on Intelligence, "Report: U.S. Intelligence Performance on Central America: Achievements and Selected Instances of Concern," Committee Print, September 22, 1982, passim.

29. Gates, *From the Shadows*, 293.

30. Gates, *From the Shadows*, 296.

31. Gates Nomination Report, 121.

32. Gates, Nomination Report, 177.

33. Bob Woodward, *Veil*, 385–92, 436–38. The House Permanent Select Committee on Intelligence examined the estimate and drafts and decided that the presence of dissents in the finished paper sufficiently demonstrated that the process had been a legitimate one (Woodward, *Veil*, 438).

34. Gates Nomination Report, 128, discussed at 125–29.

35. John Prados, *Safe for Democracy: The Secret Wars of the CIA* (Chicago: Ivan R. Dee, 2006), 507–39.

36. George P. Shultz, *Turmoil and Triumph: My Years as Secretary of State* (New York: Charles Scribner's Sons, 1993), 1113, 1116, 1119.

37. Prados, *Safe for Democracy*, 467–92.

38. Charles Moser, ed., *Combat on Communist Territory* (Lake Bluff, Ill.: Regnery Gateway, 1985).

39. Gates, *From the Shadows*, 212.

40. Joseph Lelyveld, "The Director: Running the CIA," *New York Times Magazine*, January 20, 1985, 16.

41. Prados, "The Strategic Defense Initiative."

42. Gates, *From the Shadows*, 260.

43. Gates, *From the Shadows*, 287.

44. Gates, *From the Shadows*, 282.

45. Shultz, *Turmoil and Triumph*, 691.

46. John Prados, "The War Scare of 1983," in *The Cold War: A Military History*, ed. Robert Cowley (New York: Random House, 2005), 438–54.

47. Prados, *Safe for Democracy*, 499–503, 536–71.

· 7 ·

Colin Powell: The Rise and Fall of the Powell Doctrine

Walter LaFeber

$\mathcal{A}$s Texas Governor George W. Bush moved toward the presidency in the late 1990s, public opinion polls regularly revealed that Colin Powell not only was better known and liked than Bush but also ranked among the most admired of all Americans. When the United States invaded Iraq in March 2003, the polls again showed that Americans continued to admire and trust Powell, now their secretary of state. Twenty months later, the president forced Powell to resign. By then, November 2004, the secretary of state's gilded reputation had been badly tarnished by the terrible course of the bloody conflict in Iraq and the role he played before the war in justifying the invasion.

It is not one of the happier chapters in American biography but one of the most instructive. The story began in 1937 when Powell was born in New York City's Bronx neighborhood to parents who had left Jamaica to find opportunities in the city's teeming garment district. Colin had no desire to follow his father into the clothing industry. Resembling many immigrants' children, he went to the City College of New York (CCNY), an inexpensive but a demanding and remarkably successful institution. Powell was little more than a mediocre student, majoring for vague reasons in geology, until he discovered the Reserve Officers Training Corps (ROTC) program at CCNY. He quickly took to its order, hierarchy, and physical and mental demands. By his graduation, the six-foot-one-inch second-generation immigrant, on his way to an adult weight of 200 pounds, was an outstanding student commander of his 1,000-strong ROTC unit.

ROTC required a further three-year commitment beyond graduation. When that term was up in 1961, Powell quickly reenlisted. "I was in a profession that would allow me to go as far as my talents would take me," he recalled, "and for a black, no other avenue in American society offered so much opportunity"[1] That same year, he met (and in 1962 married) Alma Johnson, a gifted woman from an upper-class Birmingham, Alabama African American family. Shortly after the wedding, Powell went to South Vietnam. President John F. Kennedy was escalating, as secretly as possible, the U.S. war effort against the North Vietnamese communist government, which was attempting to unite the country. Powell loved the experience. He believed that only the best and brightest were being sent at this point to wage a stealth war against the North and that his assignment signaled that the army saw him, in his words, as one of the "comers, walk-on water types being groomed for bright futures."[2] He was wounded but remained through his one-year term. In 1968, he returned for a second tour. He now was one of the half million U.S. troops trying to win an unwinable, fourteen-year-long U.S. war. He received a medal for heroism when, despite a broken ankle, he dragged three soldiers, including a general, from a downed helicopter.

The U.S. retreat from Vietnam between 1973 and the communist victory in 1975 was the lowest point in modern U.S. military history to that point. Powell was one of the young officers who determined to learn from the experience. He obtained a master's degree in business, then became a commander in one of the most fabled U.S. military units, the 101st Airborne Division. By the early 1980s, his record had attracted invitations to serve in several important positions in Washington. Powell had established himself as that rare person who somehow understood both the civilian and the military sides of the Capitol. Even as a low-ranking Pentagon official, he also proved to be a quick learner when it came to moving the usually slow bureaucracies. In 1984, during the presidency of Ronald Reagan, now Major-General Powell became an assistant to Secretary of Defense Caspar Weinberger. The secretary was about to issue a declaration that proved to be historic and, for Powell, life shaping.

Since the U.S. military had been forced to leave Vietnam in the mid-1970s, its officers had conducted quiet, intensive studies to discover what had gone wrong. Powell played a small role in some of these discussions but a more important part in shaping Weinberger's thinking. A Middle East crisis that destroyed hundreds of American lives led the secretary of defense to decide it was time to announce the results of the nearly decade-long military studies. The crisis had developed in 1982 when Israel invaded neighboring Lebanon. Syria, the dominant power in Lebanon, and Syria's allies kept the war escalating brutally into 1983. Then the Reagan administration, over the strong dissent of Weinberger and the American military, decided to send in 1,800 troops to help stabilize the ever more dangerous situation. In October 1983, a truck bomb exploded in the encampment killing 241 Americans—the worst single-day U.S. military death toll since the last days of World War II.

Since those 1945 days, Washington officials had largely fixed their attention on the Cold War against the Soviet Union. But beginning in the late 1970s and early 1980s, the Middle East was moving to the forefront of U.S. diplomacy. The region had become the center of the world's oil production. The area had also been the center of ongoing conflicts between newly founded (in 1948) Israel and its neighboring Islamic nations. And since the 1950s, it was a region into which U.S. presidents sent their military forces, perhaps all too easily, until 241 of them had been slaughtered in a moment of 1983. In late November 1984, Weinberger responded to this tragedy as well as to the destructive effects of the Vietnam experience on the U.S. military in a Washington speech.

It became known as the Weinberger Doctrine and, later and more famously, as the Powell Doctrine. The secretary of defense began by declaring that the military must no longer be placed in killing fields when there seemed to be no overriding national interest at stake and no intention of fighting to win a complete victory. Weinberger announced that six major tests should be applied before civilian officials blithely deployed men and women into battle.

First, the "engagement" must be "deemed vital to our national interest or that of our allies." Second, U.S. forces should only be sent "with the clear intention of winning." Third, in putting American lives at stake, "we should have clearly defined political and military obligations." Fourth, the size and purpose of the force sent out to fight should be "continually reassessed and adjusted if necessary"—as had clearly not occurred when the situations in Vietnam and Lebanon rapidly changed. Fifth, troops should be assured, before they go abroad to fight and possibly die, that they have "the support of the American people and . . . Congress." Finally, and what would become of special importance to Powell over the next twenty years, Weinberger declared that "the commitment of U.S. forces to combat should be a last resort."[3]

American military officials quickly put this doctrine to work in the mid-1980s to counter civilian demands that troops be sent into the maelstrom of Central American revolutions. In 1987, Powell became involved in this struggle—and continued successfully to insist that the troops not be sent—when he became the top deputy in the National Security Council (NSC). Stationed in the White House, the NSC had been created in 1947 so that the president could better coordinate and ensure the carrying out of foreign policy decisions. It was a job for which Powell had immense talent, and later in 1987 he became the first African American to hold the top post, NSC adviser. When George H. W. Bush became president in 1989 and appointed his own NSC staff, Powell notably chose to stay in the military rather than possibly make a small fortune as a civilian. Later that year, the newly promoted four-star general was chosen by Bush over dozens of older generals to the most exalted and powerful military position, Chairman of the Joint Chiefs of Staff. He now became the first African American to head the U.S. military.

Powell's initial major crisis erupted when President Bush moved to overthrow the Panamanian regime of Manuel Noriega. As a result of a 1977 U.S.–Panama treaty, the great U.S.-built canal linking the Atlantic and Pacific oceans was slowly coming under Panama's control. Bush, however, increasingly condemned Noriega's drug running, violent acts against Americans, and threats against the canal. As the president determined to intervene, it became a test of the Weinberger Doctrine. Powell insisted that the overthrow of Noriega be a quick, overwhelming strike carried out by a force of 20,000 Americans, accompanied by the U.S. Air Force, against a handful of Panamanians who had no air force. In December 1989, the American operation quickly forced Noriega to flee, finally captured him after a series of almost comic failures, and installed a friendlier government. Powell became widely known as the highly articulate general who often explained on television why the operation was going so well.

Along with this not surprising success of the Weinberger Doctrine, the months of 1989–1990 marked another milestone of much greater importance: the collapse of the Soviet Union's East European empire and the rapid ending of the nearly half-century-long Cold War. The Soviet Union itself was enduring sometimes bloody internal division as it headed for its death, finally, on Christmas Day 1991. The United States emerged as the world's unchallenged, supreme power. Indeed, some overly imaginative American observers claimed their nation was nothing less than the most powerful force in world affairs since the Roman Empire of 1900 years before. Despite the ending of the Cold War, moreover, U.S. military budgets remained around the $300 billion mark, or more than the combined military spending of the next twenty most powerful nations.

Powell headed this juggernaut. In 1990, he spectacularly put it to work. The general did so by carefully following the six points of the Weinberger Doctrine as the United States went to war against a most surprising enemy: Saddam Hussein, the unquestioned, brutal ruler of Iraq since 1978. Saddam was a surprising enemy in 1990 because during the previous decade he had been an ally of President Ronald Reagan. Both men and their people had one strong tie: they feared and despised the religious rulers of Iran who had overthrown the U.S.-supported government in 1979 and taken more than 50 Americans hostage. Saddam, an ambitious secular Sunni Muslim, had quickly declared war in 1980 on neighboring Iran, now a fervently religious Shiia Muslim regime. The bloody eight-year war that followed claimed more than a million casualties. Despite Reagan's heavy economic support for Saddam, however, the long conflict ended in stalemate. Massive U.S. aid to Saddam nevertheless continued, even though the Iraqi leader supported the Palestinians who fought Israel, the leading U.S. ally in the Middle East, and even though he ruthlessly executed and jailed those Iraqis he suspected of opposing him.

All this suddenly changed in July 1990. Frustrated by falling oil prices and determined to obtain ports giving him greater access to the Persian Gulf, Saddam struck south and seized oil-rich Kuwait. Fear now arose that he was in position to attack or at least effectively threaten his eastern neighbor Saudi Arabia. The Saudis held one-quarter of the globe's known oil reserves. They had also been a highly valued U.S. ally since 1945. After some hesitation (Saddam, after all, had also been a longtime American ally), President Bush decided the Iraqis had to be driven from Kuwait.

The question was how, and Powell was at the center of the debate in late 1990. Secretary of Defense Richard Cheney and Undersecretary of Defense Paul Wolfowitz wanted to launch a massive military attack to drive Saddam's forces out of Kuwait and, indeed, set in motion Saddam's overthrow. The United States had never intervened massively, with hundreds of thousands of troops, in the Middle East. Unless perfectly conducted, the military feared that such a campaign could become a Vietnam-like morass. And it was questionable whether Kuwait was worth it: "I think we'd go to war over Saudi Arabia, but I doubt we'd go to war over Kuwait," Powell said privately.[4]

In his eyes, Kuwait did not fit the Weinberger Doctrine's demand that U.S. forces face death only to defend the most important national interests. Nor did a Kuwaiti campaign fit the doctrine's requirement that sending troops into battle must be the last resort—that is, after political and economic pressures on Saddam were tried and failed. Neither Cheney nor Wolfowitz had served in the military. Both had been able to avoid the draft during the Vietnam War years. They viewed the services not through the prism of Weinberger's Doctrine but as flexible instruments that should automatically be on call to carry out the nation's foreign policy. Cheney and Wolfowitz's determination to destroy Weinberger's (and soon Powell's) principles thus began in 1990, then reappeared with even greater intensity after the September 11, 2001, terrorist strikes on the United States.

Powell lost the first part of the debate in 1990–1991. He could not convince the president to use economic pressures against Saddam instead of immediately dispatching military forces. In late 1990, President Bush ordered several hundred thousand troops to the Middle East. He also dramatically built a coalition of major powers that, for the most part, not only committed their own military forces but also sent so much money for the effort that in the end the United States had to spend virtually none of its own dollars.

Powell and the Weinberger Doctrine did succeed in shaping the next part of the debate. Bush slowly built up overwhelming American, especially congressional, support for the operation. The president also decided on a carefully limited invasion and then—most importantly—closely followed Powell's advice by committing overwhelming force to achieve the single specific goal: the liberation of Kuwait. In the 100-hour war of late February 1991, the U.S.-led forces of 550,000 soldiers destroyed large numbers of badly outgunned Iraqi troops. The road to Iraq's capital, Baghdad, lay open. Bush refused to take it. He and Powell had achieved their primary objectives. Kuwait was liberated, and Saudi Arabia was no longer in danger. Many of Bush's allies, moreover, wanted nothing to do with an attack on Baghdad and the overthrow of Saddam. Led by the Saudis themselves, these allies feared a civil war might erupt in Iraq and destabilize the entire region. It would be better to let the Iraqis and Iranians continue to balance each other so neither could again threaten their neighbors. Perhaps, as Bush and his advisers hoped, the weakened Saddam might in any case be overthrown by his enemies within Iraq.

The Gulf War of 1991 was, on one level, a breathtaking military triumph televised around the globe. It dramatically demonstrated that the old Cold War had been replaced by a "new order," as President Bush liked to call it—a new world dominated by U.S. wishes and power. Americans happily accepted Bush's rosy analysis as they set out in the 1990s to enjoy the new world they believed they largely controlled—by the international popularity of their music, Coca-Cola, McDonald's, and Nike shoes as well as by their military. In the middle of the decade, they paid more attention to their president's private life than to his foreign policies. Televised newscasts helped Americans escape into an unreal, parochial world as coverage of overseas affairs was cut by at least one-third during the 1990s. Many Americans became narrow intellectual isolationists, moreover, just as terrorist attacks worldwide multiplied between 1993 and 2001.

The Weinberger/Powell Doctrine inadvertently helped to generate this intellectual isolationism. The quick, overwhelming military success in the 1991 Gulf War seemed to show conclusively that Americans and their friends had both the power to maintain world order and the leadership to decide wisely when that power should be deployed. Powell, their top military leader, had not wanted to rush into war. He indeed seemed to differ from many other commanders in history by wanting no war at all, at least not until all six of Weinberger's 1984 requirements were met. And in 1990–1991, Powell had added a seventh point: before troops were committed to battle, U.S. officials must have worked out an "exit strategy," in a definite time frame, so the soldiers would not be expected to stay anywhere and fight indefinitely. Again: no more Vietnams. The 1991 invasion had worked perfectly in this respect. The doctrine was now wholly associated with Powell.

If that was one result of the conflict, however, there was another. Cheney and Wolfowitz led a group that drew quite different lessons from the war than did Powell. The secretary of defense and his top civilian assistant loyally supported, at the time, Bush's decisions not to attack Baghdad itself and not to overthrow Saddam. They, like Bush and Powell, hoped the Iraqis themselves would destroy Saddam. But that did not occur. Saddam ruthlessly killed those he suspected of trying to remove him. Reports circulated that the dictator was reviving his programs to develop nuclear, biological, and chemical weapons— programs that he had begun in the 1970s but that had been partially destroyed by a precise Israeli air attack in 1981. By 1992, one could wonder who had won the 1991 war. Saddam was firmly in power, while George Bush lost the U.S. presidential election to an upstart Arkansas Democratic governor, William Jefferson Clinton.

In the last months of the Bush presidency, Cheney and Wolfowitz undertook a full analysis of the nation's future strategy. The result was the Defense Planning Guidance (DPG), a supposedly top-secret document quickly leaked to the press. The DPG was as far from the Powell Doctrine as Powell's battlefield experiences in the 1960s had been from Cheney and Wolfowitz's student days. The leaked DPG draft created a sensation when it stated that the United States not only intended to dominate the raw material and oil-producing areas, especially in the Middle East, but also would actively prevent anyone (and anyone included allies) from even moving toward a position that might threaten U.S. supremacy.

The Cold War with the Soviets was now to be replaced, apparently, by a Cold War against everyone else. This first draft was rewritten under public pressure but only slightly. Allies were no longer singled out. The document nevertheless remained clear that the U.S. military would not wait for a great power (say, China) to emerge as a threat but would take early steps so that no such threat could emerge—steps that became known as "preemption" after 2001. Nor would the United States necessarily depend on allies, as it had so successfully in the 1991 war. The supposedly all-powerful Americans would be willing to move alone.

This DPG directly challenged the Powell Doctrine. It used vague terms to describe vague challenges but concluded that the commitment of American men and women to fight emerging threats would be assumed. There would not be a checklist, as Weinberger had stipulated, to be met before U.S. troops went into battle. This approach of the DPG eerily anticipated Cheney and Wolfowitz's policies a decade later.

In his last months as Chairman of the Joint Chiefs (he retired in September 1993), General Powell repeatedly had to defend his doctrine against the demands of the new Clinton administration. It was an incredible nine months for Clinton, who, like Cheney and Wolfowitz, had received student deferments, not military training, in the 1960s. The president from Arkansas deployed U.S. forces to more locations on more occasions during his presidency (1993–2001) than any of his predecessors in the White House had dispatched them during any other eight-year period of the Cold War. The collapse of the Soviet Union and the apparently unquestioned supremacy of U.S. military power allowed Clinton to use the military extravagantly.

The commitments began in the last days of the Bush presidency when the outgoing and incoming chief executives agreed that small U.S. forces should land under UN auspices in Somalia, the East African country where raging tribal wars were killing many civilians and starving others. In December 1992, the first of some 25,000 U.S. troops landed. They did so as Hollywood Kleig lights set up by American television crews turned night into midday on the landing beaches. Resembling not a life-and-death situation but a blurry Saturday afternoon movie, the episode made a major splash on U.S. television screens and gave Americans a dangerously misleading view of the civil bloodshed—and thus further undermined the Powell Doctrine's emphasis on the need for great care before putting soldiers' lives at stake. But then, if Hollywood said so, U.S. forces must be unbeatable.

As Clinton entered the presidency in January 1993, the ethnically and religiously complex state of Yugoslavia was also coming apart. The dominant Orthodox Christians were "ethnically cleansing" (i.e., slaughtering or driving out) Muslims in the area of Bosnia. At a Clinton cabinet meeting, U.S. Ambassador to the United Nations Madeleine Albright urged committing U.S. forces to stop the "cleansing." Powell opposed such a sudden move. He demanded that the political preconditions of his doctrine be met—what, for example, would be the specific political objectives of the troops? Albright lashed back, "What's the point of having this superb military that you're [Powell] always talking about if we can't use it?" As the general later recalled, "I thought I would have an aneurysm. American GIs were not toy soldiers to be moved around on some sort of global game board." He gave Albright a stunning statistic: "our armed forces" had been committed "more than two dozen times in the preceding three years" for war and humanitarian missions. Powell, however, had first obtained "a clear goal" before they were sent.[5] There were to be no more vague, endless commitments as in Vietnam. No troops went to Yugoslavia in 1993.

Somalia turned out to be quite another story. Powell understood that the U.S. forces were to help open up food supply routes for the starving. In June 1993, Clinton and the United Nations changed the mission. The president ordered the troops to track down troublemaking clan chiefs, that is, to become directly involved in the conflict. As Powell recorded in his memoirs, the objective was now "'nation building,' the phrase I had first heard when we went into Vietnam. From what I have observed of history, the will to build a nation originates from within its people, not from the outside."[6]

The general wanted little to do with the growing American idea, spread most notably by Woodrow Wilson and Ronald Reagan, that the United States had a manifest destiny to spread democracy around the world—with military force if necessary. Somalia became blood-soaked evidence for his doubts. In the early autumn of 1993, a Somalia chieftain's forces shot down a U.S. helicopter and killed eighteen Americans. Television now showed not a Disney scene but the mutilated bodies of the U.S. victims being dragged by gleeful Somalis through dusty streets. Several months later, a beleaguered Clinton pulled out the remaining U.S. troops even though Somalia was sinking into chaos.

For the U.S. forces, this experience was a stunning case study of what could happen when the Powell Doctrine was not followed, especially when the political situation was not understood and the political objectives not thought through. But the tragedy did little to restrain Americans' growing belief that they could exercise their unmatched military power anywhere they saw their interests in danger. American troops went into the fragmenting Yugoslavia between 1995 and 1999 along with UN forces. With Powell retired, his doctrine was not closely followed. There was not, for example, any understanding about an "exit strategy" for the forces. Consequently, a dozen years after the commitment, American troops remained in parts of the former Yugoslavia.

Retired, Powell watched all this as a civilian for the first time in thirty-five years. After living on a government salary, he set out to make money for his family. He succeeded spectacularly. The retired general received a $6 million advance for his autobiography, then more millions when it became a best-seller in 1995 and helped enable him to charge high five-figure fees for public speeches. The Powells particularly devoted their time and new wealth to city youth organizations. In 1996, "the most trusted man in America," according to polls, considered running for president.[7] He finally decided not to after his wife, Alma, threatened, "If you run, I'm gone."[8] Among other reasons, she feared that this first serious African American candidate for the White House might have attempts made on his life.

He said little publicly about Clinton foreign policies. Those who had opposed him in 1990–1991, especially Wolfowitz and Cheney, were less restrained. Wolfowitz, now a dean at Johns Hopkins University, kept up a drumbeat of criticism, especially in regard to what he interpreted as the president's supposed restraint in using force and also in Clinton's failure to destroy Saddam Hussein's regime in Iraq. In the 2000 presidential election campaign,

Wolfowitz led a so-called neoconservative movement committed to reshaping the foreign policy debate. The neocons' media outlet was *The Weekly Standard*, edited by William Kristol.

This movement emphasized the need to freely use U.S. military forces to ensure that no rivals (China was particularly fingered) could even approach the point when they could challenge the United States. The neoconservatives also emphasized that a goal of U.S. policy must be the spreading of democracy. Democracies, the argument went, were more peaceful than other forms of government, and global stability in the interest of the United States could best be assured by their expansion. It thus was justifiable, the neocons added, to use force to extend democracy. As one phrased it, "The best democracy program ever invented is the U.S. Army."[9] (That statement, among its other problems, had already been disproved by a full century of the U.S. Army's post-1890 interventions in Central American and Caribbean nations.) It followed that the Middle East should become a case study where democracy could take over not only to topple Saddam but also to protect the more democratic Israel, the major U.S. ally in the region and a special concern of the neoconservatives. Powell agreed about Israel's importance, but he wanted nothing to do with the other two objectives—using military force more freely and attempting to reform key (and chaotic) parts of the world by somehow making them more democratic.

By 2000, the Republican presidential nominee, Texas Governor George W. Bush, had put together a foreign policy advisory panel that included three groups. The first was the neoconservatives' leading voice, Wolfowitz. The second was made up of so-called realists who largely agreed on the importance of Israel and the need to use technology so that the military could move even more quickly and effectively. In other words, they, like the neocons, wanted to destroy some of the restraints that the Powell Doctrine had imposed on this marvelous force. But the realists had little interest in the idea of expanding democracy. They were, after all, realists and thus were willing to settle for regimes that were stable and pro-American. Cheney and his close friend, former (and future) Secretary of Defense Donald Rumsfeld, as well as Condoleezza Rice, a former Stanford University political scientist who was especially close to the Bush family, belonged in the realist category.

The third group advising Bush was a group of one, Colin Powell. He wanted little to do with the neocon–realist happy acceptance of using force. Nor was Powell willing to embrace the highly complex—and often destabilizing—goal of spreading democracy; he especially had no illusions after his Vietnam experience that the U.S. Army was "the best democracy program ever invented." Bush and Powell were congenial in 2000 not because they shared foreign policy views. The highly parochial Texas governor knew little about international affairs. Nor were they especially compatible personally. Between 2001 and early 2005 when Powell finally resigned, the two men had remarkably few private conversations.

They joined forces in 2000 because Bush badly needed Powell's public support to win the White House. The Democratic Party candidate, Vice President Al Gore, won more popular votes in the election, but, thanks finally to a highly controversial Supreme Court decision, Bush won the all-important Electoral College count.

Not surprisingly, neither the new president nor his chief political adviser, Karl Rove, was enthusiastic about giving much credit for the victory to Powell. Bush did pay his political debt and made the obvious choice on its merits by appointing him secretary of state. Powell became the first African American to hold this highest of cabinet ranks. Then trouble began. Cheney, now the vice president, had helped convince Bush to name Rumsfeld secretary of defense. Cheney and Rumsfeld's intimate friendship went back a quarter century when both had served under President Gerald Ford. They now set out to remake U.S. military forces and policy.

By using new, highly expensive technology, Rumsfeld believed that the American military could be reduced in size and thus be more nimble and easier to deploy to any trouble spot. Such a belief, of course, ran directly against the Powell Doctrine's emphasis on learning from Vietnam (and Somalia) that the considerable political problems (such as obtaining U.S. support and having a definite date for the American troops to depart from the commitment) be carefully ironed out before committing men and women to battle—and then committing them in overwhelming numbers. "Rumsfeld's Rules," as they became known, included the command "Reserve the right to interfere into anything, and exercise it."[10] Nothing could have been farther from Powell's rules.

The new secretary of state had good reason to think the president himself was the true son of his father who a decade earlier had certainly deployed military power but had done so in the 1991 Iraqi conflict within carefully marked limits and in alliance with long-term (and wealthy) friends. The senior Bush wanted no part of unilateralism and nation building, nor, the son repeatedly said during the 2000 campaign, did he. In mid-December 2000, the newly elected president, with Powell at his side, promised to "conduct our foreign policy in the spirit of national unity and friendship." He emphasized that the new secretary of state "believes, as I do, that we must work closely with our allies and friends. . . . He believes, as I do, that our nation is best when we project strength and our purpose with humility." Powell then stepped to the microphone to underline the point: strong cooperation with allies was to be "the center of our foreign policy activities."[11]

It was not to be. In his first months in office, Bush retracted Clinton's pledge and pulled the United States out of the much-lauded Kyoto treaty, which aimed to improve the environment through international cooperation. Longtime European allies had shaped the pact, but that made no difference to Bush, who only wanted to have maximum freedom of action, especially on economic issues. The president next reversed Clinton's cooperative policies toward a key Asian ally, South Korea. The North Korean communist regime's ambition to become a nuclear power had supposedly been contained in a 1994 treaty pieced together by the United States, along with considerable support from South Korea. The agreement had broken down by 2001, and Bush embarrassed the South Korean president, who happened to be standing beside him, by declaring that there would be no further talks with North Korea. The next January, the president termed the North Koreans a member of "the axis of evil." (North Korea responded with a nuclear test and an experimental missile launching. In 2006, Bush, sinking in a Middle East war and feeling intense pressure from China and South Korea, finally gave in and negotiated with this "axis of evil" a preliminary pact in which North Korea promised to stop its growing nuclear program in return for massive U.S. economic aid.)

On both issues, the Kyoto treaty and the North Korean crisis, Bush and Cheney largely ignored the secretary of state—and of course, all the closest allies of the United States. Powell's top aide and close friend, Deputy Secretary of State Richard Armitage, remarked that Bush had put Powell in the "refrigerator" and was to be taken out only when Powell served the president's purposes, not when he threatened to confuse Bush.[12] The secretary of state complained but not publicly. Cheney was considerably more important in making foreign policy, although as time passed it became clear he was not making it very well. The vice president followed a U.S. tradition of wanting to go it alone, to have obligations to no one, to conduct foreign policy secretly as if it were no one else's (as the secretary of state's) business, to dictate and not negotiate, to use force easily and with bombastic threats, to ignore (or simply curse, sometimes profanely) members of Congress and informed critics, and to divide the world too simplistically between the good and the bad. These characteristics sometimes fit the United States when it fought Indians and Mexicans in the nineteenth century. They turned out to be tragically out of place in a complex, atom bomb–laden, twenty-first-century world.

But Powell, the team player with a soldier's loyalty to the president, did little as Bush continually bypassed his secretary of state. Powell later said that Bush had no system or regular procedure for making life-and-death foreign policy decisions, by which he meant that the president made decisions after private meetings with Cheney and, increasingly, Rumsfeld but not with him. The former soldier fervently believed in proper procedure; it was absolutely necessary for the adequate examination of all perspectives and possibilities as well as politically imperative to obtain as many pledges of cooperation from overseas friends as possible.

Only in one major crisis during the first half of 2001 did Bush push Powell to the front. In April, a U.S. EP-3 plane was spying on China when a Chinese fighter plane that was trying to scare it off collided with the EP-3. The fighter plane crashed in the South China Sea, the pilot never found. The U.S. aircraft made an emergency landing in China. Its twenty-four-person crew was captured. Beijing claimed the plane was flying in Chinese airspace. Washington correctly responded that the aircraft was sixty-two miles from land, that is, in territory that everyone but China recognized as common international air space. The neoconservatives, led by Wolfowitz and Kristol, wanted to get tough. They had condemned Clinton's cooperative attitude toward Beijing and continually warned that China was a dangerous military as well as economic competitor. Bush, for his part, simply wanted to free the Americans and get back to normal with 1.5 billion people who were increasingly enrapturing American investors, traders, and manufacturers who hoped to exploit that vast market. Powell worked out language that diplomatically expressed an apology to the Chinese and freed the Americans. Led by Kristol's *Weekly Standard*, neoconservatives condemned the deal as humiliating. In reality, the deal was not humiliating, but it was the first and last time that Bush allowed Powell to define the policy in settling a potentially explosive problem—and three and a half years remained in the president's first term.

"I'm not a textbook player, I'm a gut player," Bush proudly—and most revealingly—told a reporter.[13] Why in a nuclear world the president wanted to follow an unpredictable "gut" instead of carefully thought-out and more predictable "textbook" approaches was not clear. After promising in the 2000 campaign that he would be humble and work closely with allies, Bush had moved rapidly in the opposite direction of unilateralism. Much to Powell's displeasure, the president took the same approach to Russia. Determined to escape from a 1972 Anti-Ballistic Missile (ABM) treaty with the Soviets (which had sharply limited ABM sites in order to avoid an accelerated nuclear race), Bush announced that he would junk the pact. The United States would build more ABM systems. The implication was that the systems would guard against possible Chinese or North Korean nuclear strikes. The Russians were angry but had no choice but accept the American pullout. On September 11, 2001, Condoleezza Rice, the national security adviser, was to give a speech attacking the Clinton administration for not properly dealing with the great threat to the United States: a too-limited antimissile defense.

Instead of giving the speech, however, she spent the day in a bunker underneath the White House. In a series of attacks, Islamic terrorists seized, in flight, four U.S. passenger jets on that bright, clear September morning. Two planes flew into and destroyed New York City's 110-story World Trade Center buildings. Another was driven at 300 miles per hour into the Pentagon. The fourth was probably to hit another Washington, D.C., target, but courageous passengers fought for control of the plane until it crashed in Pennsylvania and killed everyone aboard. Nearly 3,000 persons died in the attacks.

Within hours, U.S. officials knew that the terrorists had been trained and directed by Osama bin Laden's al-Qaeda organization. Bin Laden, from a rich Saudi Arabian family, had once fought with Americans in the 1980s against the Soviets in Afghanistan. But the U.S. decision in 1991 to keep troops in Saudi Arabia, site of some of Islam's holiest shrines, had infuriated the fanatically religious bin Laden. He had launched a series of attacks between 1993 and 2000 that claimed hundreds of lives, including many Americans. Bush had condemned Clinton for not responding more forcefully, but despite many warnings from his own intelligence officers during the first eight months of 2001, the new president did nothing.

The day after the attacks, Americans entered a new era in their history. It was especially new in the sense that the enemy was not, as had always been the case in the past, a particular nation. Bin Laden's al-Qaeda had moved among a number of countries during the 1990s. No longer did destroying a nation (such as obliterating Germany or Japan in World War II) mean destroying this new enemy. The terrorism, moreover, was inspired by a religious fanaticism, the kind resulting in a willingness to commit suicide—as, indeed, had the September 11 Muslims who drove the planes into buildings at high speeds. Bin Laden aimed to expel the United States and Israel from the Middle East, then impose a religious "caliphate" (ruler) over victorious Islam. The overwhelming number of the world's 1 billion Muslims, however, wanted no part of bin Laden's religious fanaticism, and many had long been pro-American.

In 1996, al-Qaeda established training bases in Afghanistan when that country came under the control of fellow Sunni Muslims, the Taliban. Immediately after the 9/11 attacks, Bush and his advisers, including Powell, determined to invade Afghanistan, destroy the terrorist bases, replace the Taliban with a democratic regime, and capture bin Laden. Aided by longtime allies, including especially Europeans, Canadians, and Latin Americans, U.S.-led forces moved swiftly into Afghanistan in October 2001, just weeks after the 9/11 attacks. Powell's diplomacy played an essential role. Bush needed the help of Pakistan, Afghanistan's next-door neighbor. Pakistan, however, had long worked with the Taliban. Of equal importance, in 1999 a Pakistani military general, Pervez Musharraf, had seized power and replaced an elected government. Washington had condemned the takeover and attempted to isolate Pakistan.

Powell now changed the U.S. course. He told Musharraf, a fellow military officer, that Pakistan and the United States needed each other. The Pakistanis had their own terrorists sitting on their border with Afghanistan and could use U.S. military help. To make his point clear, Powell threatened Musharraf with more U.S. economic and political sanctions if the Pakistanis did not cooperate. Musharraf came aboard. He became perhaps the most important (if not always cooperative) of American allies in the wars against terrorism. Bush later admitted that Powell deserved the credit for bringing the Pakistanis over to the American side.

The invasion of Afghanistan was not conducted according to the Powell Doctrine. There was no overwhelming force committed, and, as it turned out, there was little understanding among Washington officials about what they wanted to achieve other than destroying al-Qaeda's training bases and removing the Taliban regime. The U.S. military indeed depended on larger Afghan forces, who had their own separate and often conflicting interests. At one point in late 2001, it seemed that bin Laden and the top al-Qaeda leadership were surrounded, but—despite Bush's Texas cowboy boast that he would get bin Laden dead or alive—the terrorist leader escaped into the mountains of the Afghan–Pakistani border. Contrary to Bush's 2000 campaign promises, moreover, the United States was now necessarily committed to nation building—the building, no less, of one of the most primitive and divided nations on earth. At this point in early 2002, Bush began to pull U.S. Special Forces and Arabic-speaking experts out of Afghanistan. He had another, much more important target for them.

The target was Iraq. In the first days of the administration, long before the 9/11 attacks, Paul Wolfowitz, now holding the number two position in the Defense Department under Rumsfeld, had pushed his long-held idea that the United States should overthrow Saddam Hussein. By September 20, nine days after the attacks in New York and Washington, U.S. officials, led by Wolfowitz, were considering the invasion of Iraq. Three motives emerged. The first was the belief that Saddam Hussein was producing or was about to produce nuclear, chemical, and/or biological weapons of mass destruction (WMD). This became the all-important argument and fear that Bush later used to convince Americans that an invasion was necessary. The second motive was to install in Iraq a democratic government that would be the necessary first step in overthrowing other authoritarian regimes in the area and making much of the Middle East politically resemble the region's only declared democracy, Israel. That possibly replacing authoritarian governments in, say, Egypt and Saudi Arabia meant replacing two of the most pro-American regimes did not seem to disturb most U.S. officials. Third, replacing Saddam, who offered $25,000 to families whose children carried out suicide bombings of Israelis, would help protect the leading U.S. ally in the region.

Powell understood this third point, but he strongly opposed the first two motives. The secretary of state doubted that Saddam was making WMD and believed that if he was, the programs could be controlled and even destroyed by internationally imposed economic and political sanctions. Indeed, the secretary of state had concluded—correctly as it turned out—that Saddam was not a military threat. Iraq, Powell declared in early 2001, "is fundamentally a broken, weak country—[with] one-third the military force it had some 10 years ago. We really did what we said we were going to do [in 1991]—bring them down to size."[14]

As for turning the Middle East into Jeffersonian democracies, Powell knew too much about the region to try to follow that pipe dream. He admired flourishing democracies but understood that democracy meant not merely casting votes. A democracy had to rest at least on a fair, enforceable legal system and a political consensus that agreed on political and economic rules. An equitable, widely accepted distribution of property also had to exist as a foundation on which political democracy could rest. Little of this existed in the Middle East outside of Israel.

Powell might have been the most admired of Washington officials, but he had become the odd man out of the Bush administration. In 2002, Cheney and Rumsfeld followed Wolfowitz's lead in claiming that Saddam had to be removed, especially because of his supposed WMD programs. National Security Council Adviser Condoleezza Rice's job was to ensure that the president received complete and informed advice from all sides. She was too weak, however, to confront Cheney and Rumsfeld, who, it was later learned, constantly and secretly met with Bush—quite unlike Powell. The secretary of state later bitterly complained that there existed no regular, systematic, agreed-on policy process, as there had been in the 1990–1991 run-up to war and even later under the supposedly disorganized Clinton. Rice was unable to create a procedure through which the president could listen to Powell and Rumsfeld or Cheney systematically argue out matters of life and death. Such a system did not appear because Bush was uninterested in such fundamental debates. He and his political advisers were frantic to present a unified government. One method for accomplishing that was to prevent arguments. And, as noted, the president boasted that he followed his gut instincts, not textbooks. Powell, the good soldier, went along.

Until August 2002. Earlier that summer, word spread around Washington that the president had decided to invade Iraq. In his January 2002 State of the Union Address, Bush had caused a sensation by defining Iraq, North Korea, and Iran as the "axis of evil." Everyone knew what had happened in

World War II to the last Axis powers, Germany and Japan. In a June speech at West Point, the president issued what became known as the Bush Doctrine: the United States need not wait to be attacked (as in 1917 and 1941) but had the right to launch a preemptive strike on any nation that might be preparing for war against Americans. (Bush did not note that to make such a preemptive attack necessary and justifiable, full and sound intelligence information about the grave threat the targeted nation posed was absolutely essential.) In July 2002, top British officials in Washington reported to London that they had learned Bush had made the decision to strike Iraq.[15] The public declarations of Cheney and Rumsfeld grew more warlike. They not only claimed that Saddam Hussein had WMD but also intimated that he was significantly linked to the 9/11 attacks and al-Qaeda—a claim no one ever proved and U.S. intelligence flatly denied.

On August 5, 2002, Powell finally obtained help from Rice, who arranged a long dinner conversation with Bush. An attack on Iraq, the secretary of state warned, could dangerously destabilize the Middle East, including such good allies as Saudi Arabia and Egypt. It would also divert attention and resources from the real enemy: al-Qaeda terrorists who remained safe and hidden along the Pakistan–Afghanistan border. You will be responsible for "25 million people" in Iraq, Powell told the president, "you'll own it all." The invasion will dominate everything else in the Bush presidency. Privately the secretary of state called this "the Pottery Barn rule: you break it, you own it."[16] He further warned Bush that the United States had to have strong international support, especially the United Nations and a coalition of powerful friends. Clearly, he saw this warning (i.e., take all this to the United Nations and our closest European allies of the United States) as a way to avoid, not make, war and to apply joint pressure on Iraq. Bush apparently saw it quite differently: an approach to the United Nations would give the organization and U.S. allies a chance to join an invasion that he seemed to believe was inevitable. He agreed with Powell's urgent request to go to the United Nations for support.

The secretary of state thought he had checked the Cheney–Rumsfeld–Wolfowitz drive toward war. He had not. In late August, the vice president gave a speech which warned that UN inspections of Iraq would be useless. Cheney said it flatly: there was "no doubt"—Saddam possessed weapons of mass destruction (WMD).[17] When Powell tried to counter by publicly coming out in favor of UN inspections, at least seven U.S. newspaper editorials (as he later noted) suggested that he should consider resigning. Leading American newspapers, columnists, historians, and television commentators joined an accelerating—and unquestioning—demand for war. They were led by the Fox News Network and several newspapers that had picked up often highly questionable information from Cheney. The vice president would then neatly quote Fox or the journals as authoritative sources for the information when he was, in reality, only passing on his own ideas to innocent listeners. Powell could not keep up with such tactics.

In September 2002, Bush seemed to be following Powell's advice by going to the United Nations to demand full inspection of Iraq's possible WMD sites. Powell worked to follow up the speech with a tough UN resolution. The November 8 resolution, number 1441, warned that if Saddam continued to violate his obligations to allow open UN inspection and to destroy his WMD, "serious consequences" would follow. Powell, moreover, stunned everyone, including Bush, by obtaining unanimous support for this resolution from the fifteen Security Council members, including Russia, China, Syria, and even the highly reluctant French. But "serious consequences" did not specify war; Powell would have to come back to the United Nations to obtain that authority.

Soon after his success at the United Nations in the autumn of 2002, the secretary of state began losing what little leverage he had over U.S. policy. A National Intelligence Estimate (NIE), written by some of the government's intelligence officers, laid out details of what it termed Iraq's continuing programs for WMD. The paper had a great effect on public opinion, strengthened prowar voices, and weakened Powell. The NIE drew on suspect Central Intelligence Agency (CIA) materials. It also used documents from the Defense Department that were highly selective, prowar, and later proven mistaken. Much of the prowar intelligence had suspicious, if not weird, origins. One such source was "Curveball," an Iraqi held by the Germans. "Curveball" had told German intelligence that Saddam had mobile biological weapon laboratories. The Germans, however, would not let a U.S. agent interview "Curveball" because they considered him unreliable, a drunkard, and even "crazy."[18] But "Curveball's" made-up information helped shape the NIE, Bush's speeches, and even Powell's influential February 2003 speech to the United Nations.

Wolfowitz and Rumsfeld also drew helpful information from Ahmed Chalabi, leader of the Iraqi National Congress, who had long been exiled from Iraq. He had also fled Jordan after being convicted of fraud in a banking scandal. As a Shiia Muslim, Chalabi was close to the Shiia government of Iran, one of the axis of evil. Bush and especially the Defense Department nevertheless passed $350,000 to Chalabi, who constructed stories for the Bush administration's use about Saddam's WMD. Chalabi happily joined the chorus calling for the dictator's overthrow—a chorus that included Saddam's old enemy and Chalabi's close associate Iran. And over all the NIE intelligence stood Cheney, who, as several CIA agents bitterly recalled, visited the agency a number of times to hint it should find more evidence with which to condemn Saddam. "The administration used intelligence not to inform decision-making, but to justify a decision already made" for war, complained a top CIA official responsible for handling the Middle East.[19]

The State Department's intelligence officers were among the few in Washington who consistently raised questions about the slanted, questionable, prowar information from "Curveball," Chalabi, and the Defense Department. Nor could the top U.S. Army intelligence officer working with the forces preparing for the invasion figure out what was happening: of the 946 Iraqi sites that prowar voices claimed had WMD, this officer could not "say with confidence that there were any weapons of mass destruction or stockpiles at a single site. Not one."[20] Rumsfeld had claimed to know for certain that Saddam possessed such weapons, but when UN inspectors failed to find them and asked the secretary of defense for help in fixing the specific locations, Rumsfeld responded with generalizations that were of no help. In January 2003, Bush made several claims in his televised State of the Union Address that Saddam had WMD. The claims were largely based on "Curveball's" highly doubtful testimony to the Germans as well as stories about Saddam obtaining nuclear components from Africa, stories that State Department officials had disproved.

The president never called a cabinet meeting to debate the decision to go to war. He did personally ask Powell whether he (the secretary of state) was with him. Ever the loyal soldier, Powell said he was. Powell vividly demonstrated that loyalty on February 5, 2003. Bush had asked him to make a major speech to the United Nations to convince the world that Saddam's WMD justified an invasion. Intelligence material for Powell's speech on February 5 originally came from Cheney's chief of staff, Lewis "Scooter" Libby. The material was so weak that Powell threw most if it out and started over. He spent three days and much of the nights at the CIA working with the agency's director, George Tenet, to put together dependable evidence of Saddam's WMD. For some reason, he did not work closely with any of his own State Department intelligence group, which had severe doubts about the evidence that Cheney, the CIA, and the Defense Department had compiled. "Powell wanted to sell a rotten fish," recalled a top State Department intelligence officer who was outside the process. "He had decided there was no way to avoid war. His job was to go to war with as much legitimacy as he could scrape up."[21]

Powell began his February 5, 2003, UN speech with the words, "My colleagues, every statement I make today is backed up by sources, solid sources."[22] As he later admitted, however, a speech that was to provide irrefutable evidence that Saddam's WMD justified an invasion of Iraq turned out to be based on false and misleading information. At the time, Powell seemed to be convinced that the argument was firm enough to justify war. Because of the person who uttered it, the speech made a tremendously favorable impression worldwide. Any American reluctance about supporting the invasion now seemed to disappear. When Powell soon after testified before a U.S. Senate committee, Senator Joseph Biden, a Democrat, only half-jokingly proposed that the secretary of state should be nominated to be president of the United States. Not known to Biden or the public was that key parts of Powell's speech relied on "Curveball's" false testimony and that the day before he spoke, at least one U.S. intelligence agent tried to warn Powell about "Curveball," but the warning was blocked by a top CIA official.

The speech did not perform the necessary magic Bush needed to obtain UN support for an invasion. Following Powell's remarks, the UN inspectors who had been to Iraq laid out their own evidence: they had found no WMD, even though they admitted that many of the governments they represented believed Saddam had such weapons. There simply was no hard evidence. The United States nevertheless began to push for a UN war resolution but then dropped it when Bush realized he did not have the votes in the Security Council. On March 19, 2003, he launched the invasion without UN support.

Powell had lost the great debate of his life. He had helped stack the deck against himself by using information that could not be verified by UN members. But he lost even more. In 2002, Bush had taken advice from Cheney and others to decide that captured terrorist suspects who were not U.S. citizens would not be protected by international law under the Geneva Conventions, which the United States had ratified decades earlier and which carefully guaranteed humane treatment for prisoners. Led by Powell, U.S. military commanders bitterly protested Bush's decision: "You have to remember that as we treat them, probably so we're [U.S. soldiers who might be captured] going to be treated," a top American general warned.[23]

Bush was unmoved. Later, terrorist prisoners facing or enduring torture tried to escape it by making up information and sending Americans down useless dead ends. Stories emerged of U.S. torture and humiliating acts occurring in Iraqi and other prisons. The stories deeply embarrassed the United States and infuriated many Muslims who had once been friendly to Americans. The nation paid heavily after Bush overruled Powell's protests against ignoring the Geneva Conventions.

It again paid heavily when Rumsfeld and Cheney moved to destroy the Powell Doctrine once and for all. They wanted no restraints on the U.S. military or, more accurately, on their power to send the military wherever they wished and under conditions they alone devised. Ten years earlier, Powell had at times stopped President Clinton from using the army by warning that any intervention would require overwhelming force. The political preconditions of the Powell Doctrine, moreover, had to be met. Rumsfeld now undercut Powell by demanding that only a small, high-tech, highly mobile force be sent into Iraq, not an expensive, large force as had been dispatched in 1991. The defense secretary, in other words, did not want to have to care about the Powell Doctrine's political preconditions. Meanwhile, the overwhelming prowar American opinion, led by a Congress and a media that had largely suspended disbelief, met the doctrine's provision demanding domestic support for the troops—or at least this provision was met during the few weeks in 2003 when the invasion and occupation seemed to go well. Nor did Cheney and Rumsfeld worry about the Powell Doctrine's demand for an "exit strategy" once Saddam was toppled. Well-founded newspaper stories reported at the time of the invasion that the United States did not want to exit from Iraq. Bush planned to build four or more major U.S. bases that Washington officials could use to stabilize and democratize the Middle East, protect Israel, and enjoy access to Iraq's giant oil reserves.

"My belief is we will, in fact, be greeted as liberators," Cheney boasted on television three days before the invasion.[24] It was not to be. Saddam Hussein went into hiding until he was caught in late 2003, then hanged in 2006. Before he lost power, however, Saddam had supplies of arms and ammunition buried around the country to use in insurgency warfare against the invaders. On May 1, 2003, Bush, costumed as a fighter pilot, swaggered across an aircraft carrier's deck and, underneath the sign "Mission Accomplished," informed the world that the war was over. It actually had only begun. By the summer of 2003, the anti-U.S. insurgency claimed increasing numbers of American lives. By late 2006, the number of U.S. dead in action in Iraq exceeded 3,000, or more than the number killed by the 9/11 attacks. Al-Qaeda members represented only a tiny part of the insurgency, but Iraq was becoming—for the first time—a training base for the terrorist group that had attacked New York City and Washington.

Of paramount importance, the WMD, so trumpeted by Cheney, Bush, Powell, and others, were never found. The WMD did not exist because Saddam, out of fear of U.S. and UN reaction, had in the 1990s destroyed the few WMD weapons he possessed. Meanwhile, in Afghanistan, Bush's decision in late 2001 to pull out U.S. troops and area experts so that they could concentrate on Iraq turned out to be a disaster. After 2003, the Taliban began returning in force and taking over parts of the country. Some 22,000 U.S. troops, helped by European and other forces, proved inadequate to handle the Taliban—or the record crops of poppy flowers that were turned into opium for American and European drug users whose money then helped support the Taliban as it killed Americans and their allies. Protected by the Taliban and the mountainous terrain, Osama bin Laden continued to direct al-Qaeda from his Afghanistan–Pakistan border hideout.

Bush and many others urged Powell to obtain help from his friends in Europe and Asia. Wolfowitz, like a number of other U.S. officials, had been confident that once Saddam fell, France and others who had opposed the U.S. invasion would be most pleased to help reconstruct Iraq—in return, of course, for access to the country's vast pools of oil. Instead, as the anti-US. insurgency expanded and suicide bombers exacted heavy tolls of civilian and military lives, France, Russia, China, and other opponents of the invasion wanted even less to deal with the bloody, deteriorating results. Days before the invasion, Powell was said to be "furious . . . at . . . Rumsfeld whom he blames in private for making diplomacy difficult by hurling insults at France and Germany, whose good will he [Powell] has been trying to win." One of Powell's friends added, "Diplomacy is slipping away, and Rumsfeld needs some duct tape put over his mouth." Bush and Cheney were never interested in applying the duct tape. The secretary of defense arrogantly dismissed the doubters as "Old Europe." A UN diplomat commented, "If the United States wants to proceed on this unilateral military timetable, they should fight this war alone."[25]

Rumsfeld and Cheney succeeded in convincing Bush to forget about the Powell Doctrine in 2003, but as the insurgency dragged on, their success helped destroy the efficiency of the U.S. military. By 2004–2005, that military was stretched far beyond its ordinary capabilities. Something had gone wrong with the neoconservative belief that the great superiority of U.S. military power could democratize the Middle East. Troops who usually took one tour of duty had to endure two and three without the usual rest in between. National Guard forces were summoned so rapidly from individual states to assist the overstretched regular military that Guard commanders warned that their troops were also at the breaking point. Some National Guard soldiers, unprepared for what they found in Iraq, were implicated in the humiliation and torturing of Iraqi prisoners. Meanwhile, attacks on Americans and Iraqis, which had amounted already in June 2003 to some 200 a month, increased nine times over the next year. As inadequate U.S. forces tried unsuccessfully to impose some order, civil war was breaking out. When asked about the insurgents in July 2003, Bush foolishly proclaimed, "Bring 'em on." It was a remark he later regretted.[26]

Powell continued to be loyal to the president. In a September 2004 speech at George Washington University, he argued that Bush was not guilty of a unilateralist approach but believed in "a strategy of partnerships"—a characterization for which he had little concrete evidence.[27] Powell notably lapsed just once. In February 2004, he told the *Washington Post* that since no WMD had been found in Iraq, it "changes the political calculus"—a remark immediately interpreted as meaning the invasion should have not occurred. When this was published, Condoleezza Rice quickly ordered the secretary of state to correct his story. Rice was an extraordinarily weak national security adviser who bore large responsibility for the breakdown of the policy process that Powell was justly criticizing, but he obeyed orders. Shortly after Rice's phone call, he declared, "The president made the right decision," and then repeated that belief three more times.[28] Several months later, Anne Applebaum, a Pulitzer Prize–winning *Washington Post* journalist, wrote that "Powell is trying to have it both ways, and it is not an attractive picture. Surely true loyalty means not only swallowing your pride when you disagree with your commander in chief, but keeping quiet about it as well, at least while in office. . . . And if he doesn't want to be held responsible for a policy he dislikes—then he should have resigned a long time ago."[29]

Still the obedient soldier, Powell stayed through Bush's first term. He resigned only after the White House chief of staff, Andrew Card, called the secretary of state several days after Bush was reelected in November 2004 and said the president wanted to make a change. Bush never contacted Powell. The retired general, as Card ordered, sent his resignation letter to the White House. The president then nominated Rice as secretary of state. When Powell went to see Bush for a farewell call, the conversation was either so trivial or so strained (especially when Powell warned about the worsening of the war in Iraq) that the outgoing secretary of state was convinced, as he told a friend, that "the president didn't know why I was there."[30] In 2000, the Texan, whom Powell then called "Sonny," had badly needed the greatly respected retired general. Less than five years later, the secretary of state was removed with hardly a political ripple.

Out of office, Powell now admitted that his February 2003 speech to the United Nations would be a "lasting blot" on his record. The WMD he had told the world was in the hands of Saddam Hussein had not existed. "It was painful. It's painful now."[31] He repeatedly charged that the United States went into the war with too few troops to pacify and stabilize Iraq. In other words, he implied that this provision of the Powell Doctrine, not Rumsfeld's inadequate war and postwar planning, should have shaped the effort. In late 2006 when Iraq was in virtual chaos and civil war waged between Sunni and Shiia Muslims, Powell criticized Bush's announcement that he was going to inject another 21,000 U.S. troops in a "surge" to try to secure Baghdad and train Iraqi troops. Powell's criticism mirrored the beliefs of top U.S. military commanders whom the president had overruled so that he could make a final attempt to save one of the most disastrous foreign policy decisions in American history.

But even as he uttered the criticisms, Powell reiterated that he had supported Bush's decision to go to war in 2003. And publicly he continued to declare that it was the correct decision. After he left office, the old soldier's loyalty to the presidency continued to trump his better judgment. In 2005, his longtime friend and chief of staff at the State Department, Colonel Larry Wilkerson, condemned Bush, Cheney, Rumsfeld, and Rice, especially for ignoring and isolating the former secretary of state. Wilkerson then explained Powell's puzzling decision to stay in the administration and even (as at the United Nations in 2003) act as its voice by declaring that the retired general "is the world's most loyal soldier."[32] This form of the loyalty, in these post-9/11 circumstances, not only contradicted Powell's beliefs of the previous quarter century but specifically contradicted Powell's Doctrine, which might have saved the United States from a catastrophe.

NOTES

1. Colin L. Powell, with Joseph E. Persico, *My American Journey* (New York: Ballantine Books, 1995), 59–66.

2. Powell, *My American Journey*, 65–66.

3. Transcript of "Excerpts from Remarks by Secretary of Defense Caspar W. Weinberger to the National Press Club, Washington, D.C., November 28, 1984," in author's possession.

4. James Mann, *Rise of the Vulcans: The History of Bush's War Cabinet* (New York: Penguin Books, 2004), 184.

5. Powell, *My American Journey*, 560–61.

6. Powell, *My American Journey*, 565.

7. Karen DeYoung, "Falling on His Sword," *Washington Post*, October 1, 2006, W12.

8. Bob Woodward, *Bush at War* (New York: Simon & Schuster, 2002), 11–12.

9. Andrew J. Bacevich, *The New American Militarism: How Americans Are Seduced by War* (New York: Oxford University Press, 2005), 85.

10. Bacevich, *The New American Militarism*, 63.

11. Karen DeYoung, *Soldier: The Life of Colin Powell* (New York: Knopf, 2006), 296–97.

12. Bob Woodward, *Plan of Attack* (New York: Simon & Schuster, 2004), 79.

13. Woodward, *Bush at War*, 342.

14. Jane Perlez, "The General Picks Up Where He Left Off," *New York Times*, January 28, 2001, 5.

15. The British report can be found in many sources; note especially the quotes and context provided in Frank Rich, "The Secret Way to War," *New York Review of Books*, April 6, 2006, 53; a stunned British military response is analyzed in Richard Norton-Taylor and Julian Borger, "Iraq Attack Plans Alarm Top Military," *The Guardian* (London), July 30, 2002, 1, 4.

16. Woodward, *Plan of Attack*, 149–50.

17. Woodward, *Plan of Attack*, 442.

18. Tyler Drumheller, *On the Brink* (New York: Penguin Books, 2005), 252.

19. Quoted in Sidney Blumenthal, "The Pentagon's Not-So-Little Secret," http://www.salon.com, February 8, 2007.

20. Woodward, *State of Denial*, 92–96.

21. Sidney Blumenthal, "There Was No Failure of Intelligence," *The Guardian* (London), February 5, 2004, 1.

22. The quote and a good context can be found in Thomas E. Ricks, *FIASCO: The American Military Adventure in Iraq* (New York: Penguin Books, 2006), 90–91.

23. Woodward, *State of Denial*, 86–87.

24. Woodward, *State of Denial*, 151.

25. Steven R. Weisman, "Powell at a New Turning Point. . . ," *New York Times*, March 14, 2003, A16.

26. Woodward, *State of Denial*, 229.

27. Glenn Kessler, "Powell Strongly Defends Bush's Foreign Policy," *Washington Post*, September 6, 2003.

28. Woodward, *Plan of Attack*, 437.

29. Anne Applebaum, "Having It Both Ways," *Washington Post*, April 21, 2004, A23.

30. De Young, "Falling on His Sword," W12.

31. Steven R. Weisman, "Powell Calls His U.N. Speech a Lasting Blot on His Record," *New York Times*, September 9, 2005, A10.

32. Dana Milbank, "Colonel Finally Saw Whites of Their Eyes," *Washington Post*, October 20, 2005, A4.

Index

remainder method, 24
Research Institute of America, 132
Ribicoff, Abraham, 96, 99, 101
Rice, Condoleezza, 162, 165, 168–69, 175
Rockefeller, David, 117
Rogers, William, 83
Rolling Thunder, 67, 69
Roosevelt, Franklin Delano, 112–14
Rostow, Walt Whitman, 59–82; background of, 59–61
Rove, Karl, 163
Rowen, Henry, 139–40
Rowny, Ed, 94
Rumsfeld, Donald, 162–64, 168–74
Rusk, Dean, 64, 69, 71
Russia, 165

Sachs, Alexander, 21–22
Safire, William, 131
Sakarov, Andrei, 98
Salisbury, Robert Gascoyne-Cecil, 36, 38
SALT. *See* Strategic Arms Limitation Treaty
Saudi Arabia, 128, 157
Savage, Carlton, 13
Schuman Plan, 50n5
Schwartz, Harry H., 13
SDI. *See* Strategic Defense Initiative
Secretary of State: Powell as, 153–77
Securities Exchange Commission, 134
Senate, Jackson and, 83–106
September 11, 2001, 165–66, 169
Shaw, George Bernard, 111
Shulman, Marshall, 121
Shultz, George P., 145–46
Sick, Gary, 136–37
Sidey, Hugh, 70
SLBMs. *See* submarine-launched ballistic missiles
Smith, Gerard, 94
Smyth, Henry D., 18
SNIE. *See* Special National Intelligence Estimate

Solarium project, 35
Solzhenitsyn, Alexander, 96, 98
Somalia, 121, 160–61
Sonnefeld, Helmut, 101
South Africa, 144
South Korea, 164
Soviet Union: Basic Principles of Relations, 89; Brzezinski and, 107–30; Casey and, 131–52; collapse of, 156; and Germany, 29–57; Jackson and, 83–106; Nitze and, 5–28; and peace offensive, 35–36, 51n16; Rostow and, 61
Special National Intelligence Estimate (SNIE), 140–41
Stalin, Josef, 110–14; death of, 30, 36, 61
Star Wars. *See* Strategic Defense Initiative
State Department, 171; Bowie and, 29–57; Nitze and, 5–28; Powell and, 153–77
Stevenson, Adlai, 13, 100
Stockman, David, 136
Strategic Arms Limitation Treaty (SALT), 83, 88–90, 92–94, 117, 120, 145
Strategic Defense Initiative (SDI), 25, 141, 144–45
submarine-launched ballistic missiles (SLBMs), 88–89
Swamp Fox, 69
Szporluk, Roman, 115

Talbott, Strobe, 128
Taliban, 166, 173
Taraki, Nur Mohammed, 123–25
Taylor, Maxwell, 65, 69
Team B report, 134–35, 149n10
technology: Brzezinski on, 115; Powell and, 163; Rostow and, 61
Tenet, George, 171
terrorism: Casey and, 138–40; September 11, 2001, 165–66
Tet Offensive, 76
Thomson, James C., 73
torture, 172, 174

About the Contributors

Lloyd Gardner is the Research Professor of History at Rutgers University. He is the author or editor of many books on a variety of subjects, including *Pay Any Price: Lyndon Johnson and the War for Vietnam.* Most recently, he coedited *Iraq and the Lessons of Vietnam; or, How Not to Learn from the Past.*

Walter LaFeber is the Andrew and James Tisch University Professor Emeritus at Cornell University and also a Weiss Presidential Teaching Fellow. His books include *American Age: U.S. Foreign Relations at Home and Abroad since 1750* and *Russia and the Cold War, 1945–2006.*

Anna Kasten Nelson is the Distinguished Historian in Residence at American University, where she teaches courses related to the history of American foreign relations. Primarily a writer of articles and essays, she has published in major historical journals on a variety of subjects in both nineteenth-century diplomacy and twentieth- and twenty-first-century foreign policy. Her research has centered on the evolution of the national security process since 1947. Her most recent essay is "The Evolution of the National Security State: Ubiquitous and Endless," in Andrew Bacevich, ed., *The Long War.*

John Prados is an analyst of security, intelligence, and diplomacy with wide interests. A senior fellow at the National Security Archive, he directs both its Iraq and its Vietnam projects.

Steven L. Rearden is a historian with the Joint Chiefs of Staff. He is currently writing a history of the Joint Chiefs of Staff and national security policy during the Reagan administration. He is the coauthor of *The Origins of U.S. Nuclear Strategy, 1945–1953.*

Chris Tudda is a historian in the Declassification and Publishing Division in the Office of the Historian, Department of State, where he declassifies manuscripts for the *Foreign Relations of the United States* series. He is the author of *The Truth Is Our Weapon: The Rhetorical Diplomacy of Dwight D. Eisenhower and John Foster Dulles*.

Patrick Vaughan is an American historian and scholar, currently teaching at the Institute for American Studies and Polish Diaspora at the Jagiellonian University in Kraków, Poland.

Made in the USA
Middletown, DE
14 February 2018